SPOTLIGHT

CHARLESTON & THE SOUTH CAROLINA LOWCOUNTRY

JIM MOREKIS

D0110657

Contents

CHARLESTON & THE SOUTH CAROLINA LOWCOUNTRY

CHARLESTON

Charleston boasts so many American "firsts" that it's almost a cliché to point them out: first museum, first theater, first public library, first municipal college, first golf club, first historic preservation ordinance, and the list goes on and on.

But for the majority of visitors, the most important Charleston first is its perennial ranking at the top of the late Marjabelle Young Stewart's annual list for "Most Mannerly City in America." (Charleston has won the award so many times that Stewart's successor at the Charleston School of Protocol and Etiquette, Cindy Grosso, has retired the city from the competition.) This is a city that takes civic harmony so seriously that it boasts the country's only "Livability Court," a binding legal proceeding which meets regularly to enforce local quality-of-life ordinances.

Everyone who spends time in Charleston comes away with a story to tell about the locals' courtesy and hospitality. Mine came while walking through the French Quarter admiring a handsome old single house on Church Street, one of the few that survived the fire of 1775. To my surprise, the lady chatting with a friend nearby turned out to be the homeowner. Noticing my interest, she invited me, a total stranger, inside to check out the progress of her renovation.

To some eyes, Charleston's hospitable nature has bordered on licentiousness. From its earliest days, the city gained a reputation for vice. (The city's nickname, "The Holy City," derives from the skyline's abundance of church steeples rather than any excess of piety among its citizens.) The old drinking clubs are gone, and the

© JIM MOREKIS

HIGHLIGHTS

The Battery: Tranquil surroundings combine with beautiful views of Charleston Harbor, key historical points in the Civil War, and amazing mansions (page 16).

Rainbow Row: Painted in warm pastels, these old merchant homes near the cobblestoned waterfront take you on a journey to Charleston's antebellum heyday (page 18).

Fort Sumter: Take the ferry to this historic place where the Civil War began and take in the gorgeous views along the way (page 29).

St. Philip's Episcopal Church: A sublimely beautiful sanctuary and two historic graveyards await you in the heart of the evocative French Quarter (page 30).

Aiken-Rhett House: There are certainly more ostentatious house museums in Charleston, but none that provide such a virtually intact glimpse into real antebellum life (page 40).

Drayton Hall: Don't miss Charleston's oldest surviving plantation home and one of America's best examples of professional historic preservation (page 45).

Middleton Place: Wander in and marvel at one of the world's most beautifully landscaped gardens — and the first in North America (page 48).

CSS *Hunley*: Newly ensconced for public viewing in its special preservation tank, the first submarine to sink a ship in battle is a moving example of bravery and sacrifice (page 51).

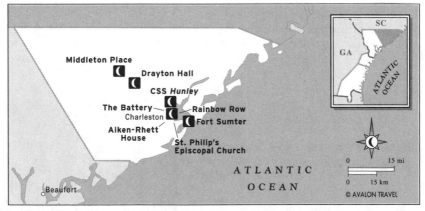

LOOK FOR **(** TO FIND RECOMMENDED SIGHTS, ACTIVITIES, DINING, AND LODGING.

yearly bacchanal of Race Week—in which personal fortunes were won or lost in seconds—is but a distant memory. But that hedonistic legacy is alive and well today in Charleston; the city is full of lovers of strong drink and serious foodies, with every weekend night finding downtown packed with partiers, diners, and show-goers.

Don't mistake the Holy City's charm and joie de vivre for weakness, however. That would be a mistake, for within Charleston's velvet glove has always been an iron fist. This is where the colonists scored their first clear victory over the British during the Revolution (another Charleston first). This is the place where the Civil War began, and which stoically endured one of the longest sieges in modern warfare during that conflict. This is the city that survived the East Coast's worst earthquake in 1886 and one of its worst hurricanes a century later.

Despite its fun-loving reputation, a martial spirit is never far from the surface in Charleston, from The Citadel military college along the Ashley River, to the aircraft carrier *Yorktown* moored at Patriots Point, to the cannonballs and mortars that children climb on at the Battery, and even to the occasional tour guide in Confederate garb.

Some of the nation's most progressive urban activity is going on in Charleston despite its often-deserved reputation for conservatism, from the renovation of the old Navy Yard in North Charleston, to impressive green start-ups, to any number of sustainable residential developments. Charleston's a leader in conservation as well, with groups like the Lowcountry Open Land Trust and the Coastal Conservation League setting an example for the entire Southeast in how to bring environmental organizations and the business community together to preserve the area's beauty and ecosystem.

While many visitors come to see the Charleston of Rhett Butler and Pat Conroy—finding it and then some, of course—they leave impressed by the diversity of Charlestonian life. It's a surprisingly cosmopolitan mix of students, professionals, and longtime inhabitants—who discuss the finer points of Civil War history as if it were last year, party on Saturday night like there's no tomorrow, and go to church on Sunday morning dressed in their finest.

But don't be deceived by these history-minded people. Under the carefully honed tradition and the ever-present ancestor worship, Charleston possesses a vitality of vision that is irrepressibly practical and forward-looking.

HISTORY

Unlike so many of England's colonies in America that were based on freedom from religious persecution, Carolina was strictly a commercial venture from the beginning. The tenure of the Lords Proprietors—the eight English aristocrats who literally owned the colony—began in 1670 when the *Carolina* finished its journey to Albemarle Creek on the west bank of the Ashley River.

Those first colonists would set up a small

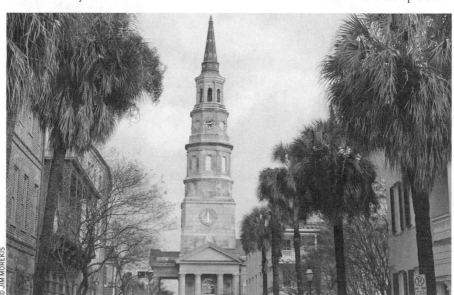

© JIM MOREKIS

The city's nickname is "The Holy City" because of its numerous church steeples.

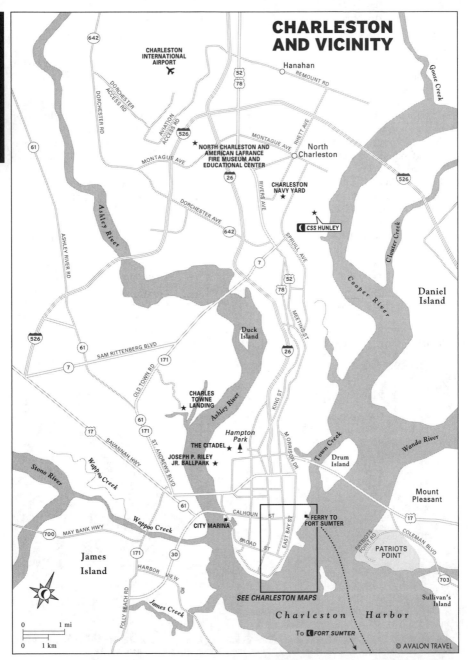

CHARLESTON AND VICINITY

CHARLESTON INTERNATIONAL AIRPORT

Hanahan

Goose Creek

REMOUNT RD

DORCHESTER ACCESS RD

DORCHESTER RD

AVIATION ACCESS RD

MONTAGUE AVE

RHETT AVE

NORTH CHARLESTON AND AMERICAN LAFRANCE FIRE MUSEUM AND EDUCATIONAL CENTER

North Charleston

MONTAGUE AVE

DORCHESTER AVE

RIVERS AVE

CHARLESTON NAVY YARD

Ashley River

ASHLEY RIVER RD

SPRUILL AVE

CSS HUNLEY

Clouter Creek

Cooper River

Daniel Island

Duck Island

MEETING ST

SAM RITTENBERG BLVD

OLD TOWN RD

CHARLES TOWNE LANDING

Ashley River

KING ST

Hampton Park

THE CITADEL

JOSEPH P. RILEY JR. BALLPARK

MORRISON DR

Town Creek

Drum Island

Wando River

ST. ANDREWS BLVD

SAVANNAH HWY

Stono River

Wappoo Creek

Mount Pleasant

CALHOUN ST

EAST BAY ST

CITY MARINA

FERRY TO FORT SUMTER

BROAD ST

PATRIOTS POINT RD

COLEMAN BLVD

PATRIOTS POINT

MAY BANK HWY

Wappoo Creek

James Island

HARBOR VIEW RD

FOLLY BEACH RD

James Creek

SEE CHARLESTON MAPS

Sullivan's Island

Charleston Harbor

To FORT SUMTER

0   1 mi
0   1 km

© AVALON TRAVEL

fortification called Charles Towne, named for Charles II, the first monarch of the Restoration. In a year they'd be joined by colonists from the prosperous but overcrowded British colony of Barbados, who brought a unique Caribbean sensibility that exists in Charleston to this day.

Finding the first Charles Towne unhealthy, not very fertile, and vulnerable to attack from Native Americans and Spanish, they moved to the peninsula and down to "Oyster Point," what Charlestonians now call White Point Gardens. Just above Oyster Point they set up a walled town, bounded by modern-day Water Street to the south (then a marshy creek, as the name indicates), Meeting Street to the west, Cumberland Street to the north, and the Cooper River on the east.

Growing prosperous as a trading center for deerskin from the great American interior, Charles Towne came into its own after two nearly concurrent events in the early 1700s: the decisive victory of a combined force of Carolinians and Native American allies against the fierce Yamasee tribe, and the final eradication of the pirate threat in the deaths of Blackbeard and Stede Bonnet.

Flushed with a new spirit of independence, Charles Towne threw off the control of the anemic, disengaged Lords Proprietors, tore down the old defensive walls, and was reborn as an outward-looking, expansive, and increasingly cosmopolitan city that came to be called Charleston. With safety from hostile incursion came the time of the great rice and indigo plantations. Springing up all along the Ashley River soon after the introduction of the crops, they turned the labor and expertise of imported Africans into enormous profit for their owners. However, the planters preferred the pleasures and sea breezes of Charleston, and gradually summer homes became year-round residences.

It was during this Colonial era that the indelible marks of Charlestonian character were stamped: a hedonistic aristocracy combining a love of carousing with a love of the arts; a code

NOT JUST A MATTER OF BLUE AND GRAY

While this area is most well known for its role in the Civil War – Charleston's as the instigator of the conflict, and Savannah's as the terminus of Sherman's notorious "March to the Sea" – this is a drastic oversimplification. Although South Carolina was the "cradle of secession," it also lost more men in the fight for American independence than any other colony, including Massachusetts. Here are some military history highlights from other eras:

In Charleston, go to **The Citadel** and enjoy the colorful weekly parade of cadets, the fabled "Thin Grey Line," at 3 P.M. most Fridays. In Mount Pleasant eat lunch in the mess hall of the **USS Yorktown** at the **Patriot's Point Naval Museum.** Visit historic **Middleton Place,** home of one of the signers of the Declaration of Independence and where some scenes from Mel Gibson's The Patriot were filmed.

On Parris Island tour the **Marine Recruit Depot Parris Island** and see one of the old-est European archaeological sites in the United States, **Charlesfort.**

In Savannah, head to **Battlefield Park** and see the replicated British redoubt marking the failed Siege of Savannah. Visit **Old Fort Jackson,** an 1812-era installation on the Savannah River. Tour the **Mighty Eighth Air Force Museum,** which honors the contributions of the Eighth Air Force, founded in Savannah in 1942.

In Darien, Georgia, is **Fort King George,** the first English outpost in Georgia. Nearby is **Harris Neck National Wildlife Refuge,** formerly a World War II airfield.

On St. Simons Island is **Ft. Frederica,** a tabby fort built by General James Oglethorpe, and the nearby **Battle of Bloody Marsh** site, where Oglethorpe ended the Spanish threat to Georgia.

While the big U.S. Navy Trident sub base at Kings Bay, Georgia, is not open to the public, check out the **St. Marys Submarine Museum** in St. Marys, which pays tribute to the "Silent Service."

of chivalry meant both to reflect a genteel spirit and reinforce the social order; and, ominously, an ever-increasing reliance on slave labor.

As the storm clouds of civil war gathered in the early 1800s, the majority of Charleston's population was of African descent, and the city was the main importation point for the transatlantic slave trade. The worst fears of white Charlestonians seemed confirmed during the alleged plot by slave leader Denmark Vesey in the early 1820s to start a rebellion. The Lowcountry's reliance on slave labor put it front and center in the coming national confrontation over abolition, which came to a head literally and figuratively in the bombardment of Fort Sumter in Charleston Harbor in April 1861.

By war's end, not only did the city lay in ruins—mostly from a disastrous fire in 1861, as well as from a 545-day Union siege—so did its way of life. Pillaged by northern troops and freed slaves, the great plantations along the Ashley became the sites of the first strip mining in America, as poverty-stricken owners scraped away the layer of phosphate under the topsoil to sell—perhaps with a certain poetic justice—as fertilizer.

The Holy City didn't really wake up until the great "Charleston Renaissance" of the 1920s and '30s, when the city rediscovered art, literature, and music in the form of jazz and the world-famous Charleston dance. This also was the time that the world rediscovered Charleston. In the 1920s, George Gershwin read local author DuBose Heyward's novel *Porgy* and decided to write a score around the story. Along with lyrics by Ira Gershwin, the three men's collaboration became the first American opera, *Porgy and Bess,* which debuted in New York in 1935. It was also during this time that a new appreciation for Charleston's history sprang up, as the local Preservation Society spearheaded the nation's first historic preservation ordinance.

World War II brought the same economic boom that came to much of the South then, most notably with an expansion of the Navy Yard and the addition of an Air Force base. By the 1950s, the automobile suburb and a thirst for "progress" claimed so many historic buildings that the inevitable backlash came with the formation of the Historic Charleston Foundation, which continues to lead the fight to keep intact the Holy City's architectural legacy.

Civil rights came to Charleston in earnest with a landmark suit to integrate Charleston Municipal Golf Course in 1960. The biggest battle, however, would be the 100-day strike in 1969 against the Medical University of South Carolina, then, as now, a large employer of African Americans.

Charleston's next great renaissance—still ongoing today—came with the redevelopment of downtown and the fostering of the tourism industry under the 30-year-plus tenure of Mayor Joe Riley, during which so much of the current, visitor-friendly infrastructure became part of daily life here. Today, Charleston is completing the transition away from a military and manufacturing base and attracting professionals and artists to town.

PLANNING YOUR TIME

Even if you're just going to confine yourself to the peninsula, I can't imagine spending less than two nights there. You'll want at least half a day for shopping on King Street and a full day for seeing various attractions and museums. Keep in mind that one of Charleston's key sights, Fort Sumter, will take almost half a day to see once you factor in ticketing and boarding time for the ferry out to the fort and back; plan accordingly.

If you have a car, there are several great places to visit off the peninsula—especially the plantations along the Ashley. None are very far away and navigation in Charleston is a snap. The farthest site from downtown should take no more than 30 minutes, and because the plantations are roughly adjacent, you can visit all of them in a single day if you get an early start.

While a good time is never far away in Charleston, keep in mind that this is the South and Sundays can get pretty slow. While the finely honed tourist infrastructure here means that there will always be something to do, the selection of open shops and restaurants dwindles on Sundays, though most other attractions keep working hours.

But for those of us who love the old city, there's nothing like a Sunday morning in Charleston—church bells ringing, families on their way to worship, a beguiling slowness in the air, perhaps spiced with the anticipation of a particular Charleston specialty—a hearty and delicious Sunday brunch.

The real issue for most visitors boils down to two questions: How much do you want to spend on accommodations, and in which part of town do you want to stay? Lodging is generally not cheap in Charleston, but because the price differential is not that much between staying on the peninsula and staying on the outskirts, I recommend the peninsula. You'll pay more, but not *that* much more, with the bonus of probably being able to walk to most places you want to see—which, after all, is the best way to enjoy the city.

ORIENTATION

Charleston occupies a peninsula bordered by the Ashley River to the west and the Cooper River to the east, which "come together to form the Atlantic Ocean," according to the haughty phrase once taught to generations of Charleston schoolchildren.

Though the lower tip of the peninsula actually points closer to southeast, that direction is regarded locally as due south, and anything towards the top of the peninsula is considered due north.

The peninsula is ringed by islands, many of which have become heavily populated suburbs. Clockwise from the top of the peninsula they are: Daniel Island, Mount Pleasant, Isle of Palms, Sullivan's Island, Morris Island, Folly Island, and James Island. The resort island of Kiawah and the much less-developed Edisto Island are farther south down the coast.

North Charleston is not only a separate municipality, it's also a different state of mind. A sprawling combination of malls, light industry, and low-income housing, it also boasts some of the more cutting-edge urban redesign activity in the area.

While Charlestonians would scoff, the truth is that Charleston proper has a surprising amount in common with Manhattan. Both are on long spits of land situated roughly north–south. Both were settled originally at the lower end in walled fortifications— Charleston's walls came down in 1718, while Manhattan still has its Wall Street as a reminder. Both cityscapes rely on age-old north–south streets that run nearly the whole length—Charleston's King and Meeting Streets, with only a block between them, and Manhattan's Broadway and Fifth Avenue. And like Manhattan, Charleston also has its own "Museum Mile" just off of a major greenspace, in Charleston's case up near Marion Square—though certainly its offerings are not as expansive as those a short walk from New York's Central Park.

Unfortunately, also like Manhattan, parking is at a premium in downtown Charleston. Luckily the city has many reasonably priced parking garages, which I recommend that you use. But cars should only be used when you have to. Charleston is best enjoyed on foot, both because of its small size and the cozy, meandering nature of its old streets, designed not for cars and tour buses but for boots, horseshoes, and carriage wheels.

Charleston is made up of many small neighborhoods, many of them quite old. The boundaries are confusing, so your best bet is to simply look at the street signs (signage in general is excellent in Charleston). If you're in a historic neighborhood, such as the French Quarter or Ansonborough, a smaller sign above the street name will indicate that.

Other key terms you'll hear are "the Crosstown," the portion of U.S. 17 that goes across the peninsula; "Savannah Highway," the portion of U.S. 17 that traverses "West Ashley," which is the suburb across the Ashley River; "East Cooper," the area across the Cooper River including Mount Pleasant, Isle of Palms, and Daniel and Sullivan's Islands; and "the Neck," up where the peninsula narrows. These are the terms that locals use, and hence what you'll see in this guide.

Sights

Though most key sights in Charleston do indeed have some tie to the city's rich history, house museums are only a subset of the attractions here. Charleston's sights are excellently integrated into its built environment, and often the enjoyment of nearby gardens or a lapping river is part of the fun.

SOUTH OF BROAD

As one of the oldest streets in Charleston, the east-west thoroughfare of Broad Street is not only a physical landmark, it's a mental one as well. The first area of the Charleston peninsula to be settled, the area south of Broad Street—often shortened to the mischievous acronym "SOB" by local wags—features older homes, meandering streets (much of them built on "made land" filling in former wharfs), and a distinctly genteel, laid-back feel.

As you'd expect, it also features more affluent residents, sometimes irreverently referred to as "SOB Snobs." This heavily residential area has no nightlife to speak of and gets almost eerily quiet after hours, but rest assured that plenty of people live here.

While I highly recommend just wandering among these narrow streets and marveling at the lovingly restored old homes, keep in mind that almost everything down here is in private hands. Don't wander into a garden or take photos inside a window unless you're invited to do so (and given Charleston's legendary hospitality, that can happen).

◖ The Battery

For many, the Battery (E. Battery St. and Murray Blvd., 843/724-7321, 24 hrs., free) is the single most iconic Charleston spot, drenched in history and boasting dramatic views in all directions. A look to the south gives you the sweeping expanse of the Cooper River, with views of Fort Sumter, Castle Pinckney, Sullivan's Island, and, off to the north, the old carrier *Yorktown* moored at Mount Pleasant. A landward look gives you a view of the

adjoining, peaceful **White Point Gardens,** the sumptuous mansions of the Battery, and a beguiling peek behind them into some of the oldest neighborhoods in Charleston.

But if you had been one of the first European visitors to this tip of the peninsula about 400 years ago, you'd have seen how it got its first name, Oyster Point: This entire area was once home to an enormous outcropping of oysters. Their shells glistened bright white in the harsh Southern sun as a ship approached from seaward, hence its subsequent name, White Point. Though the oysters are long gone and much of the area you're walking on is actually reclaimed marsh, the Battery and White Point Gardens are still a balm for the soul.

Once the bustling (and sometimes seedy) heart of Charleston's maritime activity, the Battery was where pirate Stede Bonnet and 21 of his men were hanged in 1718. As you might

statue at the Battery

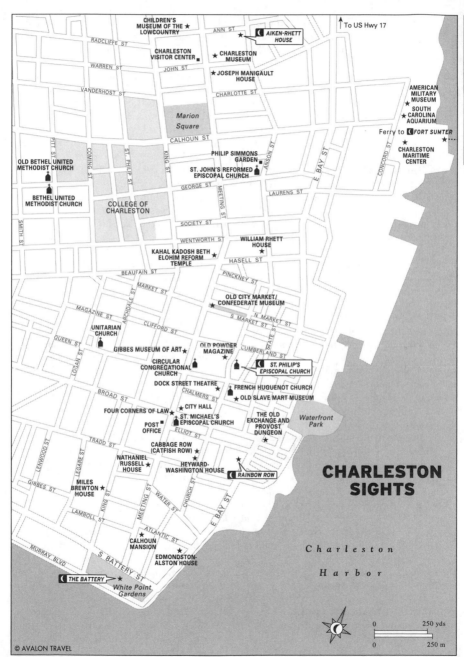

CHARLESTON SIGHTS

Charleston Harbor

0   250 yds
0   250 m

© AVALON TRAVEL

imagine, the area got its name for hosting cannon during the War of 1812, with the current distinctive seawall structure built in the 1850s.

Contrary to popular opinion, no guns fired from here on Fort Sumter at the beginning of the Civil War, as they would have been out of range. However, many thankfully inoperable cannons, mortars, and piles of shot still reside here, much to the delight of boys of all ages. This is where Charlestonians gathered in a giddy, party-like atmosphere to watch the shelling of Fort Sumter in 1861, blissfully ignorant of the horrors to come. A short time later the North would return the favor, as the Battery and all of Charleston up to Broad Street would bear the brunt of shelling during the long siege of the city (the rest was out of reach of Union guns).

But now, the Battery is a place to relax, not fight. The relaxation starts with the fact that there's usually plenty of free parking all along Battery Street. A promenade all around the periphery is a great place to stroll or jog. Add the calming, almost constant sea breeze and the meditative influence of the wide, blue Cooper River, and you'll see why this land's end—once so martial in nature—is now a favorite place for after-church family gatherings, tourists, lovestruck couples, and weddings (about 200 a year at the gazebo in White Point Gardens).

Still, military history is never far away in Charleston, and one of the chief landmarks at the Battery is the USS *Hobson* Memorial, remembering the sacrifice of the men of that vessel when it sank after a collision with the carrier USS *Wasp* in 1952.

Look for the three-story private residence where East Battery curves northward. You won't be taking any tours of it, but you should be aware that it's the **DeSaussure House** (1 E. Battery St.), best known in Charleston history for hosting rowdy, celebratory crowds on the roof and the piazzas to watch the 34-hour shelling of Fort Sumter in 1861.

Edmondston-Alston House

The most noteworthy single attraction on the Battery is the 1825 Edmondston-Alston House (21 E. Battery St., 843/722-

7171, www.middletonplace.org, Tues.–Sat. 10 a.m.–4:30 p.m., Sun. 1:30–4:30 p.m., Mon. 1–4:30 p.m., $10 adults, $8 students), the only Battery home open to the public for tours. This is one of the most unique and well-preserved historic homes in the United States, thanks to the ongoing efforts of the Alston family, who acquired the house from shipping merchant Charles Edmondston for $15,500 after the Panic of 1837 and still live on the third floor (tours only go to the first two stories).

Over 90 percent of the home's furnishings are original items from the Alston era, a percentage that's almost unheard of in the world of house museums. (Currently the House is owned and administered by the Middleton Place Foundation, best known for its stewardship of Middleton Place along the Ashley River.)

You can still see the original paper bag used to store the house's deeds and mortgages. There's also a copy of the Ordinance of Secession and some interesting memorabilia from the golden days of Race Week, that time in February when all of Charleston society came out to bet on horses, carouse, and show off their finery.

The Edmondston-Alston House has withstood storm, fire, earthquake, and Yankee shelling, due in no small part to its sturdy construction; its masonry walls are two-bricks thick and it features both interior and exterior shutters. Originally built in the Federal style, second owner Charles Alston added several Greek Revival elements, notably the parapet, balcony, and piazza, where General Beauregard watched the attack on Fort Sumter.

(Rainbow Row

From 79–107 East Bay, between Tradd and Elliot Streets, is one of the most photographed sights in the United States, colorful Rainbow Row. The reason for its name becomes obvious when you see the array of pastel-colored mansions, all facing the Cooper River. The bright, historically accurate colors—nine of them, to be exact—are one of the many vestiges you'll see around town of Charleston's Caribbean heritage, a legacy of the English settlers from

© J M MOREKIS

Rainbow Row

the colony of Barbados who were among the city's first citizens.

The homes are unusually old for this fire-, hurricane-, and earthquake-ravaged city, with most dating from 1730 to 1750. As you admire Rainbow Row from across East Battery, keep in mind you're actually walking on what used to be water. These houses were originally right on the Cooper River, their lower stories serving as storefronts on the wharf. The street was created later on top of landfill, or "made land" as it's called locally.

Besides its grace and beauty, Rainbow Row is of vital importance to American historic preservation. These were the first Charleston homes to be renovated and brought back from early-20th-century seediness. The restoration projects on Rainbow Row directly inspired the creation of the Charleston Preservation Society, the first such group in the United States.

Continue walking up the High Battery past Rainbow Row and find Water Street. This aptly named little avenue was in fact a creek in the early days, acting as the southern border of the original walled city. The large brick building on the seaward side housing the Historic Charleston Foundation sits on the site of the old Granville bastion, a key defensive point in the wall.

Nathaniel Russell House

Considered one of Charleston's grandest homes despite being built by an outsider from Rhode Island, the Nathaniel Russell House (51 Meeting St., 843/724-8481, www.historic charleston.org, Mon.–Sat. 10 A.M.–5 P.M., Sun. 2–5 P.M., last tour begins 4:30 P.M., $10 adults, $5 children) is now a National Historic Landmark and one of America's best examples of neoclassicism. Built in 1808 for the then-princely sum of $80,000 by Nathaniel Russell, a.k.a., "King of the Yankees," the home is furnished as accurately as possible to represent not only the lifestyle of the Russell family, but the 18 African American servants who shared the premises. The house was eventually bought by the Allson family, who amid the poverty of Civil War and Reconstruction decided in 1870 to sell it to the Sisters of Charity of Our Lady of Mercy as a school for young Catholic women.

Restorationists have identified 22 layers of paint within the home, which barely survived a tornado in 1811, got away with only minimal damage in the 1886 earthquake, but was damaged extensively by Hurricane Hugo in 1989 (and since repaired). As with fine antebellum homes throughout coastal South Carolina and Georgia, the use of faux finishing is prevalent

KNOW YOUR CHARLESTON HOUSES

As architects and historic preservationists have long known, Charleston's homes boast not only a long pedigree, but quite an interesting and unique one as well. Here are some key terms you should be familiar with.

Single House: A direct legacy of the early Barbadian planters among the very first settlers here, the Charleston single house is named for the fact that it's a single room wide – the better to fit deep, narrow downtown lots. The phrase refers to layout, not style, which can range from Georgian to Federal to Greek Revival, or even a combination. Furnished with full-length piazzas on the south side to take advantage of southerly breezes, the single house is perhaps America's first sustainable house design. The house sits lengthwise on the lot, with the main entrance on the side of the house. This of course means that the "backyard" is actually the side yard. Entry from the street is by a gate on one end of the lower piazza. A typical single house has three floors: a ground floor for business; a main floor for entertaining, living, and dining; and a top floor for sleeping. You can find them everywhere, but Church Street has some great examples, including 90, 92, and 94 Church Street, and the oldest single house in town, the 1730 Robert Brewton House (71 Church St.).

Double House: This layout is two rooms wide with a central hallway and a porched facade facing the street. Double houses often had separate carriage houses, the top floor of which was often reserved for servants' quarters. The Aiken-Rhett and Heyward-Washington houses are good examples of this more affluent, ostentatious design.

Piazza: The long porch or veranda of a single house. There is usually one piazza for each floor and with southern exposure so that prevailing winds can sweep the length of the house. The roof of the piazza shades the windows on that side of the house. Room doors are also on the piazza side so that they can be left open if need be. The typical dearth of windows on the north side exemplifies the so-called "northside manner," protecting the privacy of the house next door. Another Caribbean trait via Barbados, piazzas sometimes feature balconies on top.

Charleston Green: This distinctively Charlestonian color – an extremely dark green that looks pitch black in low light or at a casual glance – has its roots in the penurious aftermath of the Civil War. The federal government distributed thousands of gallons of surplus black paint to contribute to reconstruction of the shell-and-fire-ravaged peninsula, but Charlestonians were too proud (not to mention too tasteful) to use it as is. So they added the tiniest bit of yellow to each gallon, producing the distinctive, historic color we now know as Charleston Green.

Earthquake Bolt: Structural damage after the 1886 earthquake was so extensive that many buildings were retrofitted with one or more long iron rod running from wall to wall to keep the house stable. After installation the rod was then capped at both ends by a "gib plate," which was often disguised with a decorative element such as a lion's head, an S or X shape, or other design. Opinion among preservationists and engineers differs as to the efficacy of the bolts. Earthquake bolts can be seen all over town, but notable examples are at 235 Meeting Street, 198 East Bay Street, 407 King Street, 51 East Battery (rare star design), and 190 East Bay Street is unusual for having both an X and an S plate on the same building.

Joggling Board: This long (10 15 ft.), flexible plank of cypress, palm, or pine with a handle at each end served various recreational purposes for early Charlestonians depending on their age. As babies, they might be gently bounced to sleep. As small children, they might use it as a trampoline. Later, it was a method of courtship, whereby a couple would start out at opposite ends and bounce up and down until they met in the middle. Painted black or

Charleston Green, joggling boards have made quite a comeback as decorative furnishings at many local homes.

Carolopolis Award: For over 50 years, the Preservation Society of Charleston has handed out these little black badges, to be mounted near the doorway of the winning home, to local homeowners who have renovated historic properties downtown. On the award you'll see "Carolopolis," the Latinized name of the city; "Condita A.D. 1670," the Latin word for founding with the date of Charleston's inception; and another date referring to when the award was given. Don't try counting them; well over 1,000 Carolopolis Awards have been given out since the Preservation Society came up with the idea in 1953.

Ironwork: Before the mid-19th century, wrought iron was a widely used ornament in Charleston, with the oldest surviving ex-amples going back to the Revolutionary War period. Charleston's best-known blacksmith, the late Philip Simmons, made a life's work of continuing the ancient craft of working in wrought iron, and his masterpieces are visible throughout the city, most notably at the Philip Simmons Garden (91 Anson St.), a specially commissioned gate for the Visitors Center (375 Meeting St.), and the Philip Simmons Children's Garden at Josiah Smith Tennent House (corner of Blake and East Bay Sts.). Mass-produced cast iron became more common after the mid-1800s. Chevaux-de-frise, an early security device of sorts, comprises an iron bar on top of a wall, through which project some particularly menacing iron spikes. Chevaux-de-frise became popular after the Denmark Vesey slave revolt conspiracy of 1822. The best existing example is on the perimeter wall of the Miles Brewton House (27 King St).

detail of ironwork at the Philip Simmons Garden

© JIM MOREKIS

throughout, mimicking surfaces from marble to wood to lapis lazuli.

Visitors are often most impressed by the Nathaniel Russell House's magnificent "flying" spiral staircase, a work of such sublime carpentry and engineering that it needs no external support, twisting upwards of its own volition.

When you visit, keep in mind that you're in the epicenter of not only Charleston's historic preservation movement, but perhaps the nation's as well. In 1955, the Nathaniel Russell House was the first major project of the Historic Charleston Foundation, which raised $65,000 to purchase it. Two years later, admission fees from the house would support Historic Charleston's groundbreaking revolving fund for preservation, the prototype for many such successful programs. For an extra $6, you can gain admission to the Aiken-Rhett House farther uptown, also administered by the Historic Charleston Foundation.

Calhoun Mansion

The single largest of Charleston's surviving grand homes, the 1876 Calhoun Mansion (16 Meeting St., 843/722-8205, www.calhoun mansion.net, tours daily 11 A.M.–5 P.M., $15) boasts 35 opulent rooms (with 23 fireplaces!) in a striking Italianate design taking up a whopping 24,000 square feet. The grounds feature some charming garden spaces. Though the interiors at this privately run house are packed with antiques and furnishings, be aware that not all of them are accurate or period.

Miles Brewton House

A short distance from the Nathaniel Russell House but much less viewed by tourists, the circa-1769 Miles Brewton House (27 King St.), now a private residence, is maybe the best example of Georgian-Palladian architecture in the world. The almost medieval wrought-iron fencing, or chevaux-de-frise, was added in 1822 after rumors of a slave uprising spread through town.

This imposing double house was the site of not one but two headquarters of occupying armies, British General Clinton in the Revolution and the federal garrison after the

the Miles Brewton House, host to two occupying army headquarters

end of the Civil War. The great Susan Pringle Frost, principal founder of the Charleston Preservation Society and a Brewton descendant, grew up here.

Heyward-Washington House

The Heyward-Washington House (87 Church St., 843/722-0354, www.charlestonmuseum .org, Mon.–Sat. 10 A.M.–5 P.M., Sun. 1–5 P.M., $10 adults, $5 children, combo tickets to Charleston Museum and Manigault House available) takes the regional practice of naming a historic home for the two most significant names in its pedigree to its logical extreme.

Built in 1772 by the father of Declaration of Independence signer Thomas Heyward Jr., the house also hosted George Washington himself during the president's visit to Charleston in 1791. It's now owned and operated by the Charleston Museum.

The main attraction at the Heyward-Washington House is its masterful woodwork, exemplified by the cabinetry of legendary Charleston carpenter Thomas Elfe. You'll see

his work all over the house from the mantles to a Chippendale chair. Look for his signature of a figure eight with four diamonds.

Cabbage Row

You know these addresses from 89–91 Church Street better as "Catfish Row" of Gershwin's opera *Porgy and Bess* (itself based on the book *Porgy* by the great Charleston author DuBose Heyward, who lived at 76 Church St.). Today this complex—which once housed 10 families—next to the Heyward-Washington House is certainly upgraded from years past, but the row still has the humble appeal of the tenement housing it once was, primarily for freed African Americans after the Civil War. The house nearby at 94 Church Street was where John C. Calhoun and others drew up the infamous Nullification Acts that eventually led to the South's secession.

St. Michael's Episcopal Church

The oldest church in South Carolina, St. Michael's Episcopal Church (71 Broad St., 843/723-0603, mass Sun. 8 A.M. and

© JIM MOREKIS

view of St. Michael's Episcopal Church from the Mills House Hotel

THE GREAT CHARLESTON EARTHQUAKE

The Charleston peninsula is bordered by three faults, almost like a picture frame: the Woodstock Fault above North Charleston, the Charleston Fault running along the east bank of the Cooper River, and the Ashley Fault to the west of the Ashley River. On August 31, 1886, one of them buckled, causing one of the most damaging earthquakes ever to hit the United States.

The earthquake of 1886 was actually signaled by several shocks earlier that week. Residents of the nearby town of Summerville, South Carolina, 20 miles up the Ashley River, felt a small earthquake after midnight on Friday, August 27. Most slept through it. But soon after dawn a larger shock came, complete with a loud bang, causing many to run outside their houses. That Saturday afternoon another tremor hit Summerville, breaking windows and throwing a bed against a wall in one home. Still, Charlestonians remained unconcerned.

Then, that Tuesday at 9:50 P.M. came the big one. With an epicenter somewhere near the Middleton Place plantation, the Charleston earthquake is estimated to have measured about 7 on the Richter scale. Tremors were felt across half the country, with the ground shaking in Chicago

Earthquake bolts are a common sight.

© JIM MOREKIS

10:30 A.M., tours available after services) is actually the second sanctuary on this spot. The first church here was made out of black cypress and called St. Philip's, or "the English Church," which was later rebuilt on Church Street.

Though the designer is not known, we do know that work on this sanctuary in the style of Sir Christopher Wren began in 1752 as a response to the overflowing congregation at the rebuilt St. Philips, and it didn't finish until 1761. Other than a small addition on the southeast corner in 1883, the St. Michael's you see today is virtually unchanged, including the massive pulpit, outsized in the style of the time.

Worship services here over the years hosted such luminaries as Marquis de Lafayette, George Washington, and Robert E. Lee, the latter two of whom are known to have sat in the "governor's pew." Two signers of the U.S.

Constitution, John Rutledge and Charles Cotesworth Pinckney, are buried in the sanctuary.

The 186-foot steeple, painted black during the Revolution in a futile effort to disguise it from British guns, actually sank eight inches after the earthquake of 1886. Inside the tower, the famous "bells of St. Michael's" have an interesting story to tell, having made seven transatlantic voyages for a variety of reasons. They were forged in London's Whitechapel Foundry and sent over in 1764, only to be brought back as a war prize during the Revolution, after which they were returned to the church. Damaged during the Civil War, they were sent back to the foundry of their birth to be recast and returned to Charleston. In 1989 they were damaged by Hurricane Hugo, sent back to Whitechapel yet again, and returned to St.

and a church damaged in Indianapolis. A dam 120 miles away in Aiken, South Carolina, immediately gave way, washing a train right off the tracks. Cracks opened up parallel to the Ashley River, with part of the riverbank falling into the water. Thousands of chimneys all over the state either fell or were rendered useless.

A Charleston minister at his summer home in Asheville, North Carolina, described a noise like the sound of wheels driving straight up the mountain, followed by the sound of many railroad cars going by. A moment later, one corner of his house lifted off the ground and slammed back down again. The quake brought a series of "sand blows," a particularly disturbing phenomenon whereby craters open up and spew sand and water up into the air like a small volcano. In Charleston's case, some of the craters were 20 feet wide, shooting debris another 20 feet into the air.

The whole event lasted less than a minute. In crowded Charleston, the damage was horrific: over 2,000 buildings destroyed, a quarter of the city's value gone, 27 killed immediately and almost 100 more to die from injuries and disease. Because of the large numbers of newly homeless, tent cities sprang up in every available park and greenspace. The American Red Cross's first field mission soon brought some relief, but the scarcity of food, and especially fresh water, made life difficult for everyone.

Almost every surviving building had experienced structural damage, in some cases severe, so a way had to be found to stabilize them. This led to the widespread use of the "earthquake bolt" now seen throughout older Charleston homes. Essentially acting as very long screws with a washer on each end, the idea of the earthquake bolt is simple: Poke a long iron rod through two walls that need stabilizing, and cap the ends. Charleston being Charleston, of course, the end caps were often decorated with a pattern or symbol.

The seismic activity of Charleston's earthquake was so intense that more than 300 aftershocks occurred in the 35 years after the event. In fact, geologists think that most seismic events measured in the region today – including a large event in December 2008, also centering near Summerville – are probably also aftershocks.

Michael's in 1993. Throughout the lifespan of the bells, the clock tower has continued to tell time, though the minute hand wasn't added until 1849.

St. Michael's offers informal, free guided tours to visitors after Sunday worship services; contact the greeter for more information.

Four Corners of Law

No guidebook is complete without a mention of this famous intersection of Broad and Meeting Streets, so named for its confluence of federal law (the Post Office building), state law (the state courthouse), municipal law (City Hall), and God's law (St. Michael's Episcopal Church). That's all well and good, but no matter what the tour guides may tell you, the phrase "Four Corners of Law" was actually popularized by *Ripley's Believe It or Not!*

Still, there's no doubt that this intersection has been key to Charleston from the beginning. Meeting Street was laid out around 1672 and takes its name from the White Meeting House of early Dissenters, i.e., non-Anglicans. Broad Street was also referred to as Cooper Street in the early days. Right in the middle of the street once stood the very first statue in America, a figure of William Pitt erected in 1766.

WATERFRONT

Charleston's waterfront is a place where tourism, history, and industry coexist in a largely seamless fashion. Another of the successful—if at one time controversial—developments spearheaded by Mayor Joe Riley, the centerpiece of the harbor area as far as tourists are concerned is Waterfront Park up toward the High Battery. Farther up the Cooper River is

Aquarium Wharf, where you'll find the South Carolina Aquarium, the American Military Museum, the Fort Sumter Visitor Education Exhibit, and the dock where you take the various harbor ferries, whether to Fort Sumter or just a calming ride on the Cooper River.

The Old Exchange and Provost Dungeon

It's far from glamorous, but nonetheless the Old Exchange and Provost Dungeon (122 E. Bay St., 843/727-2165, www.oldexchange.com, daily 9 A.M.–5 P.M., $7 adults, $3.50 children and students) at the intersection of East Bay and Meeting Streets is brimming with history. It's known as one of the three most historically significant colonial buildings in the United States (Philadelphia's Independence Hall and Boston's Faneuil Hall being the other two). This is actually the old Royal Exchange and Custom House, with the cellar serving as a British prison, all built in 1771 over a portion of the old 1698 fortification wall, some of which you can see today.

Three of Charleston's four signers of the Declaration of Independence did time downstairs for sedition against the crown. Later, happier times were experienced upstairs in the Exchange, as it was here that the state selected its delegates to the Continental Congress and ratified the U.S. Constitution, and it's where George Washington took a spin on the dance floor. Nearly a victim of early 20th-century shortsightedness—it was almost demolished for a gas station in 1913—the building now belongs to the Daughters of the American Revolution.

Fans of kitsch will get a hoot out of the animatronic, "Hall of the Presidents"–style figures. Kids might especially get a scary kick out of the basement dungeon, where the infamous pirate Stede Bonnet was imprisoned in 1718 before being hanged with his crew on the Battery.

Waterfront Park

Dubbing it "this generation's gift to the future," Mayor Joe Riley made this eight-acre

the Old Exchange and Provost Dungeon

© JIM MOREKIS

© JIM MOREKIS

the Pineapple Fountain at Waterfront Park

project another part of his downtown renovation. Situated on Concord Street roughly between Exchange Street and Vendue Range, Waterfront Park (843/724-7327, daily dawn–dusk, free) was, like many waterfront locales in Charleston, built on what used to be marsh and water. This particularly massive chunk of "made land" juts about a football field's length farther out than the old waterline.

Visitors and locals alike enjoy the relaxing vista of Charleston Harbor, often from the many swinging benches arranged in an unusual front-to-back, single-file pattern all down the pier. On the end you can find viewing binoculars to see the various sights out on the Cooper River, chief among them the USS *Yorktown* at Patriot's Point and the big bridge to Mount Pleasant.

Children will enjoy the large "Vendue" wading fountain at the Park's entrance off Vendue Range, while a bit farther south is the large and quite artful Pineapple Fountain with its surrounding wading pool. Contemporary art lovers of all ages will appreciate the nearby

Waterfront Park City Gallery (34 Prioleau St., Mon.–Fri. noon–5 P.M., free).

South Carolina Aquarium

Honestly, if you've been to the more expansive aquariums in Monterey or Boston, you might be disappointed at the breadth of offerings at the South Carolina Aquarium (100 Aquarium Wharf, 843/720-1990, www.scaquarium.org, March–Aug. daily 9 A.M.–5 P.M., Sept.–Feb. daily 9 A.M.–4 P.M., $17.95 adults, $10.95 kids, combo tickets with Fort Sumter tour available). But nonetheless, it's clean and well done and is a great place for the whole family to have some fun while educating themselves on the rich aquatic life not only off the coast, but throughout this small but ecologically diverse state.

When you enter you're greeted with the 15,000-gallon Carolina Seas tank, with placid nurse sharks and vicious-looking moray eels. Other exhibits highlight the five key South Carolina ecosystems: beach, salt marsh, coastal plain, piedmont, and mountain forest. Another neat display is the Touch Tank, a hands-on collection of invertebrates found along the coast, such as sea urchins and horseshoe crabs. The pièce de résistance, however, is certainly the three-story Great Ocean Tank with literally hundreds of deeper-water marine creatures, including sharks, pufferfish, and sea turtles.

Speaking of sea turtles: A key part of the Aquarium's research and outreach efforts is the Turtle Hospital, which attempts to rehabilitate and save sick and injured specimens. The hospital has so far saved 20 sea turtles, the first one being a 270-pound female affectionately known as "Edisto Mama."

Keep in mind that on weekdays during the school year the place is often chockablock with local schoolchildren on field trips. Also note that you might run across some information about an IMAX movie theater near the Aquarium when researching your trip. No matter what you read or hear elsewhere, this IMAX location is now closed.

American Military Museum

Slightly out of place thematically with the

MARY CHESNUT'S DIARY

I have always kept a journal after a fashion of my own, with dates and a line of poetry or prose, mere quotations, which I understood and no one else, and I have kept letters and extracts from the papers. From today forward I will tell the story in my own way.

— Mary Boykin Chesnut

She was born in the middle of the state. But Mary Boykin Chesnut's seminal Civil War diary — originally titled *A Diary From Dixie* and first published in 1905 — provides one of the most extraordinary eyewitness accounts of antebellum life in Charleston you'll ever read.

By turns wise and witty, fiery and flirtatious, Chesnut's writing is a gripping, politically savvy, and dryly humorous chronicle of a life lived close to the innermost circles of Confederate decision-makers. Her husband, James Chesnut Jr., was a U.S. Senator until South Carolina seceded from the Union, whereupon he became a key aide to Confederate President Jefferson Davis and a general in the Confederate Army.

The diary spans from February 1861 — three months before the firing on Fort Sumter, which she witnessed — to August 1865, after the Confederate surrender. In between, the diary shifts to and from various locales, including Montgomery, Alabama; Richmond, Virginia; Columbia, South Carolina; and of course Charleston. A sample excerpt is typical of her high regard for the Holy City:

On the Battery with the Rutledges, Captain Hartstein was introduced to me. He has done some heroic things — brought home some ships and is a man of mark. Afterward he sent me a beautiful bouquet, not half so beautiful, however, as Mr. Robert Gourdin's, which already occupied the place of honor on my center table. What a dear, delightful place is Charleston!

Chesnut was a Southern patriot, and as you might imagine some of her observations are wildly politically incorrect by today's standards. But while supportive of slavery and suspicious of the motives of abolitionists — "People in those places expect more virtue from a plantation African than they can insure in practise among themselves with all their own high moral surroundings," she says of white Northern abolitionists — she does allow for a few nuanced looks at the lives of African Americans in the South, as in this observation about her own house servants after the fall of Fort Sumter:

You could not tell that they even heard the awful roar going on in the bay, though it has been dinning in their ears night and day. People talk before them as if they were chairs and tables. They make no sign. Are they stolidly stupid? or wiser than we are; silent and strong, biding their time?

While the diary begins on a confident note regarding the South's chances in the war, as the news from the battlefield gets worse we see how Southerners cope with the sure knowledge that they will lose:

I know how it feels to die. I have felt it again and again. For instance, some one calls out, "Albert Sidney Johnston is killed." My heart stands still. I feel no more. I am, for so many seconds, so many minutes, I know not how long, utterly without sensation of any kind — dead; and then, there is that great throb, that keen agony of physical pain, and the works are wound up again. The ticking of the clock begins, and I take up the burden of life once more.

Southern historian C. Vann Woodward compiled an annotated edition of the Chesnut diary in 1981, *Mary Chesnut's Civil War*, which won a Pulitzer Prize the following year. Her words came to even wider national exposure due to extensive quotations from her diary in Ken Burns' PBS miniseries *The Civil War*.

Aquarium, the American Military Museum (360 Concord St., 843/577-7000, www.americanmilitarymuseum.org, Mon.–Sat. 10 A.M.–6 P.M., Sun. 1–5 P.M., $7 adults, $3 students) is one of those under-the-radar types of small, quaint museums that can be unexpectedly enriching. Certainly its location near the embarkation point for the Fort Sumter ferry hasn't hurt its profile. It's heavy on uniforms, with a wide range all the way from the Revolution to the modern day. My favorite is the 1907 naval uniform from the cruiser USS *Charleston,* part of Teddy Roosevelt's Great White Fleet. There's also a good collection of rare military miniatures.

【 Fort Sumter

This is it: the place that brought about the beginning of the Civil War, a Troy for modern times. Though many historians insist the war would have happened regardless of President Lincoln's decision to keep Fort Sumter (843/883-3123, www.nps.gov/fosu, hours seasonal) in federal hands, nonetheless the stated *causus belli* was Major Robert Anderson's refusal to surrender the fort when requested to do so in the early morning hours of April 12, 1861.

A few hours later came the first shot of the war, fired from Fort Johnson by Confederate Captain George James. That 10-inch mortar shell, a signal for the general bombardment to begin, exploded above Fort Sumter, and nothing in Charleston, or the South, or America, would ever be the same again.

Notorious secessionist Edmund Ruffin gets credit for firing the first shot in anger, only moments after James's signal shell, from a battery at Cummings Point. Ruffin's 64-pound projectile scored a direct hit, smashing into the fort's southwest corner.

The first return shot from Fort Sumter was fired by none other than Captain Abner Doubleday, the father of baseball. The first death of the Civil War also happened at Fort Sumter, not from the Confederate bombardment but on the day after. U.S. Army Private Daniel Hough died when the cannon he was

loading, to be fired as part of a 100-gun surrender salute to the Stars and Stripes, exploded prematurely.

Today the battered but still-standing Fort Sumter remains astride the entrance to Charleston Harbor on a man-made, 70,000-ton sandbar. Sumter was part of the so-called Third System of fortifications ordered after the War of 1812. Interestingly, the fort was still not quite finished when the Confederate guns opened up on it 50 years later, and never enjoyed its intended full complement of 135 big guns.

As you might expect, you can only visit by boat, specifically the approved concessionaire **Fort Sumter Tours** (843/881-7337, www.fortsumtertours.com, $16 adults, $10 ages 6–11, $14.50 seniors). Once at the fort, there's no charge for admission. Ferries leave from Liberty Square at Aquarium Wharf on the peninsula three times a day during the high season; call or check the website for times. Make sure to arrive about a half-hour before the ferry departs. You can also get to Fort Sumter by ferry from Patriot's Point at Mount Pleasant through the same company.

Budget at least 2.5 hours for the whole trip, including an hour at Fort Sumter. At Liberty Square on the peninsula is the **Fort Sumter Visitor Education Center** (340 Concord St., daily 8:30 A.M.–5 P.M., free), so you can learn more about where you're about to go. Once there, you can be enlightened by the regular ranger's talks on the fort's history and construction (generally at 11 A.M. and 2:30 P.M.), take in the interpretive exhibits throughout the site, and enjoy the view of the spires of the Holy City from afar.

For many, though, the highlight is the boat trip itself, with beautiful views of Charleston Harbor and the islands of the Cooper River estuary. If you want to skip Sumter, you can still take an enjoyable 90-minute ferry ride around the harbor and past the fort on the affiliated **Spiritline Cruises** (800/789-3678, www.spiritlinecruises.com, $16 adults, $10 ages 6–11).

Some visitors are disappointed to find many of the fort's gun embrasures bricked over. This was done during the Spanish-American War, when the old fort was turned into an earthwork and the newer Battery Huger (pronounced "Huge-E") was built on top of it.

FRENCH QUARTER

Unlike the New Orleans version, Charleston's French Quarter is Protestant in origin and flavor. Though not actually given the name until a preservation effort in the 1970s, historically this area was indeed the main place of commerce for the city's population of French Huguenots, primarily a merchant class who fled religious persecution in their native country.

Today the five-block area—roughly bounded by East Bay, Market Street, Meeting Street, and Broad Street—contains some of Charleston's most historic buildings, its most evocative old churches and graveyards, its most charming, narrow streets, and its most tasteful art galleries.

◖ St. Philip's Episcopal Church

With a pedigree dating back to the colony's fledgling years, St. Philip's Episcopal Church (142 Church St., 843/722-7734, www.stphilipschurchsc.org, sanctuary open weekdays 10 A.M.–noon and 2–4 P.M., mass Sun. 8:15 A.M.) is the oldest Anglican congregation south of Virginia. That pedigree gets a little complicated and downright tragic at times, but any connoisseur of Charleston history needs to be clear on the fine points:

The first St. Philip's was built in 1680 at the corner of Meeting Street and Broad Street, the present site of St. Michael's Episcopal Church. That first St. Philip's was badly damaged by a hurricane in 1710, and the city fathers approved the building of a new sanctuary dedicated to the saint on Church Street. However, that building was nearly destroyed by yet another hurricane during construction. Fighting with local Native Americans further delayed rebuilding in 1721.

Alas, that St. Philip's burned to the ground in 1835—a distressingly common fate for so many old buildings in this area. Construction

St. Philip's Episcopal Church

© JIM MOREKIS

immediately began on a replacement, and it's that building you see today. Heavily damaged by Hurricane Hugo in 1989, a $4.5-million renovation kept the church usable.

So to recap: St. Philip's was originally on the site of the present St. Michael's. And while St. Philip's is the oldest congregation in South Carolina, St. Michael's has the oldest physical church building in the state. Are we clear?

South Carolina's great statesman John C. Calhoun—who ironically despised Charlestonians for what he saw as their loose morals—was originally buried across Church Street in the former "stranger's churchyard," or West Cemetery, after his death in 1850. (Charles Pinckney and Edward Rutledge are two other notable South Carolinians buried there.) But near the end of the Civil War, Calhoun's body was moved to an unmarked grave closer to the sanctuary in an attempt to hide its location from Union troops, who it was feared would go out of their way to wreak vengeance on the tomb of one of slavery's staunchest advocates and the man who invented the doctrine of nullification. In 1880, with Reconstruction in full swing, the state legislature directed and funded the building of the current large memorial in the West Cemetery.

French Huguenot Church

One of the oldest congregations in town, the French Huguenot Church (44 Queen St., 843/722-4385, www.frenchhuguenotchurch .org, liturgy Sun. 10:30 A.M.) also has the distinction of being the only remaining independent Huguenot Church in the country. Founded around 1681 by French Calvinists, the church had about 450 congregants by 1700. While refugees from religious persecution, they weren't destitute, as they had to pay for their passage to America.

As is the case with so many historic churches in the area, the building you see isn't the original sanctuary. The first church was built on this site in 1687, and became known as the "Church of Tides" because at that time the

FRENCH HUGUENOTS

A visitor can't spend a few hours in Charleston without coming across the many French-sounding names so prevalent in the region. Some are common surnames, such as Ravenel, Manigault (pronounced "MAN-i-go"), Gaillard, Laurens, or Huger (pronounced "Huge-E"). Some are street or place names, such as Mazyck or Legare (pronounced "Legree").

Unlike the predominantly French Catholic presence in Louisiana and coastal Alabama, the Gallic influence in Charleston was strictly of the Calvinist Protestant variety. Known as Huguenots, these French immigrants – refugees of an increasingly intolerant Catholic regime in their mother country – were numerous enough in the settlement by the 1690s that they were granted full citizenship and property rights if they swore allegiance to the British crown.

The Huguenot's quick rise in Charleston was due to two factors. Unlike other colonies, Carolina never put much of a premium on religious conformity, a trait that exists to this day despite the area's overall conservatism. And unlike many who fled European monarchies to come to the New World, the French Huguenots were far from poverty-stricken. Most had to buy their own journeys across the Atlantic and arrived already well educated and skilled in one or more useful trades. In Charleston's early days, they were mostly wheat and barley farmers or tarburners. In later times their pragmatism and work ethic would lead them

to higher positions in local society, such as lawyers, judges, and politicians.

One of the wealthiest Charlestonians of all, the merchant Gabriel Manigault, was by some accounts the richest person in America during the early 1700s. South Carolina's most famous French Huguenot of all was Francis Marion, the "Swamp Fox" of Revolutionary War fame. Born on the Santee River, Marion grew up in George-town and is now interred near Moncks Corner.

During that century a number of charitable aid organizations sprang up to serve various local groups, mostly along ethno-religious lines. The most wealthy and influential of them all was the South Carolina Society, founded in 1737 and first called "The Two Bit Club" because of the original weekly dues. The Society still meets today at its building at 72 Meeting Street, designed in 1804 by none other than Manigault's grandson, also named Gabriel, who was Charleston's most celebrated amateur architect. Another aid organization, the **Huguenot Society of Carolina** (138 Logan St., 843/723-3235, www.huguenot-society.org, Mon.-Fri. 9 A.M.-2 P.M.), was established in 1885. Their library is a great research tool for anyone interested in French Protestant history and genealogy.

To this day, the spiritual home of Charleston's Huguenots is the same one as always: the French Huguenot Church on Church Street, one of the earliest congregations in the city. Though many of the old ways have gone, the church still holds one liturgy a year (in April) in French.

the French Huguenot Church

Cooper River lapped at its property line. This sanctuary was deliberately destroyed as a firebreak during the great conflagration of 1796.

The church was replaced in 1800, but that building was in turn demolished in favor of the picturesque, stucco-coated Gothic Revival sanctuary you see today, which was completed in 1845 and subsequently survived Union shelling and the 1886 earthquake.

Does the church look kind of Dutch to you? There's a good reason for that. In their diaspora, French Huguenots spent a lot of time in Holland and became influenced by the tidy sensibilities of the Dutch people.

The history of the circa-1845 organ is interesting as well. A rare "tracker" organ, so named for its ultra-fast linkage between the keys and the pipe valves, it was built by famed organ builder Henry Erben. After the fall of Charleston in 1865, Union troops had begun dismantling the instrument for shipment to New York when the church organist, T. P. O'Neale, successfully pleaded with them to let it stay.

Sunday services are conducted in English now, but a single annual service in French is still celebrated in April. The unique Huguenot Cross of Languedoc, which you'll occasionally see ornamenting the church, is essentially a Maltese Cross, its eight points representing the eight beatitudes. Between the four arms of the cross are four fleurs-de-lis, the age-old French symbol of purity.

Dock Street Theatre

Fresh off an extensive multiyear renovation project, the Dock Street Theatre (135 Church St., 843/720-3968), right down the street from the Huguenot Church, is where any thespian or lover of the stage must pay homage to this incarnation of the very first theater ever built in the Western Hemisphere.

In a distressingly familiar Charleston story, the original 1736 Dock Street Theatre burned down. A second theater opened on the same site in 1754. That building was in turn demolished for a grander edifice in 1773, which, you guessed it, also burned down.

The current building dates from 1809, when the Planter's Hotel was built near the site of the original Dock Street Theatre. To mark the

Dock Street Theatre

theater's centennial, the hotel added a stage facility in 1835, and it's that building you see today.

For the theater's second centennial, the Works Progress Administration completely refurbished Dock Street back into a working theater in time to distract Charlestonians from the pains of the Great Depression. In addition to a very active and well-regarded annual season from the resident Charleston Stage Company, the 464-seat venue has hosted umpteen events of the Spoleto Festival over the past three decades and since its renovation continues to do so.

Old Powder Magazine

The Old Powder Magazine (79 Cumberland St., 843/722-9350, www.powdermag.org, Wed.–Sat. 10 a.m.–4 p.m., $2 adults, $1 children) may be small, but the building is quite historically significant. The 1713 edifice is the oldest public building in South Carolina and also the only one remaining of the days of the Lords Proprietors.

As the name indicates, this was where the city's gunpowder was stored during the Revolution. The magazine is designed to implode rather than explode in the event of a direct hit.

This is another labor of love of the Historic Charleston Foundation, which has leased the building—which from a distance looks curiously like an ancient Byzantine church—from The Colonial Dames since 1993. It was opened to the public as an attraction in 1997. Now directly across the street from a huge parking garage, the site has continuing funding issues, so occasionally the hours for tours can be erratic.

Inside you'll see displays, a section of the original brick, and an exposed earthquake rod. Right next door is the privately owned, circa-1709 **Trott's Cottage,** the first brick dwelling in Charleston.

Old Slave Mart Museum

Slave auctions became a big business in the South after 1808, when the United States banned importation of slaves, thus increasing both price and demand. The auctions, with slaves forced to stand on display on long tables, generally took place in public buildings where everyone could watch the wrenching spectacle of families being torn apart and lives ruined.

But in the 1850s, public auctions in

the Old Slave Mart Museum

Charleston were put to a stop when city leaders discovered that visitors from European nations—all of which had banned slavery outright years before—were horrified at the practice. So the slave trade was moved indoors to "marts" near the Cooper River waterfront where the sales could be conducted out of the public eye.

The last remaining such structure is the Old Slave Mart Museum (6 Chalmers St., 843/958-6467, www.charlestoncity.info, Mon.–Sat. 9 A.M.–5 P.M., $7 adults, $5 children, 5 and under free). Built in 1859, and originally known as Ryan's Mart after the builder, it was only in service a short time before the outbreak of the Civil War. The last auction was held in November 1863.

After the war, the Slave Mart became a tenement, and then in 1938 an African American history museum. The city of Charleston acquired the building in the 1980s and reopened it as a museum in late 2007.

There are two main areas: the orientation area, where visitors learn about the transatlantic slave trade and the architectural history of the building itself; and the main exhibit area,

where visitors can see documents, tools, and displays re-creating what happened inside during this sordid chapter in local history and celebrating the resilience of the area's African American community.

NORTH OF BROAD

This tourist-heavy part of town is sometimes called the Market area because of its proximity to the Old City Market. We'll start east at the border of the French Quarter on Meeting Street and work our way west and north toward Francis Marion Square.

Circular Congregational Church

The historic Circular Congregational Church (150 Meeting St., 843/577-6400, www.circular church.org, service Sun. 11 A.M., 10:15 A.M. during summer, tours Mon.–Fri. at 10:30 A.M.) has one of the most interesting pedigrees of any house of worship in Charleston, which is saying a lot. Originally held on the site of the "White Meeting House," for which Meeting Street is named, services were held here beginning in 1681 for a polyglot mix of Congregationalists,

Circular Congregational Church

THE NEW CHARLESTON GREEN

Most people know "Charleston Green" as a unique local color, the result of adding a few drops of yellow to post–Civil War surplus black paint. But these days the phrase might refer to all the environmentally friendly development in Charleston, which you might find surprising considering the city's location in one of the most conservative states in the country's most conservative region.

The most obvious example is the ambitious Navy Yard redevelopment, which seeks to re-purpose the closed-down facility. That project is part of a larger civic vision to re-imagine the entire 3,000-acre historic Noisette community of North Charleston, with an accompanying wetlands protection conservancy.

From its inception in 1902 at the command of President Theodore Roosevelt through the end of the Cold War, the Charleston Navy Yard was one of the city's biggest employers. Closed down in 1995 as part of a national base realignment plan, locals feared the worst. But a 340-acre section, the **Navy Yard at Noisette** (www.navyyardsc.com), now hosts an intriguing mix of green-friendly design firms, small nonprofits, and commercial maritime companies. The activity centers on the restoration of three huge former naval warehouses at 7, 10, and 11 Storehouse Row. Nearby, on the way to where the CSS *Hunley* is currently being restored, is the big Powerhouse, once the electrical station for the whole yard and now envisioned as the center of a future entertainment/retail district.

In the meantime, the Navy Yard's no-frills retro look is so realistic that it has played host to scenes of the Lifetime TV series *Army Wives*.

But the largest Navy Yard development is still to come. Clemson University – with the help of a massive federal grant, largest in the school's history – will oversee one of the world's largest wind turbine research facilities, to be built in Building 69. The project is expected to create hundreds of local jobs.

Also in North Charleston, local retail chain Half Moon Outfitters recently completed a green-friendly warehouse facility in an old Piggly Wiggly grocery store. The first LEED (Leadership in Energy and Environmental Design)

Platinum certified building in South Carolina, the warehouse features solar panels, rainwater reservoirs, and locally harvested or salvaged interiors. There's also the LEED-certified North Charleston Elementary School, as well as North Charleston's adoption of a "Night Skies" ordinance to cut down on light pollution.

But North Charleston's far from the only place in town going green. On the peninsula, the historic meeting house of the Circular Congregation Church, which gave Meeting Street its name, has a green addition with geothermal heating and cooling, rainwater cisterns, and Charleston's first vegetative roof.

In addition to walking the historic byways of the Old Village of Mount Pleasant, architecture and design buffs might also want to check out the new 243-acre I'On (www.ionvillage.com) "neotraditional" planned community, a successful model for this type of pedestrian-friendly, New Urbanist development.

On adjacent Daniel Island, the developers of that island's 4,000 acre planned residential community recently were certified as an "Audubon Cooperative Sanctuary" for using wildlife-friendly techniques on its golf and recreational grounds.

Even ultra-upscale Kiawah Island has gone green in something other than golf – the fabled Kiawah bobcats are making a comeback, thanks to the efforts of the Kiawah Conservancy.

Why has Charleston proven so adept at moving forward? Locals chalk it up to two things: affluent, well-connected Charlestonians who want to maintain the area's quality of life, and the forward-thinking leadership of Mayor Joe Riley in Charleston and Mayor Keith Summey in North Charleston.

For many Charlestonians, however, the green movement manifests in simpler things: the pedestrian and bike lanes on the new Ravenel Bridge over the Cooper River, the thriving city recycling program, or the Sustainable Seafood Initiative, a partnership of local restaurants, universities, and conservation groups that brings only the freshest, most environmentally responsible dishes to your table when you dine out in Charleston.

Presbyterians, and Huguenots. For that reason it was often called the Church of Dissenters ("Dissenters" being the common term at the time for anyone not an Anglican).

As with many structures in town, the 1886 earthquake necessitated a rebuilding, and the current edifice dates from 1891. Ironically, in this municipality called "the Holy City" for its many high spires, the Circular Church has no steeple, and instead stays low to the ground in an almost medieval fashion.

Look for the adjacent meeting house, which gave the street its name; a green-friendly addition houses the congregation's Christian outreach and has geothermal heating and cooling and boasts Charleston's only vegetative roof.

Gibbes Museum of Art

The Gibbes Museum of Art (135 Meeting St., 843/722-2706, www.gibbesmuseum.org, Tues.–Sat. 10 A.M.–5 P.M., Sun. 1–5 P.M., $9 adults, $7 students, $5 ages 6–12) is one of those rare Southern museums that manages a good blend of the modern and the traditional, the local and the international.

Beginning in 1905 as the Gibbes Art Gallery—the final wish of James Shoolbred Gibbes, who willed $100,000 for its construction—the complex has grown through the years in size and influence. The key addition to the original Beaux Arts building came in 1978 with the addition of the modern wing in the rear, which effectively doubled the museum's display space. Shortly thereafter the permanent collection and temporary exhibit space was also expanded. Serendipitously, these renovations enabled the Gibbes to become the key visual arts venue for the Spoleto Festival, begun about the same time.

The influential Gibbes Art School in the early 20th century formed a close association with the Woodstock School in New York, bringing important ties and prestige to the fledgling institution. Georgia O'Keefe, who taught college for a time in Columbia, South Carolina, brought an exhibit here in 1955. The first solo show by an African American artist came here in 1974 with an exhibit of the work of William H. Johnson.

© JIM MOREKIS

Gibbes Museum of Art

Don't miss the nice little garden and its centerpiece, the 1972 fountain and sculpture of Persephone by Marshall Fredericks.

Unitarian Church

In a town filled with cool old church cemeteries, the coolest belongs to the Unitarian Church (4 Archdale St., 843/723-4617, www.charleston uu.org, service Sun. 11 A.M., free tours Fri.–Sat. 10 A.M.–1 P.M.) As a nod to the beauty and power of nature, vegetation and shrubbery in the cemetery have been allowed to take their natural course (walkways excepted).

Virginia creeper wraps around 200-year-old grave markers, honeybees feed on wildflowers, and tree roots threaten to engulf entire headstones. The whole effect is oddly relaxing, and one of my favorite places in Charleston.

The church itself—the second-oldest such edifice in Charleston and the oldest Unitarian sanctuary in the South—is pretty nice, too. Begun in 1776 because of overcrowding at the Circular Congregational Church, the brand-new building saw rough usage by British troops during the Revolution. In 1787 the church was repaired, though it was not officially chartered as a Unitarian church until 1839.

An extensive modernization happened in 1852, during which the current English Perpendicular Gothic Revival walls were installed, along with the beautiful stained-glass windows. The church was spared in the fire of 1861, which destroyed the old Circular Church itself but stopped at the Unitarian Church's property line. Sadly, it was not so lucky during the 1886 earthquake, which toppled the original tower. The version you see today is a subsequent and less grand design.

Directly next door is **St. John's Lutheran Church** (5 Clifford St., 843/723-2426, www .stjohncharleston.org, worship Sun. 8:30 and 11 A.M.), which had its origin in 1742 when Dr. Henry Melchior Muhlenberg stopped in town for a couple of days on his way to minister to the burgeoning Salzburger colony in Ebenezer, Georgia. He would later be known as the father of the Lutheran Church in America. To see the sanctuary at times other than Sunday mornings, go by the office next door Monday–Friday 9 A.M.–2 P.M. and they'll let you take a walk through the interior.

Old City Market

Part kitschy tourist trap, part glimpse into the old South, part community gathering place, Old City Market (Meeting and Market Sts., 843/973-7236, daily 6 A.M.–11:30 P.M.) remains Charleston's most reliable, if perhaps least flashy, attraction. It is certainly the practical center of the city's tourist trade, not least because so many tours originate nearby.

Originally built on Daniel's Creek—claimed from the marsh in the early 1800s after the city's first marketplace at Broad and Meeting Streets burned in 1796—one of City Market's early features was a colony of vultures who hung around for scraps of meat from the many butcher stalls. Sensing that the carrion eaters would keep the area cleaner than any human could, city officials not only allowed the buzzards to hang around, they were protected by

law, becoming known as "Charleston eagles" in tongue-in-cheek local jargon.

No matter what anyone tries to tell you, Charleston's City Market never hosted a single slave auction. Indeed, when the Pinckney family donated this land to the city for a "Publick Market," one stipulation was that no slaves were *ever* to be sold here—or else the property would immediately revert to the family's descendants. And judging by the prevalence of the Pinckney name in these parts to this day, there has never been a shortage of potential claimants should that stipulation have been violated.

And also no matter what anyone tells you, the old train tracks around this area weren't for trolleys. During World War II, a railroad ran from port facilities up the peninsula to warehouses down here.

Confederate Museum

Located on the second floor of City Market's main, iconic building, Market Hall on Meeting Street, the small but spirited Confederate Museum (188 Meeting St., 843/723-1541, Tues.–Sat. 11 A.M.–3:30 P.M., $5 adults, $3 children, cash only) hosts an interesting collection of Civil War memorabilia, with an emphasis on the military side, and is also the local headquarters of the United Daughters of the Confederacy. Perhaps its best contribution, however, is its research library.

William Rhett House

The oldest standing residence in Charleston is the circa-1713 William Rhett House (54 Hasell St.), which once belonged to the colonel who captured Stede Bonnet the pirate. It's now a private residence, but you can admire this excellent prototypical example of a Charleston single house easily from the street and read nearby historical marker.

St. Mary of the Annunciation Church

The oldest Roman Catholic church in the Carolinas and Georgia, St. Mary of the Annunciation (89 Hasell St., 843/722-7696, www.catholic-doc.org/saintmarys) traces its roots to 1789, when the Irish priest Father Matthew Ryan was sent to begin the first Catholic parish in the colony.

The original church was destroyed in the great Charleston fire of 1838, and the present sanctuary dates from immediately thereafter. While it did receive a direct hit from a Union shell during the siege of Charleston in the Civil War—taking out the organ—the handsome Greek Revival edifice has survived the 1886 earthquake, the great hurricane of 1893, and Hurricane Hugo in fine form.

You can tour the interior most weekdays from 9:30 A.M.–3:30 P.M. Sunday mass is at 9:30 A.M.

Kahal Kadosh Beth Elohim Reform Temple

The birthplace of Reform Judaism in the United States and the oldest continuously active synagogue in the nation is Kahal Kadosh Beth Elohim Reform Temple (90 Hasell St., 843/723-1090, www.kkbe.org, service Sat. 11 A.M., tours Mon.–Fri. 10 A.M.–noon, Sun. 10 A.M.–4 P.M.). The congregation—Kahal Kadosh means "holy community" in Hebrew—was founded in 1749, with the current temple dating from 1840 and built in the Greek Revival style so popular at the time.

The church's Reform roots came about indirectly because of the great fire of 1838. In rebuilding, some congregants wanted to introduce musical instruments into the temple—previously a no-no—in the form of an organ. The Orthodox contingent lost the debate, and so the new building became the first home of Reform Judaism in the country, a fitting testament to Charleston's longstanding ecumenical spirit of religious tolerance and inclusiveness.

Technically speaking, because the Holocaust destroyed all Reform temples in Europe, this is actually the oldest existing Reform synagogue in the world.

UPPER KING AREA

For many visitors, the area around King Street north of Calhoun Street is the most happening area of Charleston, and not only because its proximity to the Visitors Center makes it the first part of town many see up close. On some days—Saturdays when the Farmers Market is open, for instance—this bustling, active area of town seems a galaxy away from the quiet grace of the older South of Broad area.

Its closeness to the beautiful College of Charleston campus means there's never a shortage of young people around to patronize the area's restaurants and bars and to add a youthful feel. And its closeness to the city's main shopping district, King Street, means there's never a shortage of happy shoppers toting bags of new merchandise.

Marion Square

While The Citadel moved lock, stock, and barrel almost a century ago, the college's old home, the South Carolina State Arsenal, still overlooks Francis Marion Square, a reminder of the former glory days when this was the institute's parade ground, the "Citadel Green" (the old Citadel is now a hotel). Interestingly, Marion Square (btwn. King and Meeting Sts. at Calhoun St., 843/965-4104) can still be used as a parade ground, under agreement with the Washington Light Infantry and the Sumter Guard, which lease the square to the city.

Seemingly refusing to give up on tradition—or perhaps just attracted by the many female College of Charleston students—uniformed cadets from The Citadel are still chockablock in Marion Square on any given weekend, a bit of local flavor that reminds you that you're definitely in Charleston.

Six-and-a-half-acre Marion Square is named for the "Swamp Fox" himself, Revolutionary War hero and father of modern guerrilla warfare Francis Marion, for whom the hotel at the square's southwest corner is also named. The newest feature of Marion Square is the Holocaust Memorial on Calhoun Street.

However, the dominant monument is the towering memorial to John C. Calhoun. Its 1858 cornerstone includes one of the more interesting time capsules you'll encounter: $100 in Continental money, a lock of John Calhoun's hair, and a cannonball from the Fort Moultrie battle.

Marion Square hosts many events, including the Farmers Market every Saturday from mid-April to late December, the Food and Wine Festival, and of course some Spoleto events.

College of Charleston

The oldest college in South Carolina and the first municipal college in America, the College of Charleston (66 George St., 843/805-5507, www.cofc.edu) boasts a fair share of history in addition to the way its 12,000-plus students bring a modern, youthful touch to so much of the city's public activities. While its services are no longer free, despite its historic moniker the College is now a full-blown, state-supported university in its own right.

Though the College has its share of modernistic buildings, a stroll around the campus will uncover some historic gems. The oldest building on this gorgeous campus, the Bishop Robert Smith House, dates from the year of the College's founding in 1770 and is now the president's house. Find it on Glebe Street between Wentworth and George.

The large Greek Revival building dominating the College's old quad off George and St. Philip's Streets is the magnificent Randolph Hall (1828), the oldest functioning college classroom in the country and now host to the president's office. The huge circular feature directly in front of it is "The Cistern," a historic reservoir that's a popular place for students to sit in the grass and enjoy the sun filtering through the live oaks.

The cistern is also where then-candidate Barack Obama spoke at a rally in January 2008. Movies that have shot scenes on campus include *Cold Mountain, The Patriot,* and *The Notebook.*

If you have an iPhone or iPod Touch, you can download a neat self-guided tour, complete with video, from the Apple iTunes App Store at www.apple.com.

The College's main claims to academic fame are its outstanding Art History and Marine Biology departments and its performing arts program. The **Halsey Institute of Contemporary Art** (54 St. Philip St.,

843/953-5680, www.halsey.cofc.edu, Mon.-Sat. 11 A.M.–4 P.M.) focuses on modern visual art and also offers film screenings and lectures. The groundbreaking **Avery Research Center for African American History and Culture** (843/953-7609, www.cofc.edu/avery, Mon.–Fri. 10 A.M.–5 P.M., Sat. noon–5 P.M.) features rotating exhibits from its permanent archive collection.

Charleston Museum

During its long history, it's moved literally all over town. It's currently housed in a noticeably modern building, but make no mistake: The Charleston Museum (360 Meeting St., 843/722-2996, www.charlestonmuseum.org, Mon.–Sat. 9 A.M.–5 P.M., Sun. 1–5 P.M., $10 adults, $5 children, combo tickets to Heyward-Washington and/or Manigault Houses available) is the nation's oldest museum, founded in 1773. It strives to stay as fresh and relevant as any new museum, with a rotating schedule of special exhibits in addition to its very eclectic permanent collection.

For a long time this was the only place to get a glimpse of the CSS *Hunley,* albeit just a fanciful replica in front of the main entrance. (Now you can see the real thing at its conservation site in North Charleston, and it's even smaller than the replica would indicate.)

Much of the Charleston Museum's collection focuses on aspects of everyday life of Charlestonians from aristocracy to slaves, like utensils, clothing, and furniture. There are quirks as well, such as the Egyptian mummy and the fine lady's fan made out of turkey feathers. A particular and possibly surprising specialty includes work and research by noted regional naturalists like John James Audubon, André Michaux, and Mark Catesby. There are also numerous exhibits chronicling the local history of Native Americans and African Americans. There's something for children too, in the hands-on, interactive "Kidstory."

The location is particularly convenient, being close not only to the excellent Charleston Visitors Center and its equally excellent parking garage, but to the Joseph Manigault House (which the Museum runs), the Children's Museum of the Lowcountry, and the Gibbes Museum of Art.

Joseph Manigault House

Owned and operated by the nearby Charleston Museum, the Joseph Manigault House (350 Meeting St., 843/723-2926, www.charleston museum.org, Mon.–Sat. 10 A.M.–5 P.M., Sun., 1–5 P.M., last tour 4:30 P.M., $10 adults, $5 children, combo tickets to Charleston Museum and/or Heyward-Washington House available) is sometimes called the "Huguenot House." Its splendor is a good reminder of the fact that the French Protestants were far from poverty-stricken, unlike so many groups who came to America fleeing persecution.

This circa-1803 National Historic Landmark was designed by wealthy merchant and investor Gabriel Manigault for his brother, Joseph, a rice planter of local repute and fortune. (Gabriel, quite the crackerjack dilettante architect, also designed Charleston City Hall.) The three-story brick townhouse is a great example of Adams, or Federal, architecture.

The furnishings are top-notch examples of 19th-century handiwork, and the rooms have been restored as accurately as possible, down to the historically correct paint colors. The foundations of various outbuildings, including a privy and slaves' quarters, are clustered around the picturesque little Gate Temple to the rear of the main house in the large enclosed garden.

Each December, the Manigault House offers visitors a special treat, as the Garden Club of Charleston decorates it in period seasonal fashion, using only flowers that would have been used in the 19th century.

(Aiken-Rhett House

One of my favorite spots in all of Charleston and a comparatively recent acquisition of the Historic Charleston Foundation, the poignant Aiken-Rhett House (48 Elizabeth St., 843/723-1159, www.historiccharleston.org, Mon.–Sat. 10 A.M.–5 P.M., Sun 2–5 P.M., last tour 4:15 P.M., $10 adults, $5 children) shows another side of that organization's mission. Whereas the Historic Charleston–run Nathaniel Russell

part of the Aiken-Rhett House

House seeks to recreate a specific point in time, work at the Aiken-Rhett House emphasizes conservation and research.

Built in 1818 and expanded by South Carolina Governor William Aiken Jr., after whom we know the house today, parts of this huge, rambling, almost Dickensian house remained sealed from 1918 until 1975 when the family relinquished the property to the Charleston Museum, providing historians with a unique opportunity to study original documents from that period.

As you walk the halls, staircases, and rooms—seeing the remains of original wallpaper and the various fixtures added through the years—you can really feel the impact of the people who lived within these walls and get a great sense of the full sweep of Charleston history.

While the docents are very friendly and helpful, the main way to enjoy the Aiken-Rhett House is by way of a self-guided mp3 player audio tour—unique in Charleston. While you might think this isolates you from the others in your party, it's actually part of the fun— you can synchronize your players and move as a unit if you'd like.

Children's Museum of the Lowcountry

Yet another example of Charleston's savvy regarding the tourist industry is the Children's Museum of the Lowcountry (25 Ann St., 843/853-8962, www.explorecml.org, Tues.– Sat. 9 A.M.–5 P.M., Sun. 1–5 P.M., $7, free for children under 12 months). Recognizing that historic homes and Civil War memorabilia aren't enough to keep a family with young children in town for long, the city established this museum in 2005 specifically to give families with kids aged 3 months to 12 years a reason to spend more time (and money) downtown.

A wide variety of hands-on activities—such as a 30-foot shrimp boat replica and a medieval castle—stretch the definition of "museum" to its limit. In truth, this is just as much an indoor playground as a museum, but no need to

quibble. The Children's Museum has been getting rave reviews since it opened, and visiting parents and their children seem happy with the city's investment.

Philip Simmons Garden

Charleston's most beloved artisan is the late Philip Simmons. Born on nearby Daniel Island in 1912, Simmons went through an apprenticeship to become one of the most sought-after decorative ironworkers in America. In 1982, the National Endowment for the Arts awarded him its National Heritage Fellowship. His work is on display at the National Museum of American History, the Smithsonian Institution, and the Museum of International Folk Art in Santa Fe, among many other places.

In 1989, the congregation at Simmons's **St. John's Reformed Episcopal Church** (91 Anson St., 843/722-4241, www.stjohnsre.org) voted to make the church garden a commemoration of the life and work of this legendary African American artisan, who passed away in 2009 at age 97. Completed in two phases, the Bell Garden and the Heart Garden, the project is a delightful blend of Simmons's signature graceful, sinuous style and fragrant flowers.

Old Bethel United Methodist Church

The history of the Old Bethel United Methodist Church (222 Calhoun St., 843/722-3470), third-oldest church building in Charleston, is a little confusing. Completed in 1807, the church once stood across Calhoun Street, until a schism formed in the black community over whether they should be limited to sitting in the galleries (in those days in the South, blacks and whites attended church together far more frequently than during the Jim Crow era).

The entire black congregation wanted out, so in 1852 it was moved aside for the construction of a new church for whites, and then entirely across the street in 1880. Look across the street and sure enough you'll see the circa-1853 **Bethel Methodist Church** (57 Pitt St., 843/723-4587, worship Sun. 9 A.M. and 11:15 A.M.).

HAMPTON PARK AREA

Expansive Hampton Park is a favorite recreation spot for Charlestonians. The surrounding area near the east bank of the Ashley River has some of the earliest suburbs of Charleston, now in various states of restoration and hosting a diverse range of residents. Hampton Park is bordered by streets all around, which can be fairly heavily trafficked because this is the main way to get to The Citadel. But the park streets are closed to traffic Saturday mornings in the spring 8 A.M.–noon so neighborhood people, especially those with young children, can enjoy themselves without worrying about the traffic. This is also where the Charleston Police stable their Horse Patrol steeds.

The Citadel

Though for many its spiritual and historic center will always be at the old state Arsenal in Marion Square, The Citadel (171 Moultrie St., 843/953-3294, www.citadel.edu, daily 8 A.M.–6 P.M.) has been at this 300-acre site farther up the peninsula along the Ashley River since 1922 and shows no signs of leaving. Getting there is a little tricky, in that the entrance to the college is situated behind beautiful Hampton Park off Rutledge Avenue, probably the main north–south artery on the western portion of the peninsula.

The Citadel (technically its full name is The Citadel, The Military College of South Carolina) has entered popular consciousness through the works of graduate Pat Conroy, especially his novel *Lords of Discipline,* starring a thinly disguised "Carolina Military Institute." Other famous Bulldog alumni include construction magnate Charles Daniel (for whom the school library is named); Ernest "Fritz" Hollings, South Carolina governor and longtime U.S. senator; and current Charleston Mayor Joe Riley.

You'll see The Citadel's living legacy all over Charleston in the person of the ubiquitous cadet, whose gray-and-white uniforms, ramrod posture, and impeccable manners all hearken back to the days of the Confederacy. But to best experience The Citadel, you should go to the campus itself.

view inside the Citadel barracks

© JIM MOREKIS

WOMEN AND THE CITADEL: THE ONGOING STRUGGLE

Though a lot has changed at The Citadel over a decade after courts mandated that it open its doors to female cadets, many of the same issues and obstacles remain at Charleston's formerly male-only military academy.

The first attempt to crack the gender barrier, by Shannon Faulkner in 1994, failed miserably when she dropped out after less than a week, to much celebration on campus. During her efforts, she endured not only the usual physical stress any Citadel cadet must face, but was also the subject of assorted cruelties – like bumper stickers all over town saying things like "Save the Males," one of the more printable slogans.

The star-crossed nature of Faulkner's effort was emphasized by the fact that her entrance came about because of a misunderstanding. School officials saw her first and middle names – Shannon Richey – and assumed she was a man!

The next episode came in 1996, when four female cadets were admitted, with two transferring out and filing suit against the school for sexual harassment. One of the two who remained, Nancy Mace, went on to become the first woman to graduate from The Citadel. While that accomplishment in 1999 was tempered somewhat by the fact that Mace's father was General James Emory Mace, Commandant of Cadets at the school at the time, it nonetheless marked a watershed moment in Citadel history.

In 2002, seven African American women cadets graduated from The Citadel, 32 years after Charles Foster first broke the racial barrier there in 1970 as the first African American graduate.

While the atmosphere has gotten a lot more progressive at this conservative bastion – a "citadel" in more ways than one – not all is rosy. A 2006 survey found that 68 percent of women students (and 17 percent of male students) said they were victims of sexual harassment on campus. About one in five women reported a sexual assault on campus. General John Rosa, president of The Citadel and former president of the U.S. Air Force Academy, said that though those numbers are not far off national numbers, they were "not good enough for us."

Currently, over 100 of The Citadel's cadets are female – or about six percent of the student body, as opposed to about 16 percent at the service academies. And freshmen women cadets routinely have not only higher SAT scores than male cadets, but higher grade point averages as well.

Interestingly, Lu Parker, crowned Miss USA in 1994, got her master's degree in education from The Citadel. But she wasn't a cadet – all grad courses at The Citadel are night classes. And they don't even make you wear a uniform or do push-ups.

There's lots for visitors to see, including **The Citadel Museum** (843/953-6779, Sun.–Fri. 2–5 P.M., Sat. noon–5 P.M., free), on your right just as you enter campus; the "Citadel Murals" in the Daniel Library; "Indian Hill," highest point in Charleston and former site of an Indian trader's home; and the grave of U.S. General Mark Clark of World War II fame, who was Citadel president from 1954 to 1966.

Ringing vast Summerall Field—the huge open space as soon as you enter campus—are the many castle-looking cadet barracks. If you peek inside their gates, you'll see the distinctive checkerboard pattern on which the cadets line up. All around the field itself are various military items such as a Sherman tank and an F-4 Phantom jet.

The most interesting single experience for visitors to The Citadel is the colorful Friday afternoon dress parade on Summerall Field, in which cadets pass for review in full dress uniform (the fabled "long gray line") accompanied by a marching band and pipers. Often called "the best free show in Charleston," the parade happens most every Friday at 3:45 P.M. during the school year; you might want to consult the website before your visit to confirm. Arrive well in advance to avoid parking problems.

The institute was born out of panic over the threat of a slave rebellion organized in 1822 by Denmark Vesey. The state legislature passed an act establishing the school to educate the strapping young men picked to protect Charleston from a slave revolt.

Citadel folks will proudly tell you they actually fired the first shots of the Civil War, when on January 9, 1861, two cadets fired from a battery on Morris Island at the U.S. steamer *Star of the West* to keep it from supplying Fort Sumter. After slavery stopped—and hence the school's original raison d'être—The Citadel continued, taking its current name in 1910 and moving to the Ashley River in 1922.

While The Citadel is rightly famous for its pomp and circumstance—as well as its now-defunct no-lock "honor system," done away with after the Virginia Tech shootings—the little-known truth is that to be one of the 2,000 or so currently enrolled Citadel Bulldogs you don't have to go through all that, or the infamous "Hell Week" either. You can just sign up for one of their many evening graduate school programs.

Joseph P. Riley Jr. Ballpark

When you hear Charlestonians talk about "The Joe" (360 Fishburne St., 843/577-3647, www.riverdogs.com, general admission $5 advance, $6 game day) they're referring to this charming minor league baseball stadium, home of the Charleston River Dogs, a New York Yankees affiliate playing April–August in the venerable South Atlantic League. It's also another part of the civic legacy of longtime Mayor Joe Riley, in this case in partnership with the adjacent Citadel. Inspired by the retro design of Baltimore's Camden Yards, The Joe opened in 1997 to rave reviews from locals and baseball connoisseurs all over the nation.

From downtown, get there by taking Broad Street west until it turns into Lockwood Drive. Follow that north until you get to Brittlebank Park and The Joe, right next to the Citadel.

WEST ASHLEY

Ironically, Charleston's first postwar automobile suburb also has roots back to the first days of the colony's settlement and was the site of some of the antebellum era's grandest plantations. As the cost of housing on the peninsula continues to rise, this area on the west bank of the Ashley River is experiencing a newfound cachet today for hipsters and young families alike.

For most visitors, though, the biggest draws are the ancient plantations and historic sites along the west bank of the river: Charles Towne Landing, Drayton Hall, Magnolia Plantation, and Middleton Place farthest north. Getting to this area from Charleston proper is easy. Take U.S. 17 ("the Crosstown") west across the Ashley River until the junction with Highway 61. Take a right north onto Highway 61; veer right to get on Highway 7 for Charles Towne Landing, or stay left on Highway 61 for the plantations.

Charles Towne Landing

Any look at West Ashley must begin where everything began, with the 600-acre historic site Charles Towne Landing (1500 Old Towne Rd., 843/852-4200, www.charlestowne.org, daily 9 A.M.–5 P.M., $5 adults, $3 students, 5 and under free). This is where Charleston's original settlers first arrived from Barbados and camped in 1670, remaining only a few years before eventually moving to the more defensible peninsula where the Holy City now resides.

For many years the site was in disrepair and borderline neglect, useful mainly as a place to ship busloads of local schoolchildren on field trips. However, a recent, long-overdue upgrade came to fruition with a grand "reopening" of sorts in 2006, which has been very well received and has given the Landing a newfound sheen of respect. A new audio tour has been instituted, where you rent an mp3 player ($5).

A life-size replica of a settlers' ship is the main new highlight, but another feature is the long interpretive trail that takes you around the long reconstructed palisade wall and the remains of some of the original structures. A

12-room visitors center has many exhibits on the history and daily life of the early settlers.

Many traces of Native American habitation have been found on-site as well, and don't miss the exhibits chronicling the 6,000 years of human history here before the Europeans arrived, including an apparent ceremonial area. Ranger-guided programs are available Wed.–Fri. at 10 A.M.; call ahead for reservations.

Not just a historic site, this is also a great place to bring the family. It features Charleston's only zoo, the "Animal Forest," featuring otters, bears, cougars, and buffalo, and 80 acres of beautiful gardens to relax in, many featuring fabulously ancient live oaks and highlighting other indigenous flora the settlers would have been familiar with.

Archaeology and renovation are ongoing at Charles Towne Landing, with a key project being the excavation of the original western palisade wall. They've even found one of the settlers' tobacco pipes, marked with the maker's name, "Wil. Evans." You can choose to participate vicariously through the "Digital Dig" interactive exhibit—or who knows, maybe you'll be inspired to join the park's archaeology volunteer program. It offers internships for college credit.

(Drayton Hall

A mecca for historic preservationists all over the country, Drayton Hall (3380 Ashley River Rd., 843/769-2600, www.draytonhall.org, Nov.–Feb. daily 9:30 A.M.–4 P.M., Mar.–Oct. daily 8:30 A.M.–5 P.M., $15 adults, $8 ages 12–18, $6 ages 6–11, $8 for grounds only) is remarkable not only for its pedigree but for the way in which it's been preserved. This stately redbrick Georgian-Palladian building, the oldest plantation home in America open to the public, has been *literally* historically preserved—as in no electricity, heat, or running water.

Since its construction in 1738 by John Drayton, son of Magnolia Plantation founder Thomas, Drayton Hall has survived almost completely intact through the ups and downs of Lowcountry history. Drayton died while fleeing the British in 1779; subsequently his house served as the headquarters of British General Clinton and later General Cornwallis. In 1782, however, American General "Mad Anthony" Wayne claimed the house as his own headquarters.

© JIM MOREKIS

Drayton Hall

During the Civil War, Drayton Hall escaped the depredations of the conquering Union Army, one of only three area plantation homes to survive. Three schools of thought have emerged to explain why it was spared the fate of so many other plantation homes: 1) A slave told the troops it was owned by "a Union Man," Drayton cousin Percival who served alongside Admiral David Farragut of "damn the torpedoes" fame; 2) General William Sherman was in love with one of the Drayton women; and 3) one of the Draytons, a doctor, craftily posted smallpox warning flags at the outskirts of the property. Of the three scenarios, the last is considered most likely.

Visitors expecting the more typical approach to house museums, i.e. subjective renovation with period furnishings that may or may not have any connection with the actual house, might be disappointed. But for others the experience at Drayton Hall is quietly exhilarating, almost in a Zen-like way.

Planes are routed around the house so that no rattles will endanger its structural integrity. There's no furniture to speak of, only bare rooms, decorated with original paint, no matter how little remains. It can be jarring at first, but after you get into it you might wonder why anyone does things any differently.

Another way the experience is different is in the almost military professionalism of the National Trust for Historic Preservation, which has owned and administered Drayton Hall since 1974. The guides hold degrees in the field, and a tour of the house—offered punctually at the top of the hour, except for the last of the day which starts on the half-hour—takes every bit of 50 minutes, about twice as long as most house tours.

A separate 45-minute program is "Connections: From Africa to America," which chronicles the diaspora of the slaves who originally worked this plantation, from their capture to their eventual freedom. "Connections" is given at 11:15 A.M., 1:15 P.M., and 3:15 P.M.

The site comprises not only the main house but two self-guided walking trails, one along the peaceful Ashley River and another along the marsh. Note also the foundations of the two "flankers," or guest wings, at each side of the main house. They survived the Yankees only for one to fall victim to the 1886 earthquake and the other to the 1893 hurricane. Also on-site is an African American cemetery with at least 33 known graves. It's kept deliberately un-tended and un-landscaped to honor the final wish of Richmond Bowens (1908–1998), the seventh-generation descendant of some of Drayton Hall's original slaves.

Magnolia Plantation and Gardens

A different legacy of the Drayton family is Magnolia Plantation and Gardens (3550 Ashley Rd., 843/571-1266, www.magnoliaplantation .com, Mar.–Oct. daily 9 A.M.–5 P.M., call for winter hours, $15 adults, $10 children, under 6 free). It claims not only the first garden in the United States, dating back to the 1680s, but also the first public garden, dating to 1872.

However, Magnolia's history spans back two full centuries before that, when Thomas Drayton Jr.—scion of Norman aristocracy, son of a wealthy Barbadian planter—came from the Caribbean to build his own fortune. He immediately married the daughter of Stephen Fox, who began this plantation in 1676. Throughout wars, fevers, depressions, earthquakes, and hurricanes, Magnolia has stayed in the possession of an unbroken line of Drayton descendants to this very day.

As a privately run attraction, Magnolia has little of the academic veneer of other plantation sites in the area, most of which have long passed out of private hands. There's a slightly kitschy feel here, the opposite of the quiet dignity of Drayton Hall. And unlike Middleton Place a few miles down the road, the gardens here are anything but manicured, with a wild, almost playful feel.

That said, Magnolia can claim fame to being one of the earliest bona fide tourist attractions in the United States and the beginning of Charleston's now-booming tourist industry. It happened after the Civil War, when John Grimke Drayton, reduced to near-poverty, sold off most of his property, including the original

© JIM MOREKIS

the maze at Magnolia Plantation

Magnolia Plantation, just to stay afloat. (In a common practice at the time, as a condition of inheriting the plantation, Mr. Grimke, who married into the family, was required to legally change his name to Drayton.)

The original plantation home was burned during the war—either by Union troops or freed slaves—so Drayton barged a colonial-era summer house in Summerville, South Carolina, down the Ashley River to this site, and built the modern Magnolia Plantation around it specifically as an attraction. Before long, tourists regularly came here by crowded boat from Charleston (a wreck of one such ferry is still on-site). Magnolia's reputation became so exalted that at one point Baedecker's listed it as one of the three main attractions in America, alongside the Grand Canyon and Niagara Falls.

The family took things to the next level in the 1970s, when John Drayton Hastie bought out his brother and set about marketing Magnolia Plantation and Gardens as a modern tourist destination, adding more varieties of flowers so that something would always

be blooming nearly year-round. While spring remains the best—and also the most crowded—time to come, a huge variety of camellias blooms in early winter, a time marked by a yearly Winter Camellia Festival.

Today Magnolia is a place to bring the whole family, picnic under the massive old live oaks, and wander the lush, almost overgrown grounds. Children will enjoy finding their way through "The Maze" of manicured camellia and holly bushes, complete with a viewing stand to look within the giant puzzle. Plant lovers will enjoy the themed gardens such as the "Biblical Garden," the "Barbados Tropical Garden," and the "Audubon Swamp Garden," complete with alligators and named after John James Audubon, who visited here in 1851. Hundreds of varieties of camellias, clearly labeled, line the narrow walkways. House tours, the 45-minute Nature Train tour, the 45-minute Nature Boat tour, and a visit to the Audubon Swamp Garden run about $7 extra per person for each offering.

Of particular interest is the poignant old Drayton Tomb, along the Ashley River, which housed many members of the family until being heavily damaged in the 1886 earthquake. Look closely at the nose of one of the cherubs on the tomb; it was shot off by a vengeful Union soldier. Nearby you'll find a nice walking and biking trail along the Ashley among the old rice paddies.

(Middleton Place

Not only the first landscaped garden in America but still one of the most magnificent in the world, Middleton Place (4300 Ashley River Rd., 843/556-6020, www.middleton place.org, daily 9 A.M.–5 P.M., $25 adults, $5 ages 7–15, guided house tour additional $10) is a sublime, unforgettable combination of history and sheer natural beauty. Nestled along a quiet bend in the Ashley River, the grounds contain a historic restored home, working stables, and 60 acres of breathtaking gardens, all manicured to perfection. A stunning piece of modern architecture, the Inn at Middleton Place completes the package in surprisingly harmonic fashion.

First granted in 1675, Middleton Place is the culmination of the Lowcountry rice plantation aesthetic. That sensibility is most immediate in the graceful Butterfly Lakes at the foot of the green, landscaped terrace leading up to the Middleton Place House itself, the only surviving remnant of the vengeful Union occupation. The two wing-shaped lakes, 10 years in the construction, seem to echo the low rice paddies that once dotted this entire landscape.

In 1741 the plantation became the family seat of the Middletons, one of the most notable surnames in U.S. history. The first head of the household was Henry Middleton, president of the First Continental Congress, who began work on the meticulously planned and maintained gardens. The plantation passed to his son Arthur, a signer of the Declaration of Independence; then on to Arthur's son Henry, governor of South Carolina; and then down to Henry's son, Williams Middleton, signer of the Ordinance of Secession.

It was then that things turned sour, both for the family and for the grounds themselves. As the Civil War wound down, on February 22, 1865, the 56th New York Volunteers burned

the gardens at Middleton Place

the main house and destroyed the gardens, leaving only the circa-1755 guest wing, which today is the Middleton Place House Museum. The great earthquake of 1886 added insult to injury by wrecking the Butterfly Lakes.

It wasn't until 1916 that renovation began, when heir J. J. Pringle Smith took on the project as his own. No one can say he wasn't successful. At the garden's bicentennial in 1941, the Garden Club of America awarded its prestigious Bulkley Medal to Middleton Place. In 1971 Middleton Place was named a National Historic Landmark, and 20 years later the International Committee on Monuments and Sites named Middleton Place one of six U.S. gardens of international importance. In 1974, Smith's heirs established the nonprofit Middleton Place Foundation, which now owns and operates the entire site.

All that's left of the great house are the remains of the foundation, still majestic in ruin. Today visitors can tour the excellently restored **Middleton Place House Museum** (4300 Ashley River Rd., 843/556-6020, www.middletonplace.org, guided tours Mon. 1:30–4:30 P.M., Tues.–Sun. 10 A.M.–4:30 P.M., $10)—actually the only remaining "flanker" building—and see furniture, silverware, china, and books belonging to the Middletons, as well as family portraits by Thomas Sully and Benjamin West.

A short walk takes you to the Plantation Stableyards, where costumed craftspeople still work using historically authentic tools and methods, surrounded by a happy family of domestic animals. The newest addition to the Stableyards is a pair of magnificent male water buffalo. Henry Middleton originally brought a pair in to work the rice fields—the first in North America—but today they're just there to relax and add atmosphere. They bear the Turkish names of Adem (the brown one) and Berk (the white one), or "Earth" and "Solid." Meet the fellas daily 9 A.M.–5 P.M.

However, if you're like most folks you'll best enjoy simply wandering and marveling at the gardens. "Meandering" is not the right word to describe them, since they're systematically laid out. "Intricate" is the word I prefer, and that sums up the attention to detail that characterizes all the garden's portions, each with a distinct personality and landscape design template.

To get a real feel for how things used to be here, for an extra $15 per person you can take a 45-minute carriage ride through the bamboo forest to an abandoned rice field. Rides start around 10 A.M. and run every hour or so, weather permitting.

The 53-room **Inn at Middleton Place,** besides being a wholly gratifying lodging experience, is also a quite self-conscious and largely successful experiment. Its bold, Wright-influenced modern design, comprising four units joined by walkways, is modern. But both inside and outside it manages to blend quite well with the surrounding fields, trees, and riverbanks. The Inn also offers kayak tours and instruction—a particularly nice way to enjoy the grounds from the waters of the Ashley—and features its own organic garden and labyrinth, intriguing modern counterpoints to the formal gardens of the plantation itself.

They still grow the exquisite Carolina Gold rice in a field at Middleton Place, harvested in the old style each September. You can sample some of it in many dishes at the **Middleton Place Restaurant** (843/556-6020, www .middletonplace.org, lunch daily 11 A.M.–3 P.M., dinner Tues.–Thurs. 6–8 P.M., Fri.–Sat. 6–9 P.M., Sun. 6–8 P.M., $15–25). Hint: You can tour the gardens for free if you arrive for a dinner reservation at 5:30 P.M. or later.

The Coburg Cow

The entire stretch of U.S. 17 (Savannah Highway) heading into Charleston from the west is redolent of a particularly Southern brand of retro Americana. The chief example is the famous Coburg Cow, a large, rotating dairy cow accompanied by a bottle of chocolate milk.

The current installation dates from 1959, though a version of it was on this site as far back as the early 1930s when this area was open countryside. During Hurricane Hugo the Coburg Cow was moved to a safe location.

In 2001 the attached dairy closed down, and the city threatened to have the cow moved or demolished. But community outcry preserved the delightful landmark, which is visible today on the south side of U.S. 17 in the 900 block. You can't miss it—it's a big cow on the side of the road!

NORTH CHARLESTON

For years synonymous with crime, blight, and sprawl, North Charleston—actually a separate municipality—was for the longest time considered a necessary evil by most Charlestonians, who generally ventured there only to shop at a mall or see a show at its concert venue, the Coliseum. But as the cost of real estate continues to rise on the peninsula in Charleston proper, more and more artists and young professionals are choosing to live here.

Make no mistake, North Charleston still has its share of crime and squalor, but some of the most exciting things going on in the metro area are taking place right here. While many insisted that the closing of the U.S. Navy Yard in the 1990s would be the economic death of the whole city, the free market stepped in and is transforming the former military facility into a hip, mixed-use shopping and residential area. This is also where to go if you want to see the raised submarine CSS *Hunley,* now in a research area on the grounds of the old Navy Yard.

In short, North Charleston offers a lot for the more adventurous traveler and will no doubt only become more and more important to the local tourist industry as the years go by. And as they're fond of pointing out up here, there aren't any parking meters.

Magnolia Cemetery

Though not technically in North Charleston, historic Magnolia Cemetery (70 Cunnington Ave., 843/722-8638, Sept.–May daily 8 A.M.–5 P.M., Jun.–Aug. daily 8 A.M.–6 P.M.) is on the way, in the area well north of the downtown tourist district called "The Neck." This historic burial ground, while not the equal of Savannah's Bonaventure, is still a stirring site

for its natural beauty and ornate memorials as well as for its historic aspects. Here are buried the crewmen who died aboard the CSS *Hunley,* re-interred after their retrieval from Charleston Harbor. In all, over 2,000 Civil War dead are buried here, including five Confederate generals and 84 rebels who fell at Gettysburg and were moved here.

Charleston Navy Yard

A vast post-industrial wasteland to some and a fascinating outdoor museum to others, the Charleston Navy Yard is in the baby steps of rehabilitation from one of the Cold War era's major military centers to the largest single urban redevelopment project in the United States.

The Navy's gone now, forced off the site during a phase of base realignment in the mid-1990s. But a 340-acre section, the **Navy Yard at Noisette** (1360 Truxtun Ave., 843/302-2100, www.navyyardsc.com, daily 24 hours), now hosts an intriguing mix of homes, green design firms, nonprofits, and commercial maritime companies that was named America's sixth-greenest neighborhood by *Natural Home* magazine in 2008. It's even played host to some scenes of the Lifetime TV series *Army Wives.*

Enter on Spruill Avenue and you'll find yourself on wide streets lined with huge, boarded-up warehouse facilities, old machine shops, and dormant power stations. A notable project is the restoration of **10 Storehouse Row** (2120 Noisette Blvd., 843/302-2100, Mon.–Fri. 9 A.M.–5 P.M.), which now hosts the American College of Building Arts, design firms, galleries, and a small café. Nearby, Clemson University will soon be administering one of the world's largest wind turbine research facilities.

At the north end lies the new **Riverfront Park** (843/745-1087, daily dawn–dusk) in the old Chicora Gardens military residential area. There's a nifty little fishing pier on the Cooper River, an excellent naval-themed band shell, and many sleekly designed, modernist sculptures paying tribute to the sailors and ships that made history here.

© JIM MOREKIS

North Charleston's Riverfront Park

From Charleston you get to the Navy Yard by taking I-26 north to exit 216-B (you can reach the I-26 junction by just going north on Meeting Street). After exiting take a left onto Spruill Avenue and a right onto McMillan, which takes you straight in.

(CSS *Hunley*

For the longest time the only glimpse of the ill-fated Confederate submarine was a not-quite-accurate replica outside the Charleston Museum. But after maritime novelist and adventurer Clive Cussler and his team finally found the *Hunley* in 1995 off Sullivan's Island, the tantalizing dream became a reality: we'd finally find out what it looked like, and perhaps even be lucky enough to bring it to the surface.

That moment came on August 8, 2000, when a team comprising the nonprofit **Friends of the Hunley** (Warren Lasch Conservation Center, 1250 Supply St., Building 255, 866/866-9938, www.hunley.org, Sat. 10 a.m.–5 p.m., Sun. noon–5 p.m., $12, children under 5 free), the federal government,

and private partners successfully implemented a plan to safely raise the vessel. It was recently moved to its new home in the old Navy Yard, named after Warren Lasch, chairman of the Friends of the Hunley.

You can now view the sub in a 90,000-gallon conservation tank on the grounds of the old Navy Yard, see the life-size model from the TNT movie *The Hunley,* and look at artifacts such as the "lucky" gold piece of the commander. You can even see facial reconstructions of some of the eight sailors who died onboard the sub that fateful February day in 1864, when it mysteriously sank right after successfully destroying the USS *Housatonic* with the torpedo attached to its bow.

So that research and conservation can be performed during the week, tours only happen on Saturdays and Sundays; it's wise to reserve tickets ahead of time. The sub itself is completely submerged in an electrolyte formula to better preserve it, and photography is strictly forbidden. (The remains of the crew lie in Magnolia Cemetery, where they were buried in 2004 with full military honors.)

RAISING THE *HUNLEY*

The amazing, unlikely raising of the Confederate submarine CSS *Hunley* from the muck of Charleston harbor sounds like the plot of an adventure novel – which makes sense considering that the major player is an adventure novelist.

For 15 years, the undersea diver and best-selling author Clive Cussler looked for the

final resting place of the *Hunley*. The sub was mysteriously lost at sea after sinking the USS *Housatonic* on February 17, 1864, with the high-explosive "torpedo" mounted on a long spar on its bow. It marked the first time a sub ever sank a ship in battle.

For over a century before Cussler, treasure-

replica of the CSS *Hunley* outside the Charleston Museum

© JIM MOREKIS

To get to the Warren Lasch Center from Charleston, take I-516 north to exit 216-B. Take a left onto Spruill Avenue and a right onto McMillan. Once in the Navy Yard, take a right on Hobson, and after about a mile take a left onto Supply Street. The Lasch Center is the low white building on your left. Secure your tickets in advance online.

Park Circle

The focus of restoration in North Charleston is the old Park Circle neighborhood (intersection of Rhett and Montague Aves., www.park circle.net). The adjacent **Olde North Charleston**

development has a number of quality shops, bars, and restaurants.

Fire Museum

It's got a mouthful of a name, but the new **North Charleston and American LaFrance Fire Museum and Educational Center** (4975 Centre Pointe Dr., 843/740-5550, www.legacyofheroes .org, Mon.–Sat. 10 A.M.–5 P.M., Sun. 1–5 P.M., last ticket 4 P.M., $6 adults, 13 and under free), right next to the huge Tanger Outlet Mall, does what it does with a lot of chutzpah—which is fitting considering that it pays tribute to fire-fighters and the tools of their dangerous trade.

seekers had searched for the sub, with P. T. Barnum even offering $100,000 to the first person to find it. But on May 3, 1995, a magnetometer operated by Cussler and his group, the National Underwater Marine Agency, discovered the *Hunley*'s final resting place – in 30 feet of water and under three feet of sediment about four miles off Sullivan's Island at the mouth of the harbor.

Using a specially designed truss to lift the entire sub, a 19-person dive crew and a team of archaeologists began a process that would result in raising the vessel on August 8, 2000. But before the sub could be brought up, a dilemma had to be solved: For 136 years the saltwater of the Atlantic had permeated its metallic skin. Exposure to air would rapidly disintegrate the entire thing. So the conservation team, with input from the U.S. Navy, came up with a plan to keep the vessel submerged in a special solution indefinitely at the specially constructed **Warren Lasch Conservation Center** (1250 Supply St., Building 255, 866/866-9938, www.hunley.org, Sat. 10 A.M.–5 P.M., Sun. noon–5 P.M., $12, 5 and under free) in the old Navy Yard while research and conservation was performed on it piece-by-piece.

And that's how you see the *Hunley* today, submerged in its special conservation tank, still largely covered in sediment. Upon seeing the almost unbelievably tiny, cramped vessel –

much smaller than most experts imagined it would be – visitors are often visibly moved at the bravery and sacrifice of the nine-man Confederate crew, who no doubt would have known that the *Hunley*'s two previous crews had drowned at sea in training accidents. Theirs was, in effect, a suicide mission. That the crew surely realized this only makes the modern visitor's experience even more poignant and meaningful.

The Warren Lasch Center, operated under the auspices of Clemson University, is only open to the public on weekends. Archaeology continues apace during the week – inch by painstaking inch, muck and tiny artifacts removed millimeter by millimeter. The process is so thorough that archaeologists have even identified an individual eyelash from one of the crew. Other interesting artifacts include a three-fold wallet with a leather strap, owner unknown; seven canteens; and a wooden cask in one of the ballast tanks, maybe used to hold water or liquor or even used as a chamber pot.

The very first order of business once the sub was brought up, however, was properly burying those brave sailors. In 2004, Charleston came to a stop as a ceremonial funeral procession took the remains of the nine to historic Magnolia Cemetery, where they were buried with full military honors.

The museum, which opened in 2007 and shares a huge 25,000-square-foot space with the North Charleston Convention and Visitors Bureau, is primarily dedicated to maintaining and increasing its collection of antique American LaFrance firefighting vehicles and equipment. The 18 fire engines here date from 1857 to 1969.

The museum's exhibits have taken on greater poignancy in the wake of the tragic loss of nine Charleston firefighters killed trying to extinguish a warehouse blaze on U.S. 17 in summer 2007—second only to the 9/11 attacks as the largest single loss of life for a U.S. firefighting department.

EAST COOPER

The main destination in this area on the east bank of the Cooper River is the island of Mount Pleasant, primarily known as a peaceful, fairly affluent suburb of Charleston—a role it's played for about 300 years now. Though few old-timers (called "hungry necks" in local lingo) remain, Mount Pleasant does have several key attractions well worth visiting—the old words of former Charleston Mayor John Grace notwithstanding: "Mount Pleasant is neither a mount, nor is it pleasant." Through Mount Pleasant is also the only land route to access Sullivan's Island, Isle of Palms, and historic Fort Moultrie.

Shem Creek, which bisects Mount Pleasant, was once the center of the local shrimping industry, and while there aren't near as many shrimp boats as there once were, you can still see them docked or on their way to and from a trawling run. (Needless to say, there are a lot of good seafood restaurants around here as well.)

The most common route for visitors is by way of U.S. 17 over the massive Arthur Ravenel Jr. Bridge.

Patriots Point Naval and Maritime Museum

Directly across Charleston Harbor from the old city lies the Patriots Point Naval and Maritime Museum complex (40 Patriots Point Rd., 843/884-2727, www.patriotspoint.org, daily 9 A.M.–6:30 P.M., $16 adults, $9 ages 6–11, free for active duty military), one of the first chapters in Charleston's tourism renaissance. The project began in 1975 with what is still its main attraction, the World War II aircraft carrier **USS Yorktown,** named in honor of the carrier lost at the Battle of Midway. Much of "The Fighting Lady" is open to the public, and kids and nautical buffs will thrill to walk the decks and explore the many stations below deck on this massive 900-foot vessel, a veritable floating city. You can even have a full meal in the C.P.O. Mess Hall just like the crew once did (except you'll have to pay $8.50 a person). And if you really want to get up close and personal, try the Navy Flight Simulator for a small added fee.

Speaking of planes, aviation buffs will be overjoyed to see that the Yorktown flight deck (the top of the ship) and the hangar deck (right below) are packed with authentic warplanes, not only from World War II but from subsequent conflicts the ship participated in. You'll see an F6F Hellcat, an FG-1D Corsair, and an SBD Dauntless such as those that fought the Japanese, on up to an F4F Phantom and an F14 Tomcat from the jet era.

Patriots Point's newest exhibit is also on the Yorktown: the **Medal of Honor Memorial Museum,** which opened in 2007 by hosting a live broadcast of the NBC Nightly News. Included in the cost of admission, the Medal of Honor museum is an interactive experience documenting the exploits of the medal's honorees from the Civil War through today.

Other ships moored beside the Yorktown and open for tours are the Coast Guard cutter USCG Ingham, the submarine USS Clamagore, and the destroyer USS Laffey, which survived being hit by three Japanese bombs and five kamikaze attacks—all within an hour. The Vietnam era is represented by a replica of an entire Naval Support Base Camp, featuring a river patrol boat and several helicopters.

A big plus is the free 90-minute guided tour. If you really want to make a family history day out of it, you can also hop on the ferry from Patriots Point to Fort Sumter and back.

Old Village

It won't blow you away if you've seen Charleston, Savannah, or Beaufort, but Mount Pleasant's old town has its share of fine colonial and antebellum homes and historic churches. Indeed, Mount Pleasant's history is almost as old as Charleston's. First settled for farming in 1680, it soon acquired cachet as a great place for planters to spend the hot summers away from the mosquitoes inland.

The main drag is Pitt Street, where you can shop and meander among plenty of shops and restaurants (try an ice cream soda at the historic Pitt Street Pharmacy). The huge meeting hall on the waterfront, Alhambra Hall, was the old ferry terminal.

Boone Hall Plantation

Visitors who've also been to Savannah's Wormsloe Plantation will see the similarity in the majestic, live oak–lined entrance avenue to Boone Hall Plantation (1235 Long Point Rd., 843/884-4371, www.boonehallplantation .com, $17.50 adults, $7.50 children). But this site is about half a century older, dating back to a grant to Major John Boone in the 1680s (the oaks of the entranceway were planted in 1743).

Unusually in this area, which made its

original fortune mostly on rice, Boone Hall's main claim to fame was as a cotton plantation as well as a noted brick-making plant. Boone Hall takes the phrase "living history" to its extreme, as it's not only an active agricultural facility but lets visitors go on "u-pick" walks through its fields, which boast succulent strawberries, peaches, tomatoes, and even pumpkins in October—as well as free hayrides.

Currently owned by the McRae family, which first opened it to the public in 1959, Boone Hall is called "the most photographed plantation in America." And photogenic it certainly is, with natural beauty to spare in its scenic location on the Wando River and its adorable Butterfly Garden. But as you're clicking away with your camera, do keep in mind that the plantation's "big house" is not original; it's a 1935 reconstruction.

While Boone Hall's most genuine historic buildings include the big Cotton Gin House (1853) and the 1750 Smokehouse, to me the most poignant and educational structures by far are the nine humble brick slave cabins from the 1790s, expertly restored and most fitted with interpretive displays. The cabins are the center of Boone Hall's educational programs, including an exploration of Gullah culture at the outdoor "Gullah Theatre" on the unfortunately named Slave Street. Summers see some serious Civil War reenacting going on.

In all, three different tours are available: a 30-minute house tour, a tour of Slave Street, and a garden tour. Boone Hall's seasonal hours are a little tricky: from Labor Day through mid-March, Boone Hall is open Monday–Saturday 9 A.M.–5 P.M. and Sunday 1–4 P.M.; from mid-March through Labor Day, it's open Monday–Saturday 8:30 A.M.–6:30 P.M. and Sunday 1–5 P.M.

Charles Pinckney National Historic Site

This is one of my favorite sights in Charleston, for its uplifting, well-explored subject matter as well as its tastefully maintained house and grounds. Though "Constitution Charlie's" old Snee Farm is down to only 28 acres from its original magnificent 700, the Charles Pinckney National Historic Site (1240 Long Point Rd., 843/881-5516, www.nps.gov/chpi, daily 9 A.M.–5 P.M., free) that encompasses it

Charles Pinckney National Historic Site

is still an important repository of local and national history.

Sometimes called "the forgotten Founder," Charles Pinckney was not only a hero of the American Revolution and a notable early abolitionist, but one of the main authors of the U.S. Constitution. His great aunt Eliza Lucas Pinckney was the first woman agriculturalist in America, responsible for opening up the indigo trade. Her son Charles Cotesworth Pinckney was one of the signers of the Constitution.

The current main house, doubling as the visitors center, dates from 1828, 11 years after Pinckney sold Snee Farm to pay off debts. That said, it's still a great example of Lowcountry architecture, replacing Pinckney's original home, where President George Washington slept and had breakfast under a nearby oak tree in 1791 while touring the south. Another highlight at this National Parks Service-administered site is the half-mile, self-guided walk around the site, some of it on boardwalks over the marsh.

No matter what anyone tells you, no one is buried underneath the tombstone in the grove of oak trees bearing the name of Constitution Charlie's father, Colonel Charles Pinckney. The marker incorrectly states the elder Pinckney's age, so it was put here only as a monument. A memorial to the colonel is in the churchyard of the 1840s-era Christ Church about a mile down Long Point Road.

Isle of Palms

This primarily residential area of about 5,000 people received the state's first "Blue Wave" designation from the Clean Beaches Council for its well-managed and preserved beaches. Like adjacent Sullivan's Island, there are pockets of great wealth here, but also a laid-back, windswept beach town vibe. You get here from Mount Pleasant by taking the Isle of Palms Connector off U.S. 17 (Johnnie Dodds/Chuck Dawley Boulevard).

Aside from just enjoying the whole scene, the main self-contained attraction here is **Isle of Palms County Park** (14th Ave., 843/886-3863, www.ccprc.com, May–Labor Day daily 9 A.M.–7 P.M., Mar.–Apr. and Sept.–Oct. daily

10 A.M.–6 P.M., Nov.–Feb. daily 10 A.M.–5 P.M. $5 per vehicle, pedestrians/cyclists free), with its oceanfront beach, complete with umbrella rental, a volleyball court, a playground, and lifeguards. Get here by taking the Isle of Palms Connector/Highway 517 from Mount Pleasant, going through the light at Palm Boulevard and taking the next left at the gate.

The island's other claim to fame is the excellent (and surprisingly affordable) **Wild Dunes Resort** (5757 Palm Blvd., 888/778-1876, www.wilddunes.com), with its two Fazio golf courses and 17 clay tennis courts.

Breach Inlet, between Isle of Palms and Sullivan's Island, is where the Confederate sub *Hunley* sortied to do battle with the USS *Housatonic.* During Hurricane Hugo the entire island was submerged.

Sullivan's Island

Part funky beach town, part ritzy getaway, Sullivan's Island has a certain timeless quality. While much of it was rebuilt after Hurricane Hugo's devastation, plenty of local character remains, as evidenced by some cool little bars in its tiny "business district" on the main drag of Middle Street.

There's a ton of history on Sullivan's, but you can also just while the day away on the quiet, windswept beach on the Atlantic, or ride a bike all over the island and back. Unless you have a boat, you can only get here from Mount Pleasant.

From U.S. 17 follow the signs for Highway 703 and Sullivan's Island. Cross the Ben Sawyer Bridge and then turn right onto Middle Street; continue for about a mile and a half.

FORT MOULTRIE

While Fort Sumter gets the vast bulk of the press, the older Fort Moultrie (1214 Middle St., 843/883-3123, www.nps.gov/fosu, daily 9 A.M.–5 P.M., $3 adults, $5 per family, under 16 free) on Sullivan's Island actually has a much more sweeping history. Furthering the irony, Major Robert Anderson's detachment at Fort Sumter at the opening of the Civil War was actually the Fort Moultrie garrison, reassigned

© JIM MOREKIS

Fort Moultrie on Sullivan's Island

to Sumter because Moultrie was thought too vulnerable from the landward side.

Indeed, Moultrie's first incarnation, a perimeter of felled palm trees, didn't even have a name when it was unsuccessfully attacked by the British in the summer of 1776, the first victory by the colonists in the Revolution. The redcoat cannonballs bounced off those soft, flexible trunks, and thus was born South Carolina's nickname, "The Palmetto State." The hero of the battle, Sergeant William Jasper, would gain immortality for putting the blue and white regimental banner—forerunner to the modern blue and white state flag—on a makeshift staff after the first one was shot away.

Subsequently named for the commander at the time, William Moultrie, the fort was captured by the British at a later engagement. That first fort fell into decay and a new one was built over it in 1798, but was soon destroyed by a hurricane.

In 1809 a brick fort was built here; it soon gained notoriety as the place where the great chief Osceola was detained soon after his capture, posing for the famous portrait by George Catlin. His captors got more than they bargained for when they jokingly asked the old guerrilla soldier for a rendition of the Seminole battle cry. According to accounts, Osceola's realistic performance scared some bystanders half to death. The chief died here in 1838 and his modest gravesite is still on-site, in front of the fort on the landward side.

Other famous people to have trod on Sullivan's Island include Edgar Allan Poe, who was inspired by Sullivan's lonely, evocative environment to write *The Gold Bug* and other works. There's a Gold Bug Avenue and a Poe Avenue here today, and the local library is named after him as well. A young Lieutenant William Tecumseh Sherman was also stationed here during his Charleston stint in the 1830s before his encounter with history in the Civil War.

Moultrie's main Civil War role was as a target for Union shot during the long siege of Charleston. It was pounded so hard and for so long that its walls fell below a nearby sand hill and were finally unable to be hit anymore.

A full military upgrade happened in the late

1800s, extending over most of Sullivan's Island (some private owners have even bought some of the old batteries and converted them into homes). It's the series of later forts that you'll visit on your trip to the Moultrie site, which is technically part of the Fort Sumter National Monument and administered by the National Park Service.

Most of the outdoor tours are self-guided, but ranger programs typically happen Memorial Day through Labor Day daily at 11 A.M. and 2:30 P.M. There's a bookstore and visitors center across the street, offering a 20-minute video on the hour and half-hour 9 A.M.–4:30 P.M. Keep in mind there's no regular ferry to Fort Sumter from Fort Moultrie; the closest ferry to Sumter leaves from Patriots Point on Mount Pleasant.

BENCH BY THE ROAD
Scholars say that about half of all African Americans alive today had an ancestor who once set foot on Sullivan's Island. As the first point of entry for at least half of all slaves imported to America, the island's "pest houses" acted as quarantine areas so slaves could be checked for communicative diseases before going to auction in Charleston proper.

But few people seem to know this. In a 1989 magazine interview, African American author and Nobel laureate Toni Morrison said about historic sites concerning slavery, "There is no suitable memorial, or plaque, or wreath or wall, or park or skyscraper lobby. There's no 300-foot tower, there's no small bench by the road."

In 2008, that last item became a reality, as the first of several planned "benches by the road" was installed on Sullivan's Island to mark the sacrifice of enslaved African Americans. It's a simple black steel bench, with an attached marker and a nearby plaque. The Bench by the Road is just near Fort Moultrie, which has also recently expanded its African American–oriented interpretation at its visitors center.

FOLLY BEACH
Though a large percentage of the town of Folly Beach was destroyed in Hurricane Hugo, enough of its funky charm is left to make it worth visiting. Called "The Edge of America"

a view of Folly Beach from the pier

© JIM MOREKIS

during its heyday from the 1930s through the '50s as a swinging resort getaway, Folly Beach is now a slightly beat, but thoroughly enjoyable, little getaway on this barrier island. Though as with all areas of Charleston, the cost of living here is rapidly increasing, Folly Beach still reminds locals of a time that once was, a time of soda fountains, poodle skirts, stylish one-piece bathing suits, and growling hot rods.

Folly's main claim to larger historic fame is playing host to George Gershwin, who stayed at a cottage on West Arctic Avenue to write the score to *Porgy and Bess,* set in downtown Charleston across the harbor. (Ironically, Gershwin's opera couldn't be performed in its original setting until 1970 because of segregationist Jim Crow laws.) Original *Porgy* author DuBose Heyward stayed around the corner at a summer cottage on West Ashley Avenue that he dubbed "Follywood."

Called Folly Road until it gets to the beach, Center Street is the main drag here, dividing the beach into east and west. In this area you'll find the **Folly Beach Fishing Pier** (101 E. Arctic Ave., 843/588-3474, Apr.–Oct. daily 6 A.M.–11 P.M., Nov. and Mar. daily 7 A.M.–7 P.M., during winter daily 8 A.M.–5 P.M., $5 parking, $8 fishing fee), which replaced the grand old wooden pier-and-pavilion structure that tragically burned down in 1960.

Back in the day, restaurants, bars, and amusement areas with rides lined the way up to the old pavilion. As the premier musical venue in the region, the pavilion hosted legends like Tommy and Jimmy Dorsey, Benny Goodman, and Count Basie. The new fishing pier, while not as grand as the old one, is worth visiting—a massive, well-built edifice jutting over 1,000 feet into the Atlantic with a large, diamond-shaped pavilion at the end. Fishing rod holders and cleaning stations line the entire thing.

Out on the "front beach," daytime activities once included boxing matches and extralegal drag races. In the old days, the "Washout" section on the far west end was where you went to go crabbing or fly-fishing or maybe even steal a kiss from your sweetie. Today though, the Washout is known as the prime surfing area in the Carolinas, with a dedicated group of diehards.

Another attraction, humble though it is, is **Folly Beach County Park** (1100 West Ashley Ave., 843/588-2426, www.ccprc.com, May–Labor Day daily 9 A.M.–7 P.M., Mar.–Apr. and Sept.–Oct. daily 10 A.M.–6 P.M., Nov.–Dec. daily 10 A.M.–5 P.M., $7 per vehicle, free for pedestrians and cyclists) at the far west end of the island. Swim, tan, and relax, maybe under a rented beach umbrella.

To get to Folly Beach from Charleston, go west on Calhoun Street and take the James Island Connector. Take a left on Folly Road/Highway 171, which becomes Center Street on into Folly Beach.

At the far east end of Folly Island, about 300 yards offshore, you'll see the **Morris Island Lighthouse,** an 1876 beacon that was once surrounded by lush, green landscape, now completely surrounded by water as the land has eroded around it. Now privately owned, there's an extensive effort to save and preserve the lighthouse (www.savethelight .org). There's also an effort to keep high-dollar condo development off of beautiful, bird-friendly Morris Island itself (www.morris island.org). To get there while there's still something left to enjoy, take East Ashley Street until it dead-ends. Park in the lot and take a quarter-mile walk to the beach.

TOURS

Because of the city's small, fairly centralized layout, the best way to experience Charleston is on foot—either yours or via hooves of equine nature. Thankfully, there's a wide variety of walking and carriage tours for you to choose from.

The sheer number and breadth of tour options in Charleston is beyond the scope of this section. For a full selection of available tours, visit the **Charleston Visitor Reception and Transportation Center** (375 Meeting St., 800/774-0006, www.charlestoncvb.com, Mon.–Fri. 8:30 A.M.–5 P.M.), where they have

DOIN' THE CHARLESTON

It's been called the biggest song and dance craze of the 20th century. Though it first entered the American public consciousness via New York City, in a 1923 Harlem musical called *Runnin' Wild*, the roots of the dance soon to be known as the Charleston were indeed in the Holy City.

Though no one is quite sure of the day and date, local lore assures us that members of Charleston's legendary Jenkins Orphanage Band were the first to start dancing that crazy "Geechie step," a development that soon became part of the band's act. The Jenkins Orphanage was started in 1891 by the African American Baptist minister Reverend D. J. Jenkins, and originally housed in the Old Marine Hospital at 20 Franklin Street (which you can see today, though it's not open to the public). To raise money, Reverend Jenkins acquired donated instruments and started a band comprising talented orphans from the house.

The orphans traveled as far away as London, where they were a hit with the locals but not with the constabulary, who unceremoniously

fined them for stopping traffic. A Charleston attorney who happened to be in London at the time, Augustine Smyth, paid their way back home, becoming a lifelong supporter of the Orphanage in the process.

From then on, playing in donated old Citadel uniforms, the Jenkins Orphanage Band frequently took its act on the road. They played at the St. Louis and Buffalo expositions, and even at President Taft's inauguration. They also frequently played in New York, and it was there that African American pianist and composer James P. Johnson heard the Charlestonians play and dance to their Gullah rhythms, considered exotic at the time. Johnson would incorporate what he heard into the tune "Charleston," one of many songs in the revue *Runnin' Wild*. The catchy song and its accompanying loose-limbed dance seemed tailor-made for the Roaring Twenties and its liberated, hedonistic spirit.

Before long the Charleston had swept the nation, becoming a staple of jazz clubs and speakeasies across America, and indeed, the world.

entire walls of brochures for all the latest tours, with local tourism experts on-site. Here are some notable highlights.

Walking Tours

If you find yourself walking around downtown soon after dark, you'll almost invariably come across a walking tour in progress, with a small cluster of people gathered around a tour guide. There are too many walking tours to list them all, but here are the best.

For more than 10 years, **Ed Grimball's Walking Tours** (306 Yates Ave., 843/762-0056, www.edgrimballtours.com, $16 adults, $8 children) has run two-hour tours on Friday and Saturday mornings, courtesy of the knowledgeable and still-sprightly Ed himself, a native Charlestonian. All of Ed's walks start from the big Pineapple Fountain in Waterfront Park and reservations are a must.

A much newer addition is the **Pat Conroy**

South of Broad Tour (843/568-0473, www .southofbroadwalkingtour.com, Tues.–Sat. 11 A.M., $25), a two-hour walking tour which came out with the launch of Conroy's new book by the same name. While it understandably deals with some of the characters from the book, it's also a good all-around tour for this historically pivotal area of town. It meets in the lobby of the Mills House Hotel at 115 Meeting St. Price includes admission to the nearby Gibbes Museum of Art (which is where the tour ends) and a cocktail at Slightly North of Broad restaurant. Advance reservations for the tour are required.

Original Charleston Walks (45 Broad St., 800/729-3420, www.charlestonwalks.com, daily 8:30 A.M.–9:30 P.M., $18.50 adults, $10.50 children) has received much national TV exposure. They leave from the corner of Market and State Streets. They have a full slate of tours, including a popular adults-only pub crawl. **Charleston Strolls Walk with History** (843/766-2080, www.charlestonstrolls.com, $18 adults, $10 children) is another popular tour good for a historical overview and tidbits. They have three daily embarkation points: Charleston Place (9:30 A.M.), the Days Inn (9:40 A.M.), and the Mills House (10 A.M.). **Architectural Walking Tours** (173 Meeting St., 800/931-7761, www.architecturalwalking toursofcharleston.com, $20) offers an 18th-century tour at 10 A.M. and a 19th-century tour at 2 P.M., daily except Tuesdays and Sundays, which are geared more toward historic preservation. They leave from the Meeting Street Inn (173 Meeting St.).

A relatively new special interest tour is **Charleston Art Tours** (53 Broad St., 843/860-3327, www.charlestonarttours.com, $49). The brainchild of local artists Karen Hagan and Martha Sharp, this tour is led by a professional artist guide and includes refreshments and a gift bag from one of the featured galleries. It leaves Tuesday–Saturday at 10 A.M. and 2 P.M. from 53 Broad Street. They also run a Charleston Renaissance tour, which includes a visit to the Gibbes Museum of Art (Tues.–Sat. 10 A.M., leaving from the Gibbes, $55).

Ghost tours are very popular in Charleston. **Bulldog Tours** (40 N. Market St., 843/722-8687, www.bulldogtours.com) has exclusive access to the Old City Jail, which features prominently in most of their tours. Their most popular tour, the Haunted Jail Tour ($18 adults, $10 children) leaves daily at 7 P.M., 8 P.M., 9 P.M., and 10 P.M.; meet at the Old City Jail. The Ghosts and Dungeons tour (not available Dec.–Feb., $18) leaves Tuesday–Saturday at 7 and 9 P.M. from 40 North Market Street. Other tours include the Ghosts and Graveyard Tour (7:30 and 9:30 P.M., $18) and the adults-only Dark Side of Charleston (daily 8 and 10 P.M., $18). **Tour Charleston** (184 E. Bay St., 843/723-1670, www.tourcharleston.com, $18) offers two paranormal tours, Ghosts of Charleston I, which leaves daily at 5:30 P.M., 7:30 P.M., and 9:30 P.M. from Waterfront Park, and Ghosts of Charleston II, which leaves at 7 P.M. and 9 P.M. from Marion Square.

Carriage Tours

The city strictly regulates the treatment and upkeep of carriage horses, so there's not a heck of a lot of difference in service or price among the various tour companies. Typically rides take 1–1.5 hours. They sometimes book up early, so call ahead.

The oldest service in town is **Palmetto Carriage Works** (40 N. Market St., 843/723-8145, www.carriagetour.com), which offers free parking at its "red barn" base near City Market. Another popular tour is **Old South Carriage Company** (14 Anson St., 843/723-9712, www.oldsouthcarriage.com, $21 adults, $13 children) with its Confederate-clad drivers. **Carolina Polo & Carriage Company** (16 Hayne St., 843/577-6767, www.cpcc.com, $20 adults, $12 children) leaves from several spots, including the Doubletree Hotel and their Hayne Street stables.

Motorized Tours

Leaving from Charleston Visitor Reception and Transportation Center at 375 Meeting Street, **Adventure Sightseeing** (843/762-0088, www.touringcharleston.com, $20 adults, $11 children) offers several comfortable 1.5–2 hour rides, including the only motorized tour to the Citadel area. Tour times are daily at 9:30 A.M., 10 A.M., 10:30 A.M., 10:45 A.M., 11:30 A.M., 12:20 P.M., 1:30 P.M., and 2:45 P.M. You can make a day of it with **Charleston's Finest Historic Tours** (843/577-3311, www .historictoursofcharleston.com, $18 adults, $9 children), which has a basic two-hour city tour each day at 10:30 A.M. plus offers some much longer tours to outlying plantations. They also offer free downtown pickup from most lodgings. The old faithful **Gray Line of Charleston** (843/722-4444, www.graylineofcharleston .com, $20 adults, $12 children) offers a 90-minute tour departing from the Visitors Center every half-hour 9:30 A.M.–3 P.M. March–November (hotel pickup by reservation). Last tour leaves at 2 P.M. during the off-season.

African American History Tours

Charleston is rich in African American history,

and a couple of operators specializing in this area are worth mentioning: Al Miller's **Sites & Insights Tours** (843/762-0051, www.sitesandinsightstours.com, $13–18) has several packages, including a Black History and Porgy & Bess Tour as well as a good combo city and island tour, all departing from the Visitors Center. Alphonso Brown's **Gullah Tours** (843/763-7551, www.gullahtours.com), featuring stories told in the Gullah dialect, all leave from Gallery Chuma at 43 John St. near the Visitors Center Monday–Friday at 11 A.M. and 1 P.M. and Saturday at 11 A.M., 1 P.M., and 3 P.M.

Water Tours

The best all-around tour of Charleston Harbor is the 90-minute ride offered by **Spiritline Cruises** (800/789-3678, www.spiritlinecruises.com, $16 adults, $10 ages 6–11), which leaves from either Aquarium Wharf or Patriots Point. Allow about a half-hour for ticketing and boarding. They also have a three-hour dinner cruise in the evening leaving from Patriots Point (about $50 per person) and a cruise to Fort Sumter.

Sandlapper Water Tours (843/849-8687, www.sandlappertours.com, $20–27) offers many types of evening and dolphin cruises on a 45-foot catamaran. They also offer Charleston's only water-borne ghost tour.

Ecotours

This aspect of Charleston's tourist scene is very well represented. The best operators include: **Barrier Island Eco Tours** (50 41st Ave., 843/886-5000, www.nature-tours.com, tours start at $30), taking you up to the Cape Romain Refuge out of Isle of Palms; **Coastal Expeditions** (514-B Mill St., 843/884-7684, www.coastalexpeditions.com, prices vary), with a base on Shem Creek in Mount Pleasant, offering several different-length sea kayak adventures; and **PaddleFish Kayaking** (843/330-9777, www.paddlefishkayaking.com, tours start at $45), offering several kinds of kayaking tours (no experience necessary) from downtown, Kiawah Island, and Seabrook Island.

Entertainment and Events

Charleston practically invented the idea of diversion and culture in America, so it's no surprise that there's plenty to do here, from museums to festivals to a brisk nightlife scene.

NIGHTLIFE

Unlike the locals vs. tourists divide you find so often in other destination cities, in Charleston it's nothing for a couple of tourists to find themselves at a table next to four or five college students enjoying themselves in true Charlestonian fashion, i.e., loudly and with lots of good food and strong drink nearby.

Indeed, the Holy City is downright ecumenical in its partying. The smokiest dives also have some of the best brunches. The toniest restaurants also have some of the most hopping bar scenes. Tourist hot spots written up in all the guidebooks also have their share of local regulars.

But through it all, one constant remains: Charleston's finely honed ability to seek out and enjoy the good life. It's a trait that comes naturally and traditionally, going back to the days of the earliest Charleston drinking and gambling clubs, like the Fancy Society, the Meddlers Laughing Club, and the Fort Jolly Volunteers.

Bars close in Charleston at 2 A.M. The old days of the "mini-bottle"—in which no free pour was allowed and all drinks had to be made from the little airline bottles—are gone, and it seems that local bartenders have finally figured out how to mix a decent cocktail. At the retail level, all hard liquor sales stop at 7 P.M., with none at all on Sundays. You can buy beer and wine in grocery stores 24/7.

Pubs and Bars

In a nod to the city's perpetual focus on well-prepared food, it's difficult to find a Charleston watering hole that *doesn't* offer really good food in addition to a well-stocked bar.

One of Charleston's favorite neighborhood spots is **Moe's Crosstown Tavern** (714 Rutledge Ave., 843/722-3287, daily 11 A.M.–2 A.M.) at Rutledge and Francis in the Wagener Terrace/Hampton Square area. A newer location, **Moe's Downtown Tavern** (5 Cumberland St., 843/577-8500, daily 11 A.M.–2 A.M.) offers a similar vibe and menu, but the original, and best, Moe's experience is at the Crosstown.

Nipping on Moe's heels for best pub food in town is **A.C.'s Bar and Grill** (467 King St., 843/577-6742, daily 11 A.M.–2 A.M.). Though this dark, quirky watering hole might seem out of place in the increasingly tony Upper King area, this only adds to its appeal. A.C.'s at its best is all things to all people: Charleston's favorite late-night bar, a great place to get a burger basket, and also one of the best (and certainly most unlikely) Sunday brunches in town, featuring chicken and waffles.

The action gets going late at **Social Wine Bar** (188 E. Bay St., 843/577-5665, daily 4 P.M.–2 A.M.), a hopping hangout near the French Quarter. While the hot and cold tapas are tasty—I like the special sashimi—the real action here, as you'd expect, is the wine. They offer at least 50 wines by the glass and literally hundreds by the bottle. My favorite thing to do here is partake of the popular "flights," triple tastes of kindred spirits, as it were. If the pricing on the menu seems confusing, ask your server to help you out.

Johnson's Pub (12 Cumberland St., 843/958-0662, daily noon–2 A.M.), a quirky but popular downtown spot, offers seven varieties of burger, all incredible, plus great pizza; it's also well known for its Caesar salad. Oh, yeah, and they keep the drinks coming, too.

The Guinness flows freely at **Tommy Condon's Irish Pub** (160 Church St., 843/577-3818, www.tommycondons.com, Sun.–Thurs. 11 A.M.–2 A.M., dinner served until 10 P.M., Fri.–Sat. 11 A.M.–2 A.M., dinner served until 11 P.M.)—after the obligatory and traditional

slow-pour, that is—as do the patriotic Irish songs performed live most nights. You have three sections to choose from in this large, low building right near City Market: the big outdoor deck, the cozy pub itself, and the back dining room with classic wainscoting.

If it's a nice day out, a good place to relax and enjoy happy hour outside is **Vickery's Bar and Grill** (15 Beaufain St., 843/577-5300, www.vickerysbarandgrill.com, Mon.–Sat. 11:30 A.M.–2 A.M., Sun. 11 A.M.–1 A.M., kitchen closes 1 A.M.), actually part of a small regional chain based in Atlanta. Start with the oyster bisque, and maybe try the turkey and Brie sandwich or crab cakes for your entrée.

Because of its commercial nature, Broad Street can get sparse when the sun goes down and the office workers disperse back to the 'burbs. But a warm little oasis can be found a few steps off Broad Street in the **Blind Tiger** (36–38 Broad St., 843/577-0088, daily 11:30–2 A.M., kitchen closes 10 P.M. Mon.–Thurs., 9 P.M. Fri.–Sun.), which takes its name from the local Prohibition-era nickname for a speakeasy. Wood panels, Guinness and Bass on tap, and some good bar-food items make this a good stop off the beaten path if you find yourself in the area. A patio out back often features live music.

Located not too far over the Ashley River on U.S. 17, Charleston institution **Gene's Haufbrau** (17 Savannah Hwy., 843/225-4363, www.geneshaufbrau.com, daily 11:30 A.M.–2 A.M.) is worth making a special trip into West Ashley. Boasting the largest beer selection in Charleston—from the Butte Creek Organic Ale from California to a can of PBR—Gene's also claims to be the oldest bar in town, established in 1952.

Though Sullivan's Island has a lot of high-dollar homes, it still has friendly watering holes like **Dunleavy's Pub** (2213-B Middle St., 843/883-9646, Sun.–Thurs. 11:30 A.M.–1 A.M., Fri.–Sat. 11:30 A.M.–2 A.M.). Inside is a great bar festooned with memorabilia, or you can enjoy a patio table. The other Sullivan's watering hole of note is **Poe's Tavern** (2210 Middle St., 843/883-0083, daily 11 A.M.–2 A.M., kitchen

Poe's Tavern on Sullivan's Island

© JIM MOREKIS

closes 10 P.M.) across the street, a nod to Edgar Allan Poe and his service on the island as a clerk in the U.S. Army. It's a lively, mostly-locals scene, set within a fun but suitably dark interior (though you might opt for one of the outdoor tables on the raised patio). Simply put, no trip to Sullivan's is complete without a stop at one (or possibly both) of these two local landmarks, each within a stone's throw of the other.

If you're in Folly Beach, enjoy the great views and the great cocktails at **Blu Restaurant and Bar** (1 Center St., 843/588-6658, www.blu follybeach.com, $10–20) inside the Holiday Inn Folly Beach Oceanfront. There's nothing like a Spiked Lemonade on a hot Charleston day at the beach.

Another notable Folly Beach watering hole is the **Sand Dollar Social Club** (7 Center St., 843/588-9498, Sun.–Fri. noon–1 A.M., Sat. noon–2 A.M.), the kind of cash-only, mostly local, and thoroughly enjoyable dive you often find in little beach towns. You have to pony up for a "membership" to this private club, but it's only a buck. There's a catch though: you can't get in until your 24-hour "waiting period" is over.

If you find yourself up in North Charleston, by all means stop by **Madra Rua Irish Pub** (1034 E. Montague Ave., 843/554-2522), an authentic watering hole with a better-than-average pub food menu that's also a great place to watch a soccer game.

Live Music

Charleston's music scene is best described as hit-and-miss. There's no distinct "Charleston sound" to speak of (especially now that the heyday of Hootie and the Blowfish is long past) and there's no one place where you're assured of finding a great band any night of the week.

The scene is currently in even more of a state of flux because the city's best-regarded live rock club, Cumberland's on King Street, closed in late 2007 after 15 years in business. The best place to find up-to-date music listings is the local free weekly *Charleston City Paper* (www.charlestoncitypaper.com).

These days the hippest music spot in town is out on James Island at **The Pour House** (1977 Maybank Hwy., 843/571-4343, www .charlestonpourhouse.com, 9 P.M.–2 A.M. on nights with music scheduled, call for info), where sometimes the local characters are just as entertaining as the acts onstage.

The venerable **Music Farm** (32 Ann St., 843/722-8904, www.musicfarm.com) on Upper King isn't much to look at from the outside, but inside, the cavernous space has played host to all sorts of bands over the past 15 years, including Talking Heads, Ween, Widespread Panic, and De La Soul.

For jazz, check out **Mistral** (99 S. Market St., 843/722-5708, Sun.–Thurs. 11 A.M.–11 P.M., Fri.–Sat. 11 A.M.–midnight). There's a constant stream of great performers from a variety of traditions, including Dixieland, every night of the week—not to mention some awesome food. Another great jazz place—and, like Mistral, a very good restaurant to boot—is **Mercato** (102 N. Market St., 843/722-6393, www.mercatocharleston.com, bar 4 P.M.–2 A.M., late night menu until 1 A.M.). Italian in menu and feel, the live jazz and R&B Wed.–Sat. at this establishment—owned by the same company that owns the five-star Peninsula Grill—is definitely all-American. The late kitchen hours are a great bonus.

Lounges

Across the street from Gene's Haufbrau, the retro-chic **Voodoo Lounge** (15 Magnolia Ln., 843/769-0228, Mon–Fri. 4 P.M.–2 A.M., Sat.–Sun. 5:30 P.M.–2 A.M., kitchen open until 1 A.M.) is another very popular West Ashley hangout. It has a wide selection of trendy cocktails and killer gourmet tacos.

The aptly named **Rooftop Bar and Restaurant** (23 Vendue Range, 843/723-0485, Tues.–Sat. 6 P.M.–2 A.M.) at the Library Restaurant in the Vendue Inn is a very popular waterfront happy hour spot from which to enjoy the sunset over the Charleston skyline. It's also a hot late-night hangout with a respectable menu.

Located in a 200-year-old building and suitably right above a cigar store, **Club Habana** (177 Meeting St., 843/853-5900, Mon.–Sat. 5 P.M.–1 A.M., Sun. 6 P.M.–midnight) is the perfect place to sink down into a big couch, warm yourself by the fireplace, sip a martini (or port, or single-malt scotch), and enjoy a good smoke in the dim light. Probably the last, best vestige of the cigar bar trend in Charleston, Club Habana remains popular. You get your cigars downstairs in Tinderbox Internationale, which features a range of rare "Legal Cuban" smokes, i.e., rolled from pre-embargo tobacco that's been warehoused for decades in Tampa, Florida.

Dance Clubs

The **Trio Club** (139 Calhoun St., 843/965-5333, Thurs.–Sat. 9 P.M.–2 A.M.) right off Marion Square is a favorite place to make the scene. There's a relaxing outdoor area with piped-in music, an intimate, sofa-filled upstairs bar for dancing and chilling, and the dark, candlelit downstairs with frequent live music.

Without a doubt Charleston's best dance club is **Club Pantheon** (28 Ann St., 843/577-2582, Fri.–Sun. 10 P.M.–2 A.M.).

Gay and Lesbian

Charleston is very tolerant by typical Deep South standards, and this tolerance extends to the gay and lesbian community as well. Most gay- and lesbian-oriented nightlife centers in the Upper King area.

Charleston's hottest and hippest dance spot of any type, gay or straight, is **Club Pantheon** (28 Ann St., 843/577-2582, Fri.–Sun. 10 P.M.–2 A.M.) on Upper King on the lower level of the parking garage across from the Visitors Center (375 Meeting St.). Pantheon's not cheap—cover charges are routinely well over $10—but it's worth it for the great DJs, the dancing, and the people-watching, not to mention the drag cabaret on Friday and Sunday nights.

Just down the street from Club Pantheon—and owned by the same people—is a totally different kind of gay bar, **Dudley's** (42 Ann St., 843/577-6779, daily 4 P.M.–2 A.M.). Mellower and more appropriate for conversation or a friendly game of pool, Dudley is a nice contrast to the thumping Pantheon a few doors down.

Though **Vickery's Bar and Grill** (15

Beaufain St., 843/577-5300, www.vickerysbar andgrill.com, Mon.–Sat. 11:30 A.M.–2 A.M., Sun. 11 A.M.–1 A.M., kitchen closes 1 A.M.) does not market itself as a gay and lesbian establishment, it's nonetheless become quite popular with that population—not least because of the good reputation its parent tavern in Atlanta has with that city's large and influential gay community.

PERFORMING ARTS
Theater

Unlike the more puritanical (literally) colonies farther up the American coast, Charleston was from the beginning an arts-friendly settlement. The first theatrical production in the western hemisphere happened in Charleston in January 1735, when a nomadic troupe rented a space at Church and Broad Streets to perform Thomas Otway's *The Orphan.*

The play's success led to the building of the Dock Street Theatre on now-Queen Street, which on February 12, 1736, held its first production, *The Recruiting Officer,* a popular play for actresses of the time because it calls for some female characters to wear tight-fitting British army uniforms. Live theater became a staple of Charleston social life, with notable thespians including both Edwin and Junius Booth (brothers of Lincoln's assassin John Wilkes) and Edgar Allan Poe's mother Eliza performing here.

Several high-quality troupes continue to keep that proud old tradition alive, chief among them being **Charleston Stage** (843/577-7183, www.charlestonstage.com), the resident company of the Dock Street Theatre. In addition to its well-received regular season of classics and modern staples, Charleston Stage has debuted more than 30 original scripts over the years, most recently *Gershwin at Folly,* recounting the composer's time at Folly Beach working on *Porgy and Bess.*

The city's most unusual players are **The Have Nots!** (843/853-6687, www.thehavenots .com), with a total ensemble of 35 comedians who typically perform their brand of edgy improv every Friday night at Theatre 99 (280 Meeting St.).

CHARLESTON NATIVES

In addition to the long list of historic figures, some notable modern personalities born in Charleston or closely associated with the city include:

- Counterculture artist Shepard Fairey, who designed the iconic "Hope" campaign sign for Barack Obama

- Actress Mabel King *(The Wiz)*

- Actress/model Lauren Hutton

- Author Nancy Friday

- Actor Thomas Gibson *(Dharma & Greg)*

- Author/lyricist DuBose Heyward

- Author Josephine Humphreys

- Author Sue Monk Kidd *(The Secret Life of Bees)*

- Actress Vanessa Minnillo (attended high school)

- Actor Will Patton *(Remember the Titans)*

- Author Alexandra Ripley

- Musician Darius Rucker (singer for Hootie and the Blowfish, now a solo country artist)

- Comedian Andy Dick

- Comedian Stephen Colbert

The players of **PURE Theatre** (843/723-4444, www.puretheatre.org) perform at the Circular Congregation Church's Lance Hall (150 Meeting St.). Their shows emphasize compelling, mature drama, beautifully performed. This is where to catch less-glitzy, more-gritty productions like *Rabbit Hole, American Buffalo,* and *Cold Tectonics,* a hit at Piccolo Spoleto. **The Footlight Players** (843/722-4487, www.footlightplayers.net) are the oldest continuously active company in town (since 1931). This community-based, amateur company performs a mix of crowd-pleasers *(The Full Monty)* and cutting-edge drama *(This War is Live)* at their space at 20 Queen Street.

Music

The forerunner to the **Charleston Symphony Orchestra** (843/554-6060, www.charleston symphony.com) performed for the first time on December 28, 1936, at the Hibernian Hall on Meeting Street. During that first season the CSO accompanied the inaugural show at the renovated Dock Street Theatre, *The Recruiting Officer.* For seven decades, the CSO continued to provide world-class orchestral music, gaining "Metropolitan" status in the 1970s, when they accompanied the first-ever local performance of *Porgy and Bess,* which despite its downtown setting couldn't be performed locally before then due to segregation laws.

Sadly, as of this writing the CSO has suspended operations and cancelled the 2010–2011 season due to ongoing financial difficulties. I suggest checking the website, which is occasionally updated, for news.

However, the separate group **Chamber Music Charleston** (843/763-4941, www .chambermusiccharleston.org), which relies on many core CSO musicians, continues to perform around town, including at Piccolo Spoleto. They play a wide variety of picturesque historic venues, including the Old Exchange (120 E. Bay St.), the Calhoun Mansion (16 Meeting St.), and the Footlight Players Theatre (20 Queen St.). They can also be found at private house concerts, which sell out quickly.

The excellent music department at the

STEPHEN COLBERT, NATIVE SON

A purist would insist that Charlestonians are born, not made. While it's true that Comedy Central star Stephen Colbert was actually born in Washington, DC, he did spend most of his young life in the Charleston suburb of James Island, attending the Porter-Gaud School. And regardless of his literal birthplace, few would dispute that Colbert is the best-known Charlestonian in American pop culture today.

While it's commonly assumed that Colbert's surname is a link to Charleston's French Huguenot heritage, the truth is that it's really an Irish name. To further burst the bubble, Colbert's father, a vice president at Charleston's Medical University of South Carolina, adopted the current French pronunciation himself – historically his family pronounced the "t" at the end.

That being said, Colbert returns quite often to Charleston, as he did in a December 2007 performance at the Sottile Theater, "I am Charleston – and So Can You!," a play on the title of his most recent book. The event included a reading from the book, an interview on growing up in Charleston, and a Q&A session with the local audience. The performance benefited Charleston Stage Company, which,

perhaps apocryphally, passed over Colbert for a role after an audition in 1981 for *Babes in Toyland.*

In summer 2007, Colbert cooperated with Ben & Jerry's Ice Cream to create a new flavor, "Americone Dream" (vanilla with fudge-covered waffle cone pieces and caramel swirl), proceeds from which went to the Coastal Community Foundation of South Carolina. To unveil the flavor, Colbert appeared at "The Joe" and threw out the first pitch at a Charleston River Dogs minor league game.

Soon after, Colbert told *Charleston* magazine that he and wife Evelyn "went to the Pig and bought eight pints" – a reference to the ubiquitous Southern grocery chain Piggly Wiggly, a.k.a., "the Pig."

Later that year, Colbert embarked on an ill-fated, tongue-in-cheek bid to get on the South Carolina presidential primary ballot, which never materialized. In a video message to the South Carolina Agricultural Summit in November he cried mock tears and said, "I wanted to be president of South Carolina so bad. I was going to be sworn in on a sack of pork ribs and I was going to institute the death penalty for eating Chinese shrimp."

College of Charleston sponsors the annual **Charleston Music Fest** (www.charleston musicfest.com), a series of chamber music concerts at various venues around the beautiful campus, featuring many faculty members of the College as well as visiting guest artists.

Other College musical offerings include: The **College of Charleston Concert Choir** (www.cofc.edu/music), which performs at various venues, usually churches, around town during the fall; the **College of Charleston Opera,** which performs at least one full-length production during the school year and often performs at Piccolo Spoleto; and the popular **Yuletide Madrigal Singers,** who sing in early December at a series of concerts in historic Randolph Hall.

Dance
The premier company in town is the 20-year-old **Charleston Ballet Theatre** (477 King St., 843/723-7334, www.charlestonballet.org). Its 18 full-time dancers perform a great mix of classics, modern pieces, and, of course, a yuletide *Nutcracker* at the Gaillard Municipal Auditorium. Most performances are at the Sottile Theatre (44 George St., just off King) and in the Black Box Theatre at their home office on Upper King.

CINEMA
The most interesting art house and indie venue in town is currently **The Terrace** (1956 Maybank Hwy., 843/762-9494, www.terrace theater.com), and not only because they offer beer and wine, which you can enjoy at your seat. Shows before 5 P.M. are $7. It's west of Charleston on James Island. Get there by taking U.S. 17 west out of Charleston and go south on Highway 171, then take a right on Maybank Highway (Highway 700).

For a generic but good multiplex experience, go over to Mount Pleasant to the **Palmetto Grande** (1319 Theater Dr., 843/216-8696).

FESTIVALS AND EVENTS
Charleston is a festival-mad city, especially in the spring and early fall. And new festivals are being added every year, further enhancing the hedonistic flavor of this city that has also mastered the art of hospitality. Here's a look through the calendar at all the key festivals in the area.

January
Held on a Sunday in late January at historic Boone Hall Plantation on Mount Pleasant, the **Lowcountry Oyster Festival** (www.charleston lowcountry.com, 11 A.M.–5 P.M., $8, food additional) features literally truckloads of the sweet shellfish for your enjoyment. Gates open at 10:30 A.M. and there's plenty of parking. Oysters are sold by the bucket and served with crackers and cocktail sauce. Bring your own shucking knife and/or glove, or buy them on-site.

February
One of the more unique events in town is the **Southeastern Wildlife Exposition** (various venues, 843/723-1748, www.sewe.com, $12.50/day, $30/three days, 12 and under free). For the last quarter century, the Wildlife Expo has brought together hundreds of artists and exhibitors to showcase just about any kind of naturally themed art you can think of, in over a dozen galleries and venues all over downtown. Kids will enjoy the live animals on hand as well.

March
Generally straddling late February and the first days of March, the four-day **Charleston Food & Wine Festival** (www.charlestonfood andwine.com, various venues and admission) is a glorious celebration of one of the Holy City's premier draws: its amazing culinary community. While the emphasis is on Lowcountry gurus like Donald Barickman of Magnolia's and Robert Carter of the Peninsula Grill, guest chefs from as far away as New York, New Orleans, and Los Angeles routinely come to show off their skills. Oenophiles, especially of domestic wines, will be in heaven as well. Tickets aren't cheap—an all-event pass is over $500 per person—but then again, this is one of America's great food cities, so you might find it worth every penny.

Coming immediately before the Festival of Houses and Gardens is the **Charleston International Antiques Show** (40 E. Bay St., 843/722-3405, www.historiccharleston.org, varied admission), held at Historic Charleston's headquarters at the Missroon House on the High Battery. It features over 30 of the nation's best-regarded dealers and offers lectures and tours.

Running mid-March through April, the perennial favorite **Festival of Houses and Gardens** (843/722-3405, www.historiccharleston.org, varied admission) is sponsored by the Historic Charleston Foundation and held at the very peak of the spring blooming season for maximum effect. In all, the Festival goes into a dozen historic neighborhoods to see about 150 homes. Each day sees a different three-hour tour of a different area, at about $45 per person. This is a fantastic opportunity to peek inside some amazing old privately owned properties that are inaccessible to visitors at all other times. A highlight is a big oyster roast and picnic at Drayton Hall.

Not to be confused with the above festival, the **Garden Club of Charleston House and Garden Tours** (843/530-5164, www.thegardenclubofcharleston.com, $35) are held over a weekend in late March. Highlights include the Heyward-Washington House and the private garden of the late great Charleston horticulturalist Emily Whaley.

One of Charleston's newest and most fun events, the five-night **Charleston Fashion Week** (www.fashionweek.charlestonmag.com, varied admission) is sponsored by *Charleston Magazine* and benefits a local women's charity. Mimicking New York's Fashion Week events under tenting in Bryant Park, Charleston's version features runway action under big tents in Marion Square—and, yes, past guests have included former contestants on *Project Runway.*

April

The annual **Cooper River Bridge Run** (www.bridgerun.com) happens the first Saturday in April (unless it's Easter weekend, in which case it runs the week before) and features a 10,000-

meter jaunt across the massive new Arthur Ravenel Bridge over the Cooper River, the longest cable span in the western hemisphere. It's not for those with a fear of heights, but it's still one of Charleston's best-attended events—with well over 30,000 participants.

The whole crazy idea started when Dr. Marcus Newberry of the Medical University of South Carolina in Charleston was inspired by an office fitness trail in his native state of Ohio to do something similar in Charleston to promote fitness. Participants can walk the course if they choose, and many do.

Signaled with the traditional cannon shot, the race still begins in Mount Pleasant and ends downtown, but over the years the course has changed to accommodate growth—not only in the event itself but in the city. Auto traffic, of course, is rerouted from the night before the race. The Bridge Run remains the only elite-level track and field event in South Carolina, with runners from Kenya typically dominating year after year. Each participant in the Bridge Run now must wear a transponder chip; new "Bones in Motion" technology allows you to track a favorite runner's exact position in real time during the race. The 2006 Run had wheelchair participants for the first time. There's now a Kid's Run in Hampton Square the Friday before, which also allows strollers.

From 1973 to 2000—except for 1976 when it was in Florida—the **Family Circle Cup** (161 Seven Farms Dr., Daniel Island, 843/856-7900, www.familycirclecup.com, varied admission) was held at Sea Pines Plantation on Hilton Head Island. But the popular Tier 1 Women's tennis tournament in 2001 moved to Daniel Island's brand-new Family Circle Tennis Center, specifically built for the event through a partnership of the magazine and the city of Charleston. (The Tennis Center is also open to the public and hosts many community events as well.)

Mount Pleasant is the home of Charleston's shrimping fleet, and each April sees all the boats parade by the Alhambra Hall & Park for the **Blessing of the Fleet** (843/884-8517, www.townofmountpleasant.com). Family events and lots and lots of seafood are also on tap.

May

Free admission and free parking are not the only draws at the outdoor **North Charleston Arts Festival** (5000 Coliseum Dr., www .northcharleston.org), but let's face it, that's important. Held beside North Charleston's Performing Arts Center & Convention Center, the Festival features music, dance, theater, multicultural performers, and storytellers. There are a lot of kids' events as well.

Held over three days at the Holy Trinity Greek Orthodox Church up towards the Neck, the **Charleston Greek Festival** (30 Race St., 843/577-2063, www.greekorthodoxchs.org, $3) offers a plethora of live entertainment, dancing, Greek wares, and of course fantastic Greek cuisine cooked by the congregation. Parking is not a problem, and there's even a shuttle to the church from the lot.

One of Charleston's newest annual events is the **Charleston International Film Festival** (various venues and prices, 843/817-1617, www .charlestonIFF.com). Despite being a relative latecomer to the film festival circuit, the event is pulled off with Charleston's usual aplomb.

Indisputably Charleston's single biggest and most important event, **Spoleto Festival USA** (843/579-3100, www.spoletousa.org, varied admission) has come a long way since it was a sparkle in the eye of the late Gian Carlo Menotti three decades ago. Though Spoleto long ago broke ties with its founder, his vision remains indelibly stamped on the event from start to finish.

There's plenty of music, to be sure, in genres from orchestral to opera to jazz to avant-garde, but you'll find something in every other performing art here, from dance to drama to spoken word, in traditions from Western to African to Southeast Asian. For 17 days from Memorial Day weekend through early June, Charleston hops and hums nearly 24 hours a day to the energy of this vibrant, cutting-edge yet accessible artistic celebration, which dominates everything and every conversation for those three weeks. Events happen in historic venues and churches all over downtown and as far as Middleton Place, which hosts the grand finale under the stars.

If you want to come to Charleston during Spoleto—and everyone should at least once— book your accommodations and your tickets far in advance. Tickets usually go on sale in early January for that summer's festival.

As if all the hubbub around Spoleto didn't give you enough to do, there's also **Piccolo Spoleto** (843/724-7305, www.piccolospoleto .com, various venues and admission), literally "little Spoleto," running concurrently. The intent of Piccolo Spoleto—begun just a couple of years after the larger festival came to town and run by the city's Office of Cultural Affairs—is to give local and regional performers a time to shine, sharing some of that larger spotlight on the national and international performers at the main event. Of particular interest to visiting families will be Piccolo's children's events, a good counter to some of the decidedly more adult fare at Spoleto USA.

June

Technically part of Piccolo Spoleto but gathering its own following, the **Sweetgrass Cultural Arts Festival** (www.sweetgrass festival.org) is held the first week in June in

© JOHN WOLLWERTH / 123RF.COM

sweetgrass baskets, celebrated at June's Sweetgrass Cultural Arts Festival

A MAN, A PLAN – SPOLETO!

Sadly, Gian Carlo Menotti is no longer with us, having died in 2007 at the age of 95. But the overwhelming success of the composer's brainchild and labor of love, **Spoleto Festival USA,** lives on, enriching the cultural and social life of Charleston and serving as the city's chief calling card to the world at large.

Menotti began writing music at age seven in his native Italy. As a young man he would move to Philadelphia to study music, where he shared classes – and lifelong connections – with Leonard Bernstein and Samuel Barber. His first full-length opera, *The Consul* would garner him the Pulitzer Prize, as would 1955's *The Saint of Bleecker Street.* But by far Menotti's best-known work is the beloved Christmas opera *Amahl and the Night Visitors,* composed especially for NBC television in 1951.

At the height of his fame in 1958, the charismatic and mercurial genius – fluent and witty in five languages – founded the "Festival of Two Worlds" in Spoleto, Italy, specifically as a forum for young American artists in Europe. But it wasn't until nearly two decades later, in 1977, that Menotti was able to make his long-imagined dream of an American counterpart a reality.

Attracted to Charleston because of its longstanding support of the arts, its undeniable good taste, and its small size – ensuring that his festival would always be the number-one activity in town while it was going on – Menotti worked closely with the man who was to become the other key part of the equation: Charleston Mayor Joe Riley, then in his first term in office. Since then, the city has built on Spoleto's success by founding its own local version, **Piccolo Spoleto** – literally, "little Spoleto" – which focuses exclusively on local and regional talent.

Things haven't always gone smoothly. Menotti and the stateside festival parted ways in 1993, when he took over the Rome Opera. Making matters more uneasy, the Italian festival – run by Menotti's longtime partner (and later adopted son) Chip – also became estranged from what was intended to be its soul mate in South Carolina. (Chip was later replaced by the Italian Culture Ministry.) And though Mayor Riley and Spoleto Mayor Massimo Brunini have gone public with their desire for reconciliation between the two events, as of this writing that possibility remains sketchy at best.

But perhaps this kind of creative tension is what Menotti intended all along. Indeed, each spring brings a Spoleto USA that seems to thrive on the inherent conflict between the festival's often cutting-edge offerings and the very traditional city that hosts it. Unlike so many of the increasingly generic arts "festivals" across the nation, Spoleto still challenges its audiences, just as Menotti intended it to do. Depending on the critic and the audience member, that modern opera debut you see may be groundbreaking or gratuitous. The drama you check out may be exhilarating or tiresome.

Still, the crowds keep coming, attracted just as much to Charleston's many charms as to the art itself. Each year, a total of about half a million people attend both Spoleto and Piccolo Spoleto. (Despite a weak economy, the 2009 edition actually broke a five-day ticket sales record.) Nearly a third of the attendees are Charleston residents – the final proof that when it comes to supporting the arts, Charleston puts its money where its mouth is.

Mount Pleasant at the Laing Middle School (2213 Hwy. 17 N.). The event celebrates the traditional sweetgrass basket-making skills of African Americans in the historical Christ Church Parish area of Mount Pleasant. If you want to buy some sweetgrass baskets made by the world's foremost experts in the field, this would be the time.

The free, weekend-long, outdoor **Charleston Harbor Fest** (www.charlestonharborfest.org, free) at the Maritime Center on the waterfront is without a doubt one of the coolest events in town for the whole family. You can see and tour working tall ships, and watch master boatwrights at work building new ones. There are free sailboat rides into the harbor and the U.S.

Navy provides displays. As if all that weren't enough, you get to witness the start of the 777-mile annual Charleston-to-Bermuda race.

July

Each year, over 30,000 people come to see the **Patriots Point Fourth of July Blast** (866/831-1720), featuring a hefty barrage of fireworks shot off the deck of the USS *Yorktown* moored on the Cooper River in the Patriots Point complex. Food, live entertainment, and kids' activities are also featured.

September

From late September into the first week of October, the city-sponsored **MOJA Arts Festival** (843/724-7305, www.mojafestival .com, varied venues and admission), highlights the cultural contributions of African Americans and people from the Caribbean with dance, visual art, poetry, cuisine, crafts, and music in genres from gospel to jazz to reggae to classical. In existence since 1984, MOJA's name comes from the Swahili word for "one," and its incredibly diverse range of offerings in so many media have made it one of the Southeast's premier events. Highlights include a Reggae Block Party and the always-fun Caribbean Parade. Some events are ticketed, while others, such as the kids' activities and many of the dance and film events, are free.

For five weeks from the last week of September into October, the Preservation Society of Charleston hosts the much-anticipated **Fall Tours of Homes & Gardens** (843/722-4630, www.preservationsociety.org, $45). The tour takes you into over a dozen local residences and is the nearly 90-year-old organization's biggest fundraiser. Tickets typically go on sale the previous June, and they tend to sell out very quickly.

October

Another great food event in this great food city, the **Taste of Charleston** (1235 Long Point Rd., 843/577-4030, www.charlestonrestaurant association.com, 11 A.M.–5 P.M., $12) is held at Boone Hall Plantation in Mount Pleasant

and sponsored by the Greater Charleston Restaurant Association. Over 50 area chefs and restaurants come together so you can sample their wares, including a wine and food pairing, with proceeds going to charity.

November

Plantation Days at Middleton Place (4300 Ashley River Rd., 843/556-6020, www .middletonplace.org, daily 9 A.M.–5 P.M., last tour 4:30 P.M., guided tour $10) happen each Saturday in November, giving visitors a chance to wander the grounds and see artisans at work practicing authentic crafts, as they would have done in antebellum days, on the grounds, with a special emphasis on the contributions of African Americans. A special treat comes on Thanksgiving, when a full meal is offered at the Middleton Place restaurant (843/556-6020, www.middletonplace.org) on the grounds (reservations highly recommended).

Though the **Battle of Secessionville** actually took place in June 1862 much farther south, November is the time the battle is re-enacted at Boone Plantation (1235 Long Point Rd., 843/884-4371, www.boonehallplantation .com, $17.50 adults, $7.50 children) on Mount Pleasant. Call for specific dates and times.

December

A yuletide in the Holy City is an experience you'll never forget, as the **Christmas in Charleston** (843/724-3705, www.charles toncity.info) events clustered around the first week of the month prove. For some reason—whether it's the old architecture, the friendly people, the churches, the carriages, or all of the above—Charleston feels right at home during Christmas. The festivities begin with Mayor Joe Riley lighting the city's 60-foot Tree of Lights in Marion Square, followed by a parade of brightly lit boats from Mount Pleasant all the way around Charleston up the Ashley River. The key event is the Sunday Christmas Parade through downtown featuring bands, floats, and performers in the holiday spirit. The Saturday Farmers Market in the square continues through the middle of the month with a focus on holiday items.

Shopping

For a relatively small city, Charleston has an impressive amount of big-name, big-city stores to go along with its charming, one-of-a-kind locally owned shops. I've never known anyone to leave Charleston without bundles of good stuff.

KING STREET

Without a doubt, King Street is by far the main shopping thoroughfare in the area. It's unique not only for the fact that so many national name stores are lined up so close to each other, but because there are so many great restaurants of so many different types scattered in and amongst all the retail outlets, ideally positioned for when you need to take a break to rest and refuel.

Though I don't necessarily recommend doing so—Charleston has so much more to offer—a visitor could easily spend an entire weekend doing nothing but shopping, eating, and carousing up and down King Street from

early morning to the wee hours of the following morning.

King Street has three distinct areas with three distinct types of merchandise: Lower King is primarily top-of-the-line antique stores (most are closed Sundays, so plan your trip accordingly); Middle King is where you'll find upscale name-brand outlets such as Banana Republic and American Apparel, as well as some excellent shoe stores; and Upper King north of Calhoun is where you'll find funky housewares shops, generally locally owned.

Antiques

A relatively new addition to Lower King's cluster of antique shops, **Alexandra AD** (156 King St., 843/722-4897, Mon.–Sat. 10 A.M.–5 P.M.) features great chandeliers, lamps, and fabrics.

As the name implies, **English Patina** (179 King St., 843/853-0380, Mon.–Sat. 10 A.M.–5 P.M.) specializes in European

© JIM MOREKIS

King Street is the center of shopping in Charleston.

MAYOR JOE'S LEGACY

Few cities anywhere have been as greatly influenced by one mayor as Charleston has by Joseph P. "Joe" Riley, re-elected in November 2007 to his ninth four-year term. Now mayor for over 30 years, "Mayor Joe," as he's called, is not only responsible for instigating the vast majority of redevelopment in the city, he continues to set the bar for its award-winning tourist industry – always a key component in his long-term plans.

Riley won his first mayoral race at the age of 32. He was the second Irish American mayor of the city, the first being the great John Grace, who was first elected in 1911 and eventually defeated by the allegedly anti-Catholic Thomas P. Stoney. Legend has it that soon after winning his first mayoral election in 1975, Riley was handed an old envelope written decades before by the Bishop of Charleston, addressed to "The Next Irish Mayor." Inside was a note with a simple message: "Get the Stoneys."

Though young, the well-regarded lawyer, Citadel grad, and former member of the state legislature had a clear vision for his administration: It would bring unprecedented numbers of women and minorities into city government, rejuvenate then-seedy King Street, and enlarge the city's tax base by annexing surrounding areas (during Riley's tenure the city has grown from 16.7 square miles to over 100).

But in order to make any of that happen, one thing had to happen first: Charleston's epidemic street crime had to be brought under control. Enter a vital and perhaps underrated partner in Riley's effort to remake Charleston – Chief of Police Reuben Greenberg. From 1982 to 2005, Greenberg – who intrigued locals and the national media not only for his dominant personality but because he was that comparative rarity, an African American Jew – turned old ideas of law enforcement in Charleston upside down through his introduction of "community policing." Charleston cops would have to have a college degree. Graffiti would not be tolerated. And for the first time in recent memory, they would have to walk beats instead of stay in their cars. With Greenberg's help, Riley was able to keep together the unusual coalition of predominantly white business and corporate interests and African American voters that brought him into office in the first place.

It hasn't all been rosy. Riley was put on the spot in 2007 after the tragic deaths of the "Charleston 9" firefighters, an episode which seemed to expose serious policy and equipment flaws in the city's fire department. And he's often been accused of being too easily infatuated with high-dollar development projects instead of paying attention to the needs of regular Charlestonians. But while every four years there's talk around town that somebody might finally be able to beat Mayor Joe, every four years the naysayers are disappointed as he's reelected again.

Here's only a partial list of the major projects and events Mayor Joe has made happen in Charleston that visitors are likely to enjoy:

· Charleston Maritime Center

· Charleston Place

· Children's Museum of the Lowcountry

· Hampton Park rehabilitation

· King Street/Market Street retail district

· Mayor Joseph P. Riley Ballpark (named after the mayor at the insistence of city council over his objections)

· MOJA Arts Festival

· Piccolo Spoleto

· The South Carolina Aquarium

· Spoleto USA

· Waterfront Park

· West Ashley Bikeway & Greenway

furniture, brought to its big James Island warehouse three times a year in shipping containers. Since 1929, **George C. Birlant & Co.** (191 King St., 843/722-3842, Mon.–Sat. 9 A.M.–5:30 P.M.) has been importing 18th- and 19th-century furniture, silver, china, and crystal, and also deals in the famous "Charleston Battery Bench."

On the 200 block, **A'riga IV** (204 King St., 843/577-3075, Mon.–Sat. 10:30 A.M.–4:30 P.M.) deals in a quirky mix of 19th-century decorative arts, including rare apothecary items. **Carlton Daily Antiques** (208 King St., 843/853-2299, Mon.–Sat. 10 A.M.–5:30 P.M.) intrigues with its unusual focus on deco and modernist pieces and furnishings.

Art Galleries

Ever since native son Joseph Allen Smith began one of America's first art collections in Charleston in the late 1700s, the Holy City has been fertile ground for visual artists.

For most visitors, the center of visual arts activity is in the French Quarter between South Market and Tradd Streets. Thirty galleries reside there within short walking distance, including: **Charleston Renaissance Gallery** (103 Church St., 843/723-0025, www.fineart south.com, Mon.–Sat. 10 A.M.–5 P.M.) specializing in 19th- and 20th-century oils and sculpture featuring artists from the American South, including some splendid pieces from the Charleston Renaissance; the city-funded **City Gallery at Waterfront** (34 Prioleau St., 843/958-6484, Tues.–Fri. 11 A.M.–6 P.M., Sat.–Sun. noon–5 P.M.); the **Pink House Gallery** (17 Chalmers St., 843/723-3608, http://pinkhousegallery.tripod.com, Mon.–Sat. 10 A.M.–5 P.M.), in the oldest tavern building in the South, circa 1694; **Helena Fox Fine Art** (12 Queen St., 843/723-0073, www.fraser foxfineart.com, Mon.–Sat. 10 A.M.–5 P.M.), dealing in 20th-century representational art; the **Anne Worsham Richardson Birds Eye View Gallery** (119-A Church St., 843/723-1276, Mon.–Sat. 10 A.M.–5 P.M.), home of

South Carolina's official painter of the state flower and state bird; and the more modern-oriented **Robert Lange Studios** (2 Queen St., 843/805-8052, www.robertlangestudios.com, daily 11 A.M.–5 P.M.).

The best way to experience the area is to go on one of the popular **French Quarter ArtWalks** (843/724-3424, www.frenchquarter arts.com), held the first Friday of March, May, October, and December between 5–8 P.M. and featuring lots of wine, food, and, of course, art. You can download a map at the website.

One of the most important single venues, the nonprofit **Redux Contemporary Art Center** (136 St. Philip St., 843/722-0697, www.redux studios.org, Wed.–Sat. noon–5 P.M.) features modernistic work in a variety of media, from illustration to video installation to blueprints to performance art to graffiti. Outreach is hugely important to this venture, including lecture series, classes, workshops, and internships.

Part art gallery, part artsy home goods store, **Plum Elements** (161½ King St., 843/727-3747, Mon.–Tues. and Fri.–Sat. 10 A.M.–6 P.M., Wed. noon–6 P.M., Thurs. 10 A.M.–7 P.M.) is the labor of love of Andrea Schenck, who was inspired to open the shop by her time in Asia. The shop offers lots of absolutely unique gift items with an Eastern twist, plus there's a bona fide art gallery in the adjacent space.

For a more modern take from local artists, check out the **Sylvan Gallery** (171 King St., 843/722-2172, www.thesylvangallery.com, Mon.–Fri. 9 A.M.–5 P.M., Sat. 10 A.M.–5 P.M., Sun. 11 A.M.–4 P.M.), which specializes in 20th-and 21st-century art and sculpture.

Right up the street and incorporating works from the estate of Charleston legend Elizabeth O'Neill Verner is **Ann Long Fine Art** (177 King St., 843/577-0447, www.annlongfine art.com, Mon.–Sat. 11 A.M.–5 P.M.), which seeks to combine the painterly aesthetic of the Old World with the edgy vision of the New.

Farther up King and specializing in original Audubon prints and antique botanical prints is **The Audubon Gallery** (190 King St.,

Blue Bicycle Books on Upper King

843/853-1100, www.audubonart.com, Mon.–Sat. 10 A.M.–5 P.M.), the sister store of the Joel Oppenheimer Gallery in Chicago.

In the Upper King area is **Gallery Chuma** (43 John St., 843/722-7568, www.gallery chuma.com, Mon–Sat. 10 A.M.–6 P.M.), which specializes in the art of the Gullah people of the South Carolina coast. They do lots of cultural and educational events about Gullah culture as well as display art on the subject.

By far Charleston's favorite art supply store is **Artist & Craftsman Supply** (434 King St., 843/579-0077, www.artistcraftsman.com, Mon.–Sat. 10 A.M.–7 P.M., Sun. noon–5 P.M.), part of a well-regarded Maine-based chain. They cater to the pro as well as the dabbler, and have a fun children's art section as well.

Books and Music

It's easy to overlook at the far southern end of retail development on King, but the excellent **Preservation Society of Charleston Book and Gift Shop** (147 King St., 843/722-4630, Mon.–Sat. 10 A.M.–5 P.M.) is perhaps the best place in town to pick up books on Charleston lore and history as well as locally themed gift items.

The charming **Pauline Books and Media** (243 King St., 843/577-0175, Mon.–Sat. 10 A.M.–6 P.M.) is run by the Daughters of St. Paul and carries Christian books, Bibles, rosaries, and images from a Roman Catholic perspective.

Housed in an extremely long and narrow storefront on Upper King, Jonathan Sanchez's funky and friendly **Blue Bicycle Books** (420 King St., 843/722-2666, www.bluebicycle books.com, Mon.–Sat. 10 A.M.–6 P.M., Sun. 1–6 P.M.) deals primarily in used books and has a particularly nice stock of local and regional books, art books, and fiction.

The local bastion of indie music and the best place to find that rare vinyl is **52.5 Records** (561 King St., 843/722-3525, Mon.–Thurs. 11 A.M.–7 P.M., Fri.–Sat. 11 A.M.–9 P.M., Sun. 1–6 P.M.).

Clothes

Cynics may scoff at the proliferation of high-end national retail chains on Middle King, but rarely will a shopper find so many so conveniently located, and in such a pleasant environment. The biggies are: **The Gap** (269 King St., 843/577-2498, Mon.–Thurs. 10 A.M.–7 P.M.,

Fri.–Sat. 10 A.M.–8 P.M., Sun. 11 A.M.–7 P.M.); **Banana Republic** (247 King St., 843/722-6681, Mon.–Fri. 10 A.M.–7 P.M., Sat. 10 A.M.–8 P.M., Sun. noon–6 P.M.); **J. Crew** (264 King St., 843/534-1640, Mon.–Thurs. 10 A.M.–6 P.M., Fri.–Sat. 10 A.M.–8 P.M., Sun. noon–6 P.M.); and **American Apparel** (348 King St., 843/853-7220, Mon.–Sat. 10 A.M.–8 P.M., Sun. noon–7 P.M.).

For a locally owned clothing shop, try the innovative **Worthwhile** (268 King St., 843/723-4418, www.shopworthwhile.com, Mon.–Sat. 10 A.M.–6 P.M., Sun. noon–5 P.M.), which has lots of organic fashion.

After living for a time in L.A., native Charlestonian Guilds Bennett brought back a fun and flirty West Coast vibe to her boutique **Miostile** (346 King St., 843/722-7073, Mon.–Sat. 10 A.M.–7 P.M., Sun. noon–5 P.M.), which offers designer items in a beautifully restored setting.

Also in this area is one of the city's most unique locally owned shops: the nationally famous **Mary Norton** (318 King St., 843/724-1081, www.marynorton.com, Mon.–Sat. 10 A.M.–6 P.M., formerly Moo Roo, where native Charlestonian Mary Norton creates and sells her one-of-a-kind designer handbags.

Big companies' losses are your gain at **Oops!** (326 King St., 843/722-7768, Mon.–Fri. 10 A.M.–6 P.M., Sat. 10 A.M.–7 P.M., Sun. noon–6 P.M.), which buys factory mistakes and discontinued lines from major brands at a discount, passing along the savings to you. The range here tends towards colorful and preppy.

If hats are your thing, make sure you visit **Magar Hatworks** (57 Cannon St., 843/577-7740, www.magarhatworks.com, leighmagar@aol.com), where Leigh Magar makes and sells her whimsical, all-natural hats, some of which she designs for Barneys New York.

Another notable locally owned clothing store on King Street is the classy **Berlins Men's and Women's** (114–120 King St., 843/722-1665, Mon.–Sat. 9:30 A.M.–6 P.M.), dating from 1883.

Health and Beauty

The Euro-style window display of **Stella Nova** (292 King St., 843/722-9797, Mon.–Sat. 10 A.M.–7 P.M., Sun. 1–5 P.M.) beckons at the corner of King and Society. Inside this locally owned cosmetics store and studio, you'll find a wide selection of high-end makeup and beauty products. There's also a Stella Nova day spa (78 Society Street, 843/723-0909, Mon.–Sat. 9 A.M.–6 P.M., Sun. noon–5 P.M.).

Inside the Francis Marion Hotel near Marion Square is **Spa Adagio** (387 King St., 843/577-2444, Mon.–Sat. 10 A.M.–7 P.M., Sun. by appointment only), offering massage, waxing, and skin and nail care. On Upper King you'll find **Allure Salon** (415 King St., 843/722-8689, Tues. and Thurs. 10 A.M.–7 P.M., Wed. and Fri. 9 A.M.–5 P.M., Sat. 10 A.M.–3 P.M.) for stylish haircuts.

Home, Garden, and Sporting Goods

With retail locations in Charleston and Savannah and a new cutting-edge, green-friendly warehouse in North Charleston, **Half Moon Outfitters** (280 King St., 843/853-0990, www.halfmoonoutfitters.com, Mon.–Sat. 10 A.M.–7 P.M., Sun. noon–6 P.M.) is something of a local legend. Here you can find not only top-of-the-line camping and outdoor gear and good tips on local recreation, but some really stylish, outdoorsy apparel as well.

Probably Charleston's best-regarded home goods store is the nationally recognized **ESD, Elizabeth Stuart Design** (314 King St., 843/577-6272, www.esdcharleston.com, Mon.–Sat. 10 A.M.–6 P.M.), with a wide range of antique and new furnishings, art, lighting, jewelry, and more.

Several great home and garden stores are worth mentioning on Upper King: **Global Awakening Market** (499 King St., 843/577-8579, www.globalawakeningmarket.com, Mon.–Sat. 11 A.M.–6 P.M.), which deals exclusively in fair trade clothing, crafts, and furnishings from all over the world; **Charleston Gardens** (650 King St., 866/469-0118, www.charlestongardens.com, Mon.–Sat. 9 A.M.–5 P.M.) for furniture and accessories; and **Haute Design Studio** (489 King

St., 843/577-9886, www.hautedesign.com, Mon.–Fri. 9 A.M.–5:30 P.M.) for upper-end furnishings with an edgy feel.

Jewelry

Joint Venture Estate Jewelers (185 King St., 843/722-6730, www.jventure.com, Mon.–Sat. 10 A.M.–5:30 P.M.) specializes in antique, vintage, and modern estate jewelry as well as pre-owned watches, including Rolex, Patek Philippe, and Cartier. Since 1919, **Croghan's Jewel Box** (308 King St., 843/723-3594, www.croghansjewelbox.com, Mon.–Fri. 9:30 A.M.–5:30 P.M., Sat. 10 A.M.–5 P.M.) has offered amazing locally crafted diamonds, silver, and designer pieces to generations of Charlestonians. An expansion in the late 1990s tripled the size of the historic location. **Art Jewelry by Mikhail Smolkin** (312 King St., 843/722-3634, Mon.–Sat. 10 A.M.–5 P.M.) features one-of-a-kind pieces by this St. Petersburg, Russia native.

Shoes

Rangoni of Florence (270 King St., 843/577-9554, Mon.–Sat. 9:30 A.M.–6 P.M., Sun. 12:30–5:30 P.M.) imports the best women's shoes from Italy, with a few men's designs as well. **Copper Penny Shooz** (317 King St., 843/723-3838, Mon.–Sat. 10 A.M.–7 P.M., Sun. noon–6 P.M.) combines hip and upscale fashion. Funky and fun **Phillips Shoes** (320 King St., 843/965-5270, Mon.–Sat. 10 A.M.–6 P.M.) deals in Dansko for men, women, and kids (don't miss the awesome painting above the register of Elvis fitting a customer). **Mephisto** (322 King St., 843/722-4666, www.mepcomfort.com, Mon.–Sat. 10 A.M.–6 P.M.) deals in that incredibly comfortable, durable brand.

The most famous locally owed place for footwear is **Bob Ellis Shoe Store** (332 King St., 843/722-2515, www.bobellisshoes.com, Mon.–Sat. 9 A.M.–6 P.M.), which has served Charleston's elite with high-end shoes since 1950.

CHARLESTON PLACE

Charleston Place (130 Market St., 843/722-4900, www.charlestonplaceshops.com, Mon.–Wed. 10 A.M.–6 P.M., Thurs.–Sat. 10 A.M.–8 P.M., Sun. noon–5 P.M.), a combined retail/hotel development begun to much controversy in the late 1970s, was the first big downtown redevelopment project of Mayor Riley's tenure. While naysayers said people would never come downtown to shop for boutique items, Riley proved them wrong, and 30 years later The Shops at Charleston Place and the Riviera (the entire complex has itself been renovated through the years) remains a big shopping draw for locals and tourists alike.

Highlights inside the large, stylish space include Gucci, Talbot's, Louis Vuitton, Yves Delorme, Everything But Water, and Godiva.

NORTH OF BROAD

In addition to the myriad of tourist-oriented shops in the Old City Market itself, there are a few gems in the surrounding area that also appeal to locals. A laid-back flea market vibe dominates at **Old City Market** (Meeting and Market Sts., 843/973-7236, daily 6 A.M.–11:30 P.M.), with the front, westward Market Hall featuring meandering halls lined with smallish, tourist-oriented shops and the subsequent, less-grand buildings purely for touristy flea market stalls. Pricier establishments, such as the famous Peninsula Grill, line the perimeter. Tip: If you must have one of the handcrafted sweetgrass baskets, try out your haggling skills—the prices have wiggle room built in.

Women come from throughout the region to shop at the incredible consignment store **The Trunk Show** (281 Meeting St., 843/722-0442, Mon.–Sat. 10 A.M.–6 P.M.). You can find one-of-a-kind vintage and designer wear and accessories. Some finds are bargains, some not so much, but there's no denying the quality and breadth of the offerings. For a more budget-conscious and counterculture vintage shop, walk a few feet next door to **Factor Five** (283 Meeting St., 843/965-5559), which has retro clothes, rare CDs, and assorted paraphernalia.

Indigo (4 Vendue Range, 800/549-2513, Sun.–Thurs. 10 A.M.–6 P.M., Fri.–Sat. 10 A.M.–7 P.M.), a favorite home accessories

The Trunk Show on Meeting Street

store, has plenty of one-of-a-kind pieces, many of them by regional artists and rustic in flavor, almost like outsider art.

Affiliated with the hip local restaurant chain Maverick Kitchens, **Charleston Cooks!** (194 East Bay St., 843/722-1212, www.charleston cooks.com, Mon.–Sat. 10 A.M.–9 P.M., Sun. 11 A.M.–6 P.M.) has an almost overwhelming array of gourmet items and kitchen ware, and even offers cooking classes.

OFF THE PENINSULA

Though the best shopping is in Charleston proper, there are some noteworthy independent stores in the surrounding areas.

Mount Pleasant boasts two fun antiques spots, **Linda Page's Thieves Mart** (1460 Ben Sawyer Blvd., 843/884-9672, Mon.–Fri., 9 A.M.–5:30 P.M., Sat. 9 A.M.–5 P.M.) and **Hungryneck Antique Mall** (401 Johnnie Dodds Blvd., 843/849-1744, Mon.–Sat. 10 A.M.–6 P.M., Sun. 1–5 P.M.) off U.S. 17.

The biggest music store in the region is **The Guitar Center** (7620 Rivers Ave., 843/572-9063, Mon.–Fri. 11 A.M.–7 P.M., Sat. 10 A.M.–7 P.M., Sun. noon–6 P.M.) in North

Charleston across from Northwood Mall. With just about everything a musician might want or need, it's part of a chain that's been around since the late 1950s, but the Charleston location is relatively new.

SHOPPING CENTERS

The newest and most pleasant mall in the area is the retro-themed, pedestrian-friendly **Mount Pleasant Towne Center** (1600 Palmetto Grande Dr., 843/216-9900, www.mtpleasant townecentre.com, Mon.–Sat. 10 A.M.–9 P.M., Sun. noon–6 P.M.), which opened in 1999 to serve the growing population of East Cooper residents tired of having to cross a bridge to get to a big mall. In addition to national chains you'll find a few cool local stores in here, like Stella Nova spa and day salon, Shooz by Copper Penny, and the men's store Jos. A. Banks.

You'll find the **Northwoods Mall** (2150 Northwoods Blvd., North Charleston, 843/797-3060, www.shopnorthwoodsmall.com, Mon.–Sat. 10 A.M.–9 P.M., Sun. noon–6 P.M.) up in North Charleston. Anchor stores include Dillard's, Belk, Sears, and J.C. Penney. North Charleston also hosts the **Tanger Outlet** (4840

Tanger Outlet Blvd., 843/529-3095, www.tangeroutlet.com, Mon.–Sat. 10 A.M.–9 P.M., Sun. 11 A.M.–6 P.M.). Get factory-priced bargains from stores such as Adidas, Banana Republic, Brooks Brothers, Corningware, Old Navy, Timberland, and more.

Citadel Mall (2070 Sam Rittenberg Blvd., 843/766-8511, www.shopcitadel-mall.com, Mon.–Sat. 10 A.M.–9 P.M., Sun. noon–6 P.M.) is in West Ashley (and curiously not at all close to the actual Citadel college). Anchors here are Dillards, Parisian, Target, Belk, and Sears.

Sports and Recreation

Because of the generally great weather in Charleston, helped immensely by the steady, soft sea breeze, outdoor activities are always popular and available. Though it's not much of a spectator sports town, there are plenty of things to do on your own, such as golf, tennis, walking, hiking, boating, and fishing.

ON THE WATER
Beaches
In addition to the charming town of Folly Beach itself, there's the modest, county-run **Folly Beach County Park** (1100 West Ashley Ave., 843/588-2426, www.ccprc.com, daily 10 A.M.–dark, open 9 A.M. Mar. and Apr., $7

per vehicle, free for pedestrians and cyclists) at the far west end of Folly Island. It has a picnic area, restrooms, outdoor showers, and beach chair and umbrella rentals. Get there by taking Highway 171/Folly Road until it turns into Center Street, and then take a right on West Ashley.

On Isle of Palms you'll find **Isle of Palms County Park** (14th Ave., 843/886-3863, www.ccprc.com, daily 10 A.M.–dark, open 9 A.M. summer, $5 per vehicle, free for pedestrians and cyclists), which has restrooms, showers, a picnic area, a beach volleyball area, and beach chair and umbrella rentals. Get there by taking the Isle of Palms Connector/Highway 517

© JASON TENCH / DREAMSTIME.COM

relaxing at the beach on Kiawah Island

to the island, go through the light at Palm Boulevard and take the next left at the park gate. There's good public beach access near the Pavilion Shoppes on Ocean Boulevard, accessed via JC Long Boulevard.

On the west end of Kiawah Island to the south of Charleston is **Kiawah Island Beachwalker Park** (843/768-2395, www.ccprc.com, Mar.– Apr. weekends only 10 A.M.–6 P.M., summer 9 A.M.–7 P.M., Sept. 10 A.M.–6 P.M., Oct. weekends only 10 A.M.–6 P.M., closed Nov.–Feb., $7 per vehicle, free for pedestrians and cyclists), the only public facility on this mostly private resort island. It has restrooms, showers, a picnic area with grills, and beach chair and umbrella rentals. Get there from downtown by taking Lockwood Avenue onto the Highway 30 Connector bridge over the Ashley River. Turn right onto Folly Road, then take a left onto Maybank Highway. After about 20 minutes you'll take another left onto Bohicket Road, which leads you to Kiawah in 14 miles. Turn left from Bohicket onto the Kiawah Island Parkway. Just before the security gate, turn right on Beachwalker Drive and follow the signs to the park.

For a totally go-it-alone type of beach day, go to the three-mile beach on the Atlantic Ocean at **Sullivan's Island.** There are no facilities, no lifeguards, strong offshore currents, and no parking lots on this residential island (park on the side of the street). There's also a lot of dog-walking on this beach since no leash is required November–February. Get there from downtown by crossing the Ravenel Bridge over the Cooper River and bearing right onto Coleman Boulevard, which turns into Ben Sawyer Boulevard. Take the Ben Sawyer Bridge onto Sullivan's Island. Beach access is plentiful and marked.

Kayaking

An excellent outfit for guided kayak tours is **Coastal Expeditions** (654 Serotina Ct., 843/881-4582, www.coastalexpeditions.com), which also runs the only approved ferry service to the Cape Romain National Wildlife Refuge. They'll rent a kayak for roughly $50 a

day. Coastal Expeditions also sells an outstanding kayaking/boating/fishing map of the area for about $12.

Barrier Island Eco Tours (50 41st Ave., 843/886-5000, www.nature-tours.com) takes you up to the Cape Romain refuge out of Isle of Palms. **PaddleFish Kayaking** (843/330-9777, www.paddlefishkayaking.com) offers several kinds of kayaking tours (no experience necessary) and is quite accommodating in terms of scheduling them. Another good tour operator is **Nature Adventures Outfitters** (1900 Iron Swamp Rd., 800/673-0679) out of Awendaw Island.

Closer to town, many kayakers put in at the **Shem Creek Marina** (526 Mill St., 843/884-3211, www.shemcreekmarina.com) or the public **Shem Creek Landing** in Mount Pleasant. From there it's a safe, easy paddle—sometimes with appearances by dolphins or manatee—to the Intracoastal Waterway. Some kayakers like to go from Shem Creek straight out into Charleston Harbor to **Crab Bank Heritage Preserve,** a prime birding island. Another good place to put in is at **Isle of Palms Marina** (50 41st Ave., 843/886-0209) on Morgan Creek behind the Wild Dunes Resort, emptying into the Intracoastal Waterway.

Local company **Half Moon Outfitters** (280 King St., 843/853-0990; 425 Coleman Blvd., 843/881-9472, www.halfmoonoutfitters.com, Mon.–Sat. 10 A.M.–7 P.M., Sun. noon–6 P.M.) sponsors an annual six-mile Giant Kayak Race at Isle of Palms Marina in late October, benefiting the Coastal Conservation League.

Behind Folly Beach is an extensive network of waterways, including lots of areas that are great for camping and fishing. The Folly River Landing is just over the bridge to the island. On Folly a good tour operator and rental house is **OceanAir Sea Kayak** (520 Folly Rd., 800/698-8718, www.seakayaksc.com).

Fishing and Boating

For casual fishing off a pier, try the well-equipped new **Folly Beach Fishing Pier** (101 E. Arctic Ave., 843/588-3474, $5 parking, $8 fishing fee, rod rentals available) on Folly

Beach or the **North Charleston Riverfront Park** (843/745-1087, www.northcharleston.org, daily dawn–dusk) along the Cooper River on the grounds of the old Navy Yard. Get onto the Navy Yard grounds by taking I-26 north to exit 216-B. Take a left onto Spruill Avenue and a right onto McMillan Avenue.

Key local marinas include **Shem Creek Marina** (526 Mill St., 843/884-3211, www.shemcreekmarina.com), **Charleston Harbor Marina** (24 Patriots Point Rd., 843/284-7062, www.charlestonharbormarina.com), **Charleston City Marina** (17 Lockwood Dr., 843/722-4968), **Charleston Maritime Center** (10 Wharfside St., 843/853-3625, www.cmcevents.com), and the **Cooper River Marina** (1010 Juneau Ave., 843/554-0790, www.ccprc.com).

Good fishing charter outfits include **Barrier Island Eco Tours** (50 41st Ave., 843/886-5000, www.nature-tours.com, about $80) out of Isle of Palms; **Bohicket Boat Adventure & Tour Co.** (2789 Cherry Point Rd., 843/559-3525, www.bohicketboat.com) out of the Edisto River; and **Reel Fish Finder Charters** (315 Yellow Jasmine Ct., Moncks Corner, 843/697-2081). Captain James picks clients up at many different marinas in the area.

For a list of all public landings in Charleston County, go to www. ccprc.com.

Diving

Diving here can be challenging because of the fast currents, and visibility can be low. But as you'd expect in this historic area, there are plenty of wrecks, fossils, and artifacts. In fact, there's an entire Cooper River Underwater Heritage Trail with the key sites marked for divers.

Offshore diving centers on the network of offshore artificial reefs (go to www.dnr.sc.gov for a list and locations), particularly the "Charleston 60" sunken barge and the new and very popular "Train Wreck," comprising 50 deliberately sunk New York City subway cars.

The longtime popular dive spot known as the "Anchor Wreck" was recently identified as the Norwegian steamer *Leif Erikkson,* which sank in 1905 after a collision with another vessel. In addition to being fun dive sites, these artificial reefs have proven to be important feeding and spawning grounds for marine life.

Probably Charleston's best-regarded outfitter and charter operator is **Charleston Scuba** (335 Savannah Hwy., 843/763-3483, www.charlestonscuba.com) in West Ashley. You also might want to check out **Cooper River Scuba** (843/572-0459, www.cooperriverdiving.com) and **Atlantic Coast Dive Center** (209 Scott St., 843/884-1500).

Surfing and Boarding

The surfing at the famous **Washout** area on the eastside of Folly Beach isn't what it used to be due to storm activity and beach erosion. But the diehards still gather at this area when the swell hits—generally about 3–5 feet (occasionally with dolphins!). Check out the conditions yourself from the three views of the Folly Surfcam (www.follysurfcam.com).

The best local surf shop is undoubtedly the historic **McKevlin's Surf Shop** (8 Center St., 843/588-2247, www.mckevlins.com) on Folly Beach, one of the first surf shops on the entire East Coast, dating to 1965 (check out an employee's "No Pop-Outs" blog at http://mckevlins.blogspot.com). Other shops include **Barrier Island Surf Shop** (2013 Folly Rd., 843/795-4545) on Folly Beach and **The Point Break** (369 King St., 843/722-4161) on the peninsula.

For lessons, **Folly Beach Shaka Surf School** (843/607-9911, www.shakasurfschool.com) offers private and group sessions at Folly; you might also try **Sol Surfers Surf Camp** (843/881-6700, www.solsurfers.net).

Kiteboarders might want to contact **Air** (843/388-9300, www.catchsomeair.us), which offers several levels of lessons, as well as **Whitecap Windsurfing** (706/833-9463, www.whitecapwindsurfing.com).

Water Parks

During the summer months, Charleston County operates three water parks, though none are on the peninsula: **Splash Island**

Waterpark (444 Needlerush Pkwy., 843/884-0832) in Mount Pleasant; **Whirlin' Waters Adventure Waterpark** (University Blvd., 843/572-7275) in North Charleston; and **Splash Zone Waterpark at James Island County Park** (871 Riverland Dr., 843/795-7275) on James Island west of town. Admission runs about $10 per person. Go to www.ccprc.com for more information.

ON LAND
Golf
America's first golf course was constructed in Charleston in 1786. The term "green fee" is alleged to have evolved from the maintenance fees charged to members of the South Carolina Golf Club and Harleston Green in what's now downtown Charleston. So as you'd expect, there's some great golfing in the area, generally in the outlying islands. Here are some of the highlights (fees are averages and subject to season and time).

The folks at the nonprofit **Charleston Golf, Inc.** (423 King St., 843/958-3629, www.charlestongolfguide.com) are your best one-stop resource for tee times and packages.

The main public course is the 18-hole **Charleston Municipal Golf Course** (2110 Maybank Hwy., 843/795-6517, www.charlestoncity.info, $40). To get there from the peninsula, take U.S. 17 south over the Ashley River, take Highway 171/Folly Road south, and then take a right onto Maybank Highway.

Probably the most renowned area facilities are at the acclaimed **Kiawah Island Golf Resort** (12 Kiawah Beach Dr., 800/654-2924, www.kiawahgolf.com) about 20 miles from Charleston. The Resort has five courses in all, the best known of which is the **Kiawah Island Ocean Course,** site of the famous "War by the Shore" 1991 Ryder Cup. This 2.5-mile course, which is walking-only until noon each day, hosted the Senior PGA Championship in 2007 and will host the 2012 PGA Championship. The Resort offers a golf academy and private lessons galore. These are public courses, but be aware that tee times are limited for golfers who aren't guests at the resort.

Two excellent resort-style public courses are at **Wild Dunes Resort Golf** (5757 Palm Blvd., 888/845-8932, www.wilddunes.com, $165) on Isle of Palms. The 18-hole **Patriots Point Links** (1 Patriots Point Rd., 843/881-0042, www.patriotspointlinks.com, $100) on the Charleston Harbor right over the Ravenel Bridge in Mount Pleasant is one of the most convenient courses in the area, and it boasts some phenomenal views.

Also on Mount Pleasant is perhaps the best course in the area for the money, the award-winning **Rivertowne Golf Course** (1700 Rivertowne Country Club Dr., 843/856-9808, www.rivertownecountryclub.com, $150) at the Rivertowne Country Club. This relatively new course, opened in 2002, was designed by Arnold Palmer.

Tennis
Tennis fans are in for a treat at the brand-new **Family Circle Tennis Center** (161 Seven Farms Dr., 800/677-2293, www.familycirclecup.com, Mon.–Thurs. 8 A.M.–8 P.M., Fri. 8 A.M.–7 P.M., Sat. 8 A.M.–5 P.M., Sun. 9 A.M.–5 P.M., $15/hr.) on Daniel Island. This multimillion-dollar facility is owned by the city of Charleston, and was built in 2001 specifically to host the annual Family Circle Cup women's competition, which was previously held in Hilton Head for many years. But it's also open to the public year-round (except when the Cup is on) with 17 courts.

The best resort tennis activity is at the **Kiawah Island Golf Resort** (12 Kiawah Beach Dr., 800/654-2924, www.kiawahgolf.com), with a total of 28 courts.

There are four free, public, city-funded facilities on the peninsula: **Moultrie Playground** (Broad St. and Ashley Ave., 843/769-8258, www.charlestoncity.info, six lighted hard courts), **Jack Adams Tennis Center** (290 Congress St., six lighted hard courts), **Hazel Parker Playground** (70 East Bay St. on the Cooper River, one hard court), and **Corrine Jones Playground** (Marlowe and Peachtree Sts., two hard courts). Over in West Ashley, the city also runs the public **Charleston Tennis**

Center (19 Farmfield Rd., 843/769-8258, www.charlestoncity.info, 15 lighted courts).

Hiking and Biking

If you're like me, you'll walk your legs off just making your way around the sights on the peninsula. Early risers will especially enjoy the beauty of dawn breaking over the Cooper River as they walk or jog along the Battery or a little farther north at Waterfront Park.

Charleston-area beaches are perfect for a leisurely bike ride on the sand. Sullivan's Island is a particular favorite, and you might be surprised at how long you can ride in one direction on these beaches.

Those desiring a more demanding use of their legs can walk or ride their bike in the dedicated pedestrian/bike lane on the massive **Arthur Ravenel Jr. Bridge** over the Cooper River, the longest cable-stayed bridge in the western hemisphere. The extra lanes are a huge advantage over the old span on the same site, and a real example for other cities to follow in sustainable transportation solutions. There's public parking on both sides of the bridge, on the Charleston side off of Meeting Street and on the Mount Pleasant side on the road to Patriots Point. **Bike the Bridge Rentals** (360 Concord St., 843/853-2453, www.bikethe bridgerentals.com) offers self-guided tours over the Ravenel Bridge and back on a Raleigh Comfort bike, and also rents road bikes for lengthier excursions.

In West Ashley, there's an urban walking/biking trail, the **West Ashley Greenway,** built on a former rail bed. The 10-mile trail runs parallel to U.S. 17 and passes parks, schools, and the Clemson Experimental Farm, ending near John Island. To get to the trailhead from downtown, drive west on U.S. 17. About a half-mile after you cross the bridge, turn left onto Folly Road (Highway 171). At the second light, turn right into South Windermere Shopping Center; the trail's behind the center on the right.

The most ambitious trail in South Carolina is the **Palmetto Trail** (www.palmetto conservation.org), begun in 1997 and eventually covering 425 miles from the Atlantic to the Appalachians. The coastal terminus near Charleston, the seven-mile Awendaw Passage through the Francis Marion National Forest, begins at the trailhead at the Buck Hall Recreational Area (843/887-3257, $5 vehicle fee), which has parking and bathroom facilities. Get there by taking U.S. 17 north about 20 miles out of Charleston and through the Francis Marion National Forest and then Awendaw. Take a right onto Buck Hall Landing Road.

Another good nature hike outside town is on the eight miles of scenic and educational trails at **Caw Caw Interpretive Center** (5200 Savannah Hwy., 843/889-8898, www.ccprc .com, Wed.–Fri. 9 A.M.–3 P.M., Sat.–Sun. 9 A.M.–5 P.M., $1) in nearby Ravenel on an old rice plantation.

One of the best outfitters in town is **Half Moon Outfitters** (280 King St., 843/853-0990, www.halfmoonoutfitters.com, Mon.–Sat. 10 A.M.–7 P.M., Sun. noon–6 P.M.). They have a Mount Pleasant location (425 Coleman Blvd., 843/881-9472) as well (and it has better parking).

Bird-Watching

Right in Charleston Harbor is the little **Crab Bank Heritage Preserve** (803/734-3886), where thousands of migratory birds can be seen depending on the season. From October to April you can either kayak there yourself or take a charter with **Nature Adventures Outfitters** (1900 Iron Swamp Rd., 800/673-0679) out of Awendaw Island.

On James Island southwest of Charleston is **Legare Farms** (2620 Hanscombe Point Rd., 843/559-0763, www.legarefarms.com), which holds migratory bird walks each Saturday in autumn at 8:30 A.M. ($6 adults, $3 children).

Ice-Skating

Ice-skating in South Carolina? Yep, 100,000 square feet of it, year-round at the two NHL-size rinks of the **Carolina Ice Palace** (7665 Northwoods Blvd., 843/572-2717, www .carolinaicepalace.com, $7 adults, $6 children) in North Charleston. This is also the practice facility for the local hockey team, the Stingrays, as well as where the Citadel hockey team plays.

SPECTATOR SPORTS

Charleston River Dogs

A New York Yankees farm team playing in the South Atlantic League, the Charleston River Dogs (360 Fishburne St., www.riverdogs.com, $5 general admission) play April–August at Joseph P. Riley Jr. Park, a.k.a., "The Joe." The park is great, and there are a lot of fun promotions to keep things interesting should the play on the field be less than stimulating (as minor league ball often can be). Because of the intimate, retro design of the park, there are no bad seats, so you might as well save a few bucks and go for the general admission ticket.

From downtown, get to The Joe by taking Broad Street west until it turns into Lockwood Drive. Follow that north until you get to Brittlebank Park and The Joe, next to the Citadel. Expect to pay $3–5 for parking.

Family Circle Cup

Moved to Daniel Island in 2001 from its long-time home in Hilton Head, the prestigious Family Circle Cup women's tennis tournament is held each April at the **Family Circle Tennis Center** (161 Seven Farms Dr., Daniel Island, 843/856-7900, www.familycirclecup.com, varied admission). Almost 100,000 people attend the multi-week event. Individual session tickets go on sale the preceding January.

Charleston Battery

The professional, A-League soccer team Charleston Battery (1990 Daniel Island Dr., 843/971-4625, www.charlestonbattery.com, about $10) play April–July at Blackbaud Stadium on Daniel Island north of Charleston. To get there from downtown, take I-26 north and then I-526 to Mount Pleasant. Take exit 23A, Clements Ferry Road, and then a left on St. Thomas Island Drive. Blackbaud Stadium is about a mile on the left.

South Carolina Stingrays

The ECHL professional hockey team the South Carolina Stingrays (843/744-2248, www.stingrayshockey.com, $15) get a good crowd out to their rink at the North Charleston Coliseum, playing October–April.

Citadel Bulldogs

The Citadel (171 Moultrie St., 843/953-3294, www.citadelsports.com) plays Southern Conference football home games at Johnson-Hagood Stadium next to the campus on the Ashley River near Hampton Park. The basketball team plays home games at McAlister Field House on campus. The school's hockey team skates home games at the Carolina Ice Palace.

Accommodations

As one of America's key national and international destination cities, Charleston has a very well-developed infrastructure for housing visitors—a task made much easier by the city's longstanding tradition of hospitality. Because the bar is set so high, few visitors experience a truly bad stay in town. Hotels and bed-and-breakfasts are generally well maintained and have a high level of service, ranging from very good to excellent. There's a 12.5 percent tax on hotel rooms in Charleston.

SOUTH OF BROAD

Over $300

On the south side of Broad Street is a great old Charleston lodging, **《 Governor's House Inn** (117 Broad St., 843/720-2070, www.governorshouse.com, $285–585). This circa-1760 building, a National Historic Landmark, is associated with Edward Rutledge, signer of the Declaration of Independence. Though most of its 11 rooms—all with four-poster beds, period furnishings, and high ceilings—go for

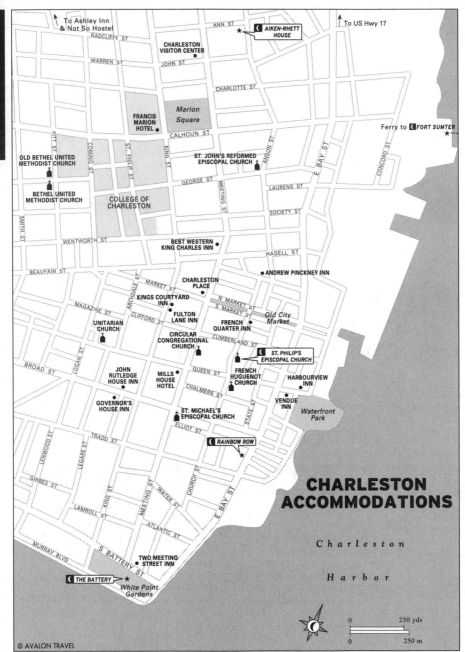

CHARLESTON ACCOMMODATIONS

Charleston

Harbor

© AVALON TRAVEL

around $300, some of the smaller rooms here can be had for closer to $200 in the off-season. The nine rooms of 🔇 **Two Meeting Street Inn** (2 Meeting St., 843/723-7322, www .twomeetingstreet.com, $220–435) down by the Battery are individually appointed, with themes like "The Music Room" and the "The Spell Room." The decor in this 1892 Queen Anne bed-and-breakfast is very traditional, with lots of floral patterns and hunt club–style pieces and artwork. It's considered by many to be the most romantic lodging in town, and you won't soon forget the experience of sitting on the veranda enjoying the sights, sounds, and breezes. Three of the rooms—the Canton, Granite, and Roberts—can be had for not much over $200.

WATERFRONT AND FRENCH QUARTER
$150-300

The rooms and the thoroughly hospitable service are the focus at the nearby 🔇 **Vendue Inn** (19 Vendue Range, 843/577-7970, www .vendueinn.com, $359). With a range of decor from Colonial to French Provincial, all rooms are sumptuously appointed in that "boutique" style, with lots of warm, rich fabrics, unique pieces, and high-end bath amenities. That said, the public spaces are cool, too, with a cozy den area with chess and checkers and a nice area in which to enjoy your excellent, made-to-order hot breakfast (complimentary!). They have a row of bikes out front for guests to use, free of charge, to roam around the city. The Inn gets a lot of traffic in the evenings because of the popular Library restaurant and its hopping Rooftop Bar, which has amazing views.

About as close to the Cooper River as a hotel gets, the **Harbourview Inn** (2 Vendue Range, 843/853-8439, www.harbourviewcharleston .com, $259) comprises a "historic wing" and a larger, newer, but still tastefully done main building. For the best of those eponymous harbor views, try to get a room on the third floor or you might have some obstructions. It's the little touches that keep guests happy here, with

wine, cheese, coffee, tea, and cookies galore and an emphasis on smiling, personalized service. The rooms are quite spacious, with big bathrooms and 14-foot ceilings. You can take your complimentary breakfast—good but not great—in your room or eat it on the nice rooftop terrace.

Over $300

Another great place in this part of town is the **French Quarter Inn** (166 Church St., 843/722-1900, www.fqicharleston.com, $359). The decor in the 50 surprisingly spacious rooms is suitably high-period French, with low-style, non-canopied beds and crisp, fresh linens. Many rooms feature fireplaces, whirlpool baths, and private balconies. One of Charleston's hottest restaurants, Tristan, is on the ground floor. You're treated to champagne on your arrival, and goodies are available all day, with wine and cheese served every night at 5 P.M.

NORTH OF BROAD
$150-300

It calls itself a boutique hotel, perhaps because each room is totally different and sumptuously appointed. But the charming 🔇 **Andrew Pinckney Inn** (199 Church St., 843/937-8800, www.andrewpinckneyinn .com, $200–290) is very nearly in a class by itself in Charleston not only for its great rates, but for its casual, West Indies–style decor, charming courtyard, gorgeous three-story atrium, and rooftop terrace on which you can enjoy your complimentary (and delicious) breakfast. For the money and the amenities, it's possibly the single best lodging package in town.

Free parking, a great location, friendly staff, and reasonable prices are the highlights of the **Best Western King Charles Inn** (237 Meeting St., 843/723-7451, www.kingcharles inn.com, $200–250). It's not where you'd want to spend your honeymoon, but it's plenty nice enough and frequent visitors to town swear by it.

If you plan on some serious shopping,

you might want to stay right on the city's main shopping thoroughfare at the **Kings Courtyard Inn** (198 King St., 866/720-2949, www.kingscourtyardinn.com, $240–270). This 1853 Greek Revival building houses a lot more rooms—more than 40—than meets the eye, and can get a little crowded at times. Still, its charming courtyard and awesome location on King Street are big bonuses, as is the convenient but cramped parking lot right next door (about $12 a day, a bargain for this part of town), with free in/out privileges.

Though a newer building by Charleston standards, the **Mills House Hotel** (115 Meeting St., 843/577-2400, www.ichotelsgroup.com, $285–380) boasts an important pedigree and still tries hard to maintain the old tradition of impeccable Southern service at this historic location. An extensive round of renovations completed in 2007 has been well-received. Dating to 1853, the first incarnation was a grand edifice that hosted luminaries such as Robert E. Lee. Through the years fire and restoration wrought their changes, and the modern version basically dates from an extensive renovation in the 1970s.

Because of its healthy banquet and event schedule—much of it centering around the very good restaurant and lounge inside—the Mills House isn't the place to go for peace and quiet. Rather, this Holiday Inn–affiliated property is where you go to feel the bustle of downtown Charleston, and be conveniently close to its main sightseeing and shopping attractions. Some of the upper floors of this seven-story building offer spectacular views.

Over $300

Considered Charleston's premier hotel, **⟨** **Charleston Place** (205 Meeting St., 843/722-4900, www.charlestonplace.com, $419–590) maintains a surprisingly high level of service and decor considering its massive, 440-room size. Now owned by the London-based Orient-Express Hotels, Charleston Place is routinely rated as one of the best hotels in North America by *Condé Nast Traveler* and other publications.

The rooms aren't especially large but they are well appointed, featuring Italian marble baths, high-speed Internet, and voice messaging—and, of course, there's a pool available. A series of suite offerings—Junior, Junior Executive, Parlor, and the 800-square-foot Senior—feature enlarged living areas and multiple TVs and phones. A Manager's Suite on the Private Club level up top comprises 1,200 square feet of total luxury that will set you back at least $1,600 a night.

It's the additional offerings that make Charleston Place closer to a lifestyle decision than a lodging decision. The on-site spa (843/937-8522) offers all kinds of massages, including couples and "mommy to be" sessions. Diners and tipplers have three fine options to choose from: the famous **Charleston Grill** (843/577-4522, dinner daily beginning at 6 P.M.) for fine dining; the breakfast, lunch, and brunch hot spot **Palmetto Cafe** (843/722-4900, breakfast daily 6:30 A.M.–11 A.M., lunch daily 11:30 A.M.–3 P.M.); and the **Thoroughbred Club** (daily 11 A.M.–midnight) for cocktails and afternoon tea.

On the north side of Broad Street, the magnificent **⟨ John Rutledge House Inn** (116 Broad St., 843/723-7999, www.johnrutledge houseinn.com, $300–442) is very close to the old South of Broad neighborhood not only in geography, but in feel. Known as "America's most historic inn," the Rutledge House boasts a fine old pedigree indeed: Built for Constitution signer John Rutledge in 1763, it's one of only 15 homes belonging to the original signers to survive. George Washington breakfasted here with Mrs. Rutledge in 1791. The interior is stunning: Italian marble fireplaces, original plaster moldings, and masterful ironwork abound in the public spaces. The inn's 19 rooms are divided among the original mansion and two carriage houses. All have antique furnishings and canopy beds, and some suites have fireplaces and whirlpool baths. A friendly and knowledgeable concierge will give you all kinds of tips and make reservations for you.

Affiliated with the Kings Courtyard—and right next door, in fact—is the smaller, cozier

© JIM MOREKIS

the John Rutledge House Inn

Fulton Lane Inn (202 King St., 866/720-2940, www.fultonlaneinn.com, $300), with its lobby entrance on tiny Fulton Lane between the two inns. Small, simple guest rooms—some with fireplaces—have comfortable beds and spacious bathrooms. This is the kind of place for active people who plan to spend most of their days out and about, but want a cozy place to come back to at night. You mark down your Continental breakfast order at night, leave it on your doorknob, and it shows up at the *exact* time you requested the next morning. Then when you're ready to shop and walk, just go down the stairs and take the exit right out onto busy King Street. Also nice is the $12-a-day parking with free in/out privileges.

UPPER KING AREA
Under $150
Stretching the bounds of the "Upper King" definition, we come to the **Ashley Inn** (201 Ashley Ave., 843/723-1848, www.charleston-sc-inns

.com, $100–125) well northwest of Marion Square, almost in the Citadel area. Though it's too far to walk from here to most any historic attraction in Charleston, the Ashley Inn does provide free bikes to its guests, as well as free off-street parking, a particularly nice touch. It also deserves a special mention not only because of the romantic, well-appointed nature of its six guest rooms, suite, and carriage house, but for its outstanding breakfasts. You get to pick a main dish, such as Carolina sausage pie, stuffed waffles, or cheese blintzes.

$150-300
In a renovated 1924 building overlooking beautiful Marion Square, the **Francis Marion Hotel** (387 King St., 843/722-0600, www.francis marioncharleston.com, $200–300) offers quality accommodation in the hippest, most bustling area of the peninsula—though be aware that it's quite a walk down to the Battery from here. The rooms are plush and big, though the bathrooms can be cramped. The hotel's parking garage costs a reasonable $12 a day, with valet parking available until about 8 P.M. A Starbucks in the lobby pleases many a guest on their way out or in. Most rooms hover around $300, but some are a real steal.

HAMPTON PARK AREA
Under $150
Charleston's least-expensive lodging is also its most unique, the ▐ **Not So Hostel** (156 Spring St., 843/722-8383, www.notsohostel .com, $21 dorm, $60 private). The already-reasonable prices also include a great make-your-own breakfast, off-street parking, bikes, high-speed Internet access in the common room, and even an airport/train/bus shuttle. The inn actually comprises three 1840s Charleston single houses, all with the obligatory piazzas to catch the breeze. (However, unlike some hostels, there's air-conditioning in all the rooms.) Because the free bike usage makes up for its off-the-beaten-path location, a stay at the Not So Hostel is a fantastic way to enjoy the Holy City on a budget, while having a great time with some cool people to boot.

WEST ASHLEY
$150-300

Looking like Frank Lloyd Wright parachuted into a 300-year-old plantation and got to work, **❰ The Inn at Middleton Place** (4290 Ashley River Rd., 843/556-0500, www.theinn atmiddletonplace.com, $215–285) is one of Charleston's most unique lodgings—and not only because it's on the grounds of the historic and beautiful Middleton Place Plantation. The four connected buildings comprising over 50 guest rooms are modern, yet deliberately blend in with the forested, neutral-colored surroundings. The spacious rooms have that same woody minimalism, with excellent fireplaces, spacious Euro-style baths, and huge, floor-to-ceiling windows overlooking the grounds and the river. Guests also have full access to the rest of the gorgeous Middleton grounds. The only downside is that you're a lengthy drive from the peninsula and all its attractions, restaurants, and nightlife.

While those who need constant stimulation will be disappointed in the deep quietude here, nature-lovers and those in search of peace and quiet will find this almost paradise. And don't worry about food—the excellent Middleton Place Restaurant is open for lunch and dinner.

ISLE OF PALMS
$150-300

One of the more accessible and enjoyable resort-type stays in the Charleston area is on the Isle of Palms at **Wild Dunes Resort** (5757 Palm Blvd., 888/778-1876, www.wilddunes.com, $254–320). This is the place to go for relaxing, beach-oriented vacation fun, either in a traditional hotel room, a house, or a villa. Bustling Mount Pleasant is only a couple of minutes away and Charleston proper not much farther.

FOLLY BEACH
$150-300

The upbeat but still cozy renovation of the **Holiday Inn Folly Beach Oceanfront** (1 Center St., 843/588-6464, $250–270) has locals raving. If you're going to stay on Folly Beach, this hotel—with its combination of attentive staff and great oceanfront views—is the place to be.

CAMPING

Charleston County runs a family-friendly, fairly boisterous campground at **James Island County Park** (871 Riverland Dr., 843/795-7275, www.ccprc.com, $31 tent site, $37 pull-through site). A neat feature here is the $5-per-person round-trip shuttle to the Visitors Center downtown, Folly Beach Pier, and Folly Beach County Park. The Park also has 10 furnished cottages for rental, sleeping up to eight people (843/795-4386, $138 a day). Reservations are recommended.

For more commercial camping in Mount Pleasant, try the **KOA of Mt. Pleasant** (3157 Hwy. 17 N., 843/849-5177, www.koa.com, $30+ tent sites, $50+ pull-through sites).

Food

If you count the premier food cities in the United States on one hand, Charleston has to be one of the fingers. Its long history of good taste and livability combines with an affluent and sophisticated population to attract some of the brightest chefs and restaurateurs in the country. Kitchens here eschew fickle trends, instead emphasizing quality, professionalism, and most of all, freshness of ingredients.

In a sort of Southern Zen, the typical Charleston chef seems to take pride in making a melt-in-your-mouth masterpiece out of the culinary commonplace—in not fixing what ain't broke, as they say down here. (I've heard Charleston's cuisine described as "competent classics," which also isn't far off the mark.)

Unlike Savannah, its more drink-oriented neighbor to the south, even Charleston's bars

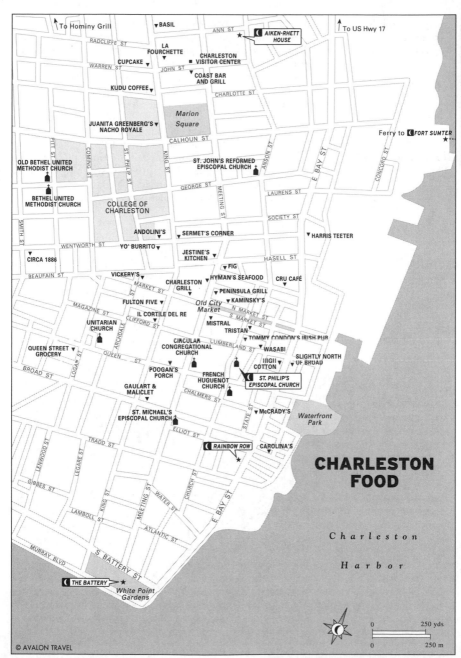

To Hominy Grill

BASIL

ANN ST

AIKEN-RHETT HOUSE

To US Hwy 17

RADCLIFFE ST

LA FOURCHETTE

CHARLESTON VISITOR CENTER

CUPCAKE

WARREN ST

JOHN ST

COAST BAR AND GRILL

KUDU COFFEE

CHARLOTTE ST

Marion Square

Ferry to FORT SUMTER

JUANITA GREENBERG'S NACHO ROYALE

CALHOUN ST

ST. JOHN'S REFORMED EPISCOPAL CHURCH

ANSON ST

E BAY ST

CONCORD ST

OLD BETHEL UNITED METHODIST CHURCH

COMING ST

ST. PHILIP ST

KING ST

GEORGE ST

MEETING ST

LAURENS ST

BETHEL UNITED METHODIST CHURCH

COLLEGE OF CHARLESTON

SOCIETY ST

SMITH ST

ANDOLINI'S

SERMET'S CORNER

HARRIS TEETER

WENTWORTH ST

YO' BURRITO

JESTINE'S KITCHEN

CIRCA 1886

HASELL ST

FIG

BEAUFAIN ST

VICKERY'S

HYMAN'S SEAFOOD

CRU CAFÉ

MARKET ST

CHARLESTON GRILL

PENINSULA GRILL

FULTON FIVE

KAMINSKY'S

MAGAZINE ST

IL CORTILE DEL RE

Old City Market

N MARKET ST

S MARKET ST

CLIFFORD ST

MISTRAL

UNITARIAN CHURCH

ARCHDALE

TRISTAN

TOMMY CONDON'S IRISH PUB

QUEEN STREET GROCERY

LOGAN ST

QUEEN ST

CIRCULAR CONGREGATIONAL CHURCH

LUMBERLAND ST

WASABI

SLIGHTLY NORTH OF BROAD

BROAD ST

POOGAN'S PORCH

HIGH COTTON

GAULART & MALICLET

FRENCH HUGUENOT CHURCH

ST. PHILIP'S EPISCOPAL CHURCH

CHALMERS ST

ST. MICHAEL'S EPISCOPAL CHURCH

STATE ST

McCRADY'S

Waterfront Park

ELLIOT ST

TRADD ST

RAINBOW ROW

CAROLINA'S

LENWOOD ST

LEGARE ST

KING ST

MEETING ST

WATER ST

CHURCH ST

E BAY ST

GIBBES ST

CHARLESTON FOOD

LAMBOLL ST

ATLANTIC ST

Charleston

MURRAY BLVD

S BATTERY ST

Harbor

THE BATTERY

White Point Gardens

Charleston

Harbor

0   250 yds

0   250 m

© AVALON TRAVEL

have great food. So don't assume you have to make reservations at a formal restaurant to fully enjoy the cuisine here. Though an entire volume could easily be written about Charleston restaurants, here's a baseline from which to start your epicurean odyssey. You'll note a high percentage of ◖ recommendations in the list; there's a good reason for that.

SOUTH OF BROAD
Classic Southern

The only bona fide restaurant in the quiet old South of Broad area is also one of Charleston's best and oldest: ◖ **Carolina's** (10 Exchange St., 843/724-3800, Sun.–Thurs. 5–10 P.M., Fri.–Sat. 5–11 P.M., $18–30). There's a new chef in town, Jeremiah Bacon, a Charleston native who spent the last seven years honing his craft in New York City. His Lowcountry take on European classics includes grilled salmon with potato gnocchi, tagliatelle with Lowcountry prosciutto, and pan-roasted diver scallops, with as many fresh ingredients as possible from the nearby Kensington Plantation.

A tried-and-true favorite that predates Bacon's tenure, however, is Perdita's fruit de mer—a recipe that goes back to the restaurant's 1950s predecessor, Perdita's, which is commonly regarded as Charleston's first fine-dining restaurant. If you can get the whole table to agree, try the $49-per-person Perdita's four-course tasting menu (wine flights extra).

A recent renovation of this Revolutionary War–era building—once the legendary Sailor's Tavern—hasn't negatively affected the romantic ambience of the three themed areas: Perdita's Room (the oldest dining area), the Sidewalk Room, and the Bar Room. Free valet parking is a nice plus.

French

If you find yourself in lodging near the Broad Street area—or if you just love crepes—you will want to acquaint yourself with the **Queen Street Grocery** (133 Queen St., 843/723-4121, Mon.–Sat. 8 A.M.–8:30 P.M., kitchen Mon.–Sat. 10 A.M.–5 P.M., Sun. 11 A.M.–3 P.M., $7–10). The kind of place frequented almost exclusively by locals, this corner store is where you can load up on light groceries, beer, wine,

Get a great crepe at the Queen Street Grocery.

© JIM MOREKIS

and cigarettes—as well as some of the tastiest made-to-order crepes this side of France.

WATERFRONT
New Southern
Few restaurants in Charleston inspire such impassioned, vocal advocates as **(McCrady's** (2 Unity Alley, 843/577-0025, www.mccradys restaurant.com, Sun.–Thurs. 5:30–10 P.M., Fri.–Sat. 5:30–11 P.M., $25–34). Housed in Charleston's oldest tavern building (circa 1788), McCrady's is also known as Charleston's best-kept secret, since despite its high quality it's managed to avoid the siege of tourists common at many local fine-dining spots. But their loss can be your gain as you enjoy the prodigious talents of young chef Sean Brock, whose *sous vide,* or vacuum cooking, is spoken of in hushed tones by his clientele.

McCrady's is not the place to gorge on usual Lowcountry fare. Portions here are small and dynamic, and range from a yam soup with marshmallow and roasted chestnuts to seared foie gras with maple syrup to seared Hawaiian tuna in a saffron-vegetable juice emulsion. The menu changes seasonally according to the local market and the chef's whim. Many diners find the seven-course, $70 Chef's Tasting a near-religious experience. For an extra $60, master sommelier Clint Sloan provides paired wine selections.

FRENCH QUARTER
New Southern
With an Art Deco–style vibe that's a refreshing change from the usual Charleston restaurant decor, **Tristan** (55 Market St., 843/534-2155, www.tristandining.com, Mon.–Thurs. 11:30 A.M.–10 P.M., Fri.–Sat. 11:30 A.M.–11 P.M., Sun. 11 A.M.–10 P.M., $18–32) inside the French Quarter Inn draws raves for its globally influenced cuisine. At last count, the copious wine list boasted over 400 labels. The real scene here is for the à la carte Sunday brunch, with crab cake benedicts, corned beef hash, frittatas, live jazz, and Bloody Marys galore. Save room for the ridiculously good fried chocolate doughnut dessert.

NORTH OF BROAD
Asian
For whatever reason, the Asian influence is not prevalent in Charleston cuisine. But **Wasabi** (61 State St., 843/577-5222, Mon.–Thurs. 11 A.M.–9:30 P.M., Fri.–Sat. 11 A.M.–11 P.M., Sun. noon–9 P.M., $10–15) has made quite a name for itself as a great place for sushi downtown, though its hibachi work is impressive as well. The bar gets hopping after dinner.

Classic Southern
Walk through the gaslit courtyard of the Planter's Inn at Market and Meeting Streets into the stately yet surprisingly intimate dining room of the **(Peninsula Grill** (112 N. Market St., 843/723-0700, www.peninsulagrill.com, nightly from 5:30 P.M., $28–35) and begin an epicurean journey you'll not soon forget. Known far and wide for impeccable service as well as the mastery of Chef Robert Carter, Peninsula Grill is perhaps Charleston's quintessential purveyor of high-style Lowcountry cuisine and the odds-on favorite as best restaurant in town.

From the lobster skillet cake and crab cake appetizer to the bourbon-grilled jumbo shrimp to the benne-crusted rack of lamb to sides like wild mushroom grits and hoppin' John, the menu reads like a "greatest hits" of regional cooking. You'll almost certainly want to start with the sampler trio of soups and finish with Carter's legendary coconut cake, a family recipe. Whatever you choose in between those bookends is almost guaranteed to be excellent.

To accompany your inevitably near-perfect meal, choose from 20 wines by the glass or from over 300 bottles. Four stars from the Mobil Travel Club, four diamonds from AAA, and countless other accolades have come this restaurant's way in its relatively brief (by Charleston standards) decade of existence. Needless to say, reservations are highly recommended.

Named for a now-deceased, beloved dog who once greeted guests, **(Poogan's Porch** (72 Queen St., 843/577-2337, www.poogansporch

.com, lunch Mon.–Fri. 11:30 A.M.–2:30 P.M., dinner daily 5–9:30 P.M., $12–20) is the prototype of a classic Charleston restaurant: Lovingly restored old home, professional but unpretentious service, great fried green tomatoes, and rich, calorie-laden Lowcountry classics. I can't decide which entrée I like best, the crab cakes or the shrimp and grits, but either one could qualify as a finalist for best dish in Charleston. Some swear that even the biscuits at Poogan's—flaky, fresh-baked, and moist—are better than some entrées around town, though that's a stretch. Brunch (Sat.–Sun. 9 A.M.–3 P.M.) is the big thing here, a bustling affair with big portions, Bloody Marys, mimosas, and soft sunlight bathing what were, after all, living and dining rooms where people once lived.

For many visitors to Charleston, there comes a point when they just get tired of stuffing themselves with seafood. If you find yourself in that situation, the perfect antidote is **☾ High Cotton** (199 E. Bay St., 843/724-3815, www .mavericksouthernkitchens.com, Mon.–Thurs. 5:30–10 P.M., Fri. 5:30–11 P.M., Sat. 11:30 A.M.–2:30 P.M. and 5:30–11 P.M., Sun. 10 A.M.–2 P.M. and 5:30–10 P.M., $20–44), a meat-lovers paradise offering some of the best steaks in town, as well as a creative menu of assorted lamb and pork dishes.

Chef Anthony Gray places heavy emphasis on using fresh local ingredients, whether they be veggies or game, and the rotating menu always reflects that. None of this comes particularly cheap, but splurges rarely do. In the woody (and popular) bar area after 6 P.M. there's usually a solo live pianist or sax player.

The long lines at Wentworth and Meeting Streets across from the fire station are waiting to follow Rachael Ray's lead and get into **Jestine's Kitchen** (251 Meeting St., 843/722-7224, Tues.–Thurs. 11 A.M.–9:30 P.M., Fri.–Sat. 11 A.M.–10 P.M., $8–15) to enjoy a simple, Southern take on such meat-and-three comfort food classics as meatloaf, pecan-fried fish, and fried green tomatoes. Most of the recipes are handed down from the restaurant's namesake, Jestine Matthews, the African American woman who raised owner Dana Berlin. Mrs. Matthews passed away in 1997 at the age of 112, her longevity perhaps a testament to the healthy qualities of traditional Southern country cooking.

French

On the north side of Broad Street itself you'll find **Gaulart & Maliclet** (98 Broad St., 843/577-9797, www.fastandfrench.org, Mon. 8 A.M.–4 P.M., Tues., Wed., and Thurs. 8 A.M.–10 P.M., Fri.–Sat. 8 A.M.–10:30 P.M., $12–15), i.e. "fast and French." As the name indicates, this is a gourmet bistro with a strong takeout component. Prices are especially reasonable for this area of town, with great lunch specials under $10 and Thursday night "fondue for two" coming in at just over $20.

Mediterranean

One of the most romantic restaurants in Charleston—which is saying a lot—**☾ Il Cortile del Re** (193A King St., 843/853-1888, Mon.–Sat. 5–10:30 P.M., $18–30) is amidst the antique stores on Lower King. Thankfully

Il Cortile del Re

© JIM MOREKIS

the Italian owners don't overdo the old country sentimentality, either in atmosphere or in menu. Sure, the tablecloths are white and the interior is warm, dark, and decorated with opera prints. But the piped-in music is long on cool jazz and short on over-the-top tenors, and the skinny wine bar in the front room is a favorite destination all its own.

Portions here manage to be simultaneously large and light, as in the overtopped mussel plate in a delightfully thin and spicy tomato sauce, or the big spinach salad with goat cheese croutons sprinkled with a subtle vinaigrette. The entrées emphasize the Tuscan countryside, focusing both on slow-roasted meats and sublime takes on traditional pasta dishes. My favorite is the perfect roasted lamb in a dark juniper and rosemary sauce, served on a bed of what are likely to be the best mashed potatoes in the world. Save room for the gelato dessert, served swimming in a pool of dark espresso.

Literally right around the corner from Il Cortile del Re is the other in Charleston's one-two Italian punch, **Fulton Five** (5 Fulton St., 843/853-5555, Mon.–Sat. from 5:30 P.M., $15–32). The cuisine of Northern Italy comes alive in this bustling, dimly lit room, from the *bresaola* salad of spinach and thin dried beef to the caper-encrusted tuna on a bed of sweet pea risotto. It's not cheap and the portions aren't necessarily the largest, but with these tasty, non-tomato-based dishes and this romantic, gusto-filled atmosphere, you'll be satiated with life itself.

One of Charleston's original hip people-watching spots and still a personal favorite is **Sermet's Corner** (276 King St., 843/853-7775, lunch daily 11 A.M.–3 P.M., dinner Sun.–Thurs. 4–10 P.M., Fri.–Sat. 4–11 P.M., $9–16), on a bustling intersection of King and Wentworth. Charismatic chef and owner Sermet Aslan—who also painted most of the artwork on the walls of this charming, high-ceilinged space—dishes up large, inexpensive portions of Mediterranean-style goodies like panini, pastas, pestos, calamari, and inventive meat dishes.

The best "regular" pizza in Charleston can be found at the multiple locations of the local chain **Andolini's** (82 Wentworth St., 843/722-7437, daily 11 A.M.–11 P.M., $2–10). One of the best deals in town at this quirky, college-friendly institution is the lunch special: six bucks even for a huge one-topping slice of their signature New York–style pies, a salad, and a soda. Or for the same money you can have two cheese slices and a Bud. Their best special, however, might be a massive 19-inch with one topping and a pitcher of beer for $20. There's a less funky but just as tasty incarnation in Mount Pleasant (414 W. Coleman Blvd., 843/849-7437) and a fun retro-style location in West Ashley (1117 Savannah Hwy., 843/225-4743), in addition to branches way out on James Island (967 Folly Rd., 843/576-7437) and up in North Charleston (6610 Rivers Ave., 843/266-7437).

Mexican

If you find yourself craving Mexican while shopping on King Street, duck about a block down Wentworth to find the cavernous, delightful **Yo' Burrito** (86 Wentworth St., 843/853-3287, www.yoburrito.com, Sun.–Thurs. 11 A.M.–10 P.M., Fri.–Sat. 11 A.M.–11 P.M., $5–8), a local legend in its own right. Order from a variety of overstuffed specialty burritos, tasty quesadillas, and stacked nachos at the counter and take a seat at one of the large, communal-style tables, perhaps enjoying a freshly squeezed lemonade while you wait. But the real kicker is the condiment bar of homemade salsas, including a smoky chipotle number that is the closest thing to real red salsa I've had this side of New Mexico.

New Southern

Don't be put off by the initials of **Slightly North of Broad** (192 East Bay St., 843/723-3424, www.mavericksouthernkitchens.com, lunch Mon.–Fri. 11:30 A.M.–3 P.M., dinner daily 5:30–11 P.M., $15–35). Its acronym "S.N.O.B." is an ironic play on the often-pejorative reference to the insular "South of Broad" neighborhood. This hot spot, routinely voted best restaurant in town in such contests,

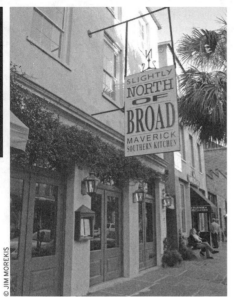

© JIM MOREKIS

Slightly North of Broad

is anything but snobby. Hopping with happy foodies for lunch and dinner, the fun is enhanced by the long, open kitchen with its own counter area.

The dynamic but comforting menu here is practically a bible of the new wave of Lowcountry cuisine, with dishes like beef tenderloin, jumbo lump crab cakes, grilled BBQ tuna—and of course the sinful Wednesday night dinner special: deviled crab-stuffed flounder. An interesting twist at SNOB is the selection of "medium plates," i.e., dishes a little more generous than an app but with the same adventurous spirit.

Just across the street from Hyman's Seafood is that establishment's diametrical opposite, the intimate bistro and stylish bar (**FIG** (232 Meeting St., 843/805-5900, www.eatatfig.com, Mon.–Thurs. 6–11 P.M., Fri.–Sat. 6 P.M.–midnight, $20–25)—but the two do share one key thing: a passion for fresh, simple ingredients. While Hyman's packs in the tourists, FIG— short for "Food Is Good"—attracts young professional scenesters, as well as the diehard

foodies. Chef Mike Lata won James Beard's Best Chef of the Southeast award in 2009. FIG is one of Charleston's great champions of the Sustainable Seafood Initiative, and the kitchen staff strives to work as closely as possible with local farmers and anglers in determining its seasonal menu.

Inside the plush Charleston Place Hotel you'll find (**Charleston Grill** (224 King St., 843/577-4522, www.charlestongrill.com, dinner daily beginning at 6 P.M., $27–50), one of the city's favorite (and priciest) fine-dining spots for locals and tourists alike. Veteran executive chef Bob Waggoner was recently replaced by his longtime *sous chef* Michelle Weaver, but the menu still specializes in French-influenced Lowcountry cuisine like a nicoise vegetable tart. There are a lot of great fusion dishes as well, such as the tuna and hamachi sashimi topped with pomegranate molasses and lemongrass oil. Reservations are a must.

A new hit with local foodies, **Cru Café** (18 Pinckney St., 843/534-2434, lunch Tues.–Sat. 11 A.M.–3 P.M., dinner Tues.–Thurs. 5–10 P.M., Fri.–Sat. 5–11 P.M., $20–24) boasts an adventurous menu within a traditional-looking Charleston single house, with a choice of interior or exterior seating. Sample entrées include a Poblano and Mozzarella Fried Chicken and Seared Maple Leaf Duck Breast.

The hard-to-define **Mistral** (99 S. Market St., 843/722-5708, Sun.–Thurs. 11 A.M.–11 P.M., Fri.–Sat. 11 A.M.–midnight, $10–25) is part seafood restaurant, part sexy French bistro, part Lowcountry living. With live, serious jazz blowing it hot Monday–Saturday nights and some of the best mussels and shrimp in the area served up fresh, all you really need to do is enjoy. If you're not a shellfish fan, try the sweetbreads or their excellent veal.

Seafood

Routinely voted the best seafood restaurant in the South, **Hyman's Seafood** (215 Meeting St., 843/723-6000, www.hymanseafood .com, Mon.–Thurs. 11 A.M.–9 P.M., Fri.–Sun. 11 A.M.–11 P.M., $14–25) is thought by many locals to border on a tourist trap. That said, this

© JIM MOREKIS

the oyster bar at Hyman's Seafood

is a genuine tradition—rest assured that some member of the same family that began Hyman's in 1890 will be on the premises any time it's open for business. To keep things manageable, Hyman's offers the same menu and prices for both lunch and dinner. After asking for some complimentary fresh boiled peanuts in lieu of bread, start with the Carolina Delight, a delicious app (also available as an entrée) involving a lightly fried cake of grits topped with your choice of delectable seafood, or maybe a half-dozen oysters from the Half Shell oyster bar. In any case, definitely try the she-crab soup, some of the best you'll find anywhere. As for entrées, the ubiquitous Lowcountry crispy scored flounder is always a good bet, as is any fish special; but the real action at Hyman's comes from anything that has a shell.

Alas, this establishment, popular with locals and tourists as well as the occasional movie star (Anthony Hopkins, Barbra Streisand, Mel Gibson), rock band (AC/DC, Metallica), and astronaut (Neil Armstrong) doesn't take reservations, so budget your time accordingly.

Lunch crowds are generally lighter, though that's a relative term.

Perhaps only in Charleston would the best-known Irish pub also be one of its better seafood restaurants. But then again, **Tommy Condon's Irish Pub** (160 Church St., 843/577-3818, www.tommycondons.com, dinner Sun.–Thurs. until 10 P.M., Fri. and Sat. until 11 P.M., bar daily until 2 A.M., $13–20) is unusual in a lot of ways: Irish in a town that tends to celebrate all things English and French, and fairly expensive in a town where pub food is surprisingly reasonable for the high quality. The best picks are the shepherd's pie and the shrimp and grits. If you're feeling particularly adventurous and/or have had a few Guinnesses, try the Irish nachos, featuring the usual ingredients but on fried potatoes instead of tortilla chips.

UPPER KING AREA
Asian
There's usually a long wait to get a table at the great Thai place **Basil** (460 King St., 843/724-3490, www.basilthairestaurant.com, lunch

Mon.–Thurs. 11:30 A.M.–2:30 P.M., dinner Mon.–Thurs. 5–10:30 P.M., Fri.–Sat. 5–11 P.M., Sun. 5–10 P.M., $15–23) on Upper King, since they don't take reservations. But Basil also has one of the hippest, most happening bar scenes in the area, so you won't necessarily mind. (Tip: Basil calls your cell phone when your table is ready, so a lot of people go across the street to Chai's to have a drink while they wait.)

Basil is a long, loud room, with big open windows for people-watching. But most of the action takes place inside, as revelers down cosmos and diners enjoy fresh, succulent takes on Thai classics like cashew chicken and pad thai, all cooked by Asian chefs. The signature dish, as you might imagine, is the basil duck.

French

A taste of the Left Bank on Upper King, the intimate bistro **La Fourchette** (432 King St., 843/722-6261, Mon.–Sat. from 6 P.M., $15–20) is regarded as the best French restaurant in town and, *naturalment,* one of the most romantic as well. You'll be pleasantly surprised by the reasonable prices as well. Cassoulet, the French national dish, is front and center among Chef Perig Goulet's concoctions, arriving in its own casserole dish on a trivet. Whatever you do, make sure you start with the *pommes frites* double-fried in duck fat. Your arteries may not thank you, but your taste buds will.

Mexican

The best quesadilla I've ever had was at **Juanita Greenberg's Nacho Royale** (439 King St., 843/723-6224, www.juanitagreenbergs.com, daily 11 A.M.–11 P.M., $6–8)—perfectly packed with Jack cheese but not overly so, full of spicy sausage, and finished with a delightful *pico de gallo*. This modest Mexican joint on Upper King caters primarily to a college crowd, as you can tell from the reasonable prices, the large patio out back, the extensive tequila list, and the bar that stays open until 2 A.M. on weekends.

Seafood

Many say the cashew-encrusted seared rare tuna on a bed of crabmeat and buckwheat noodles at **COAST Bar and Grill** (39-D John St., 843/722-8838, www.coastbarandgrill.com, nightly from 5:30 P.M., $18–30) is the single best dish in Charleston. I wouldn't go that far, but it's certainly up there. COAST makes the most of its loud, hip former warehouse setting. Beautifully textured Lowcountry-themed paintings and kitschy faux-Polynesian items ring the walls, as the clanging silverware competes with the boisterous conversation.

While the fun-loving decor in the dining room will suck you in, what keeps you happy is what goes on in the kitchen—specifically on its one-of-a-kind hickory-and-oak grill, which cooks up some of the freshest seafood in town. The raw bar is also satisfying, with a particularly nice take on and selection of ceviche. COAST is perhaps the strongest local advocate of the Sustainable Seafood Initiative, whereby restaurants work directly with local fishermen to make the most out of the area's stock while making sure it thrives for future generations.

Getting there's a little tricky: find Rue de Jean on John Street and then duck about 100 feet down the alley beside it.

COLLEGE OF CHARLESTON AREA
New Southern

Focusing on purely seasonal offerings which never stay on the menu longer than three months, **Circa 1886** (149 Wentworth St., 843/853-7828, www.circa1886.com, Mon.–Sat. 5:30–9:30 P.M., $23–32) combines the best old world tradition of Charleston with the vibrancy of its more adventurous kitchens. The restaurant—surprisingly little-known despite its four-star Mobil rating—is located in the former carriage house of the grand Wentworth Mansion B&B just west of the main College of Charleston campus. It is now the playground of Chef Marc Collins, who delivers entrées like a robust Beef Au Pivre and a shrimp-and-crab stuffed flounder, to name two recent offerings. The service here is impeccable and friendly, the ambience classy and warm, and the wine list impressive. Be sure to check the daily prixe fixe offerings; those can be some great deals.

HAMPTON PARK AREA
Classic Southern

Moe's Crosstown Tavern (714 Rutledge Ave., 843/722-3287, Mon.–Sat. 11 A.M.–midnight, bar until 2 A.M., $10–15) is not only one of the classic Southern dives, but they've got one of the best kitchens on this side of town, known for hand-cut fries, great wings, and, most of all, excellent burgers. On Tuesdays, the burgers are half-price at happy hour—one of Charleston's best deals.

With a motto like "Grits are good for you," you know what you're in store for at **❰ Hominy Grill** (207 Rutledge Ave., 912/937-0930, breakfast Mon.–Fri. 7:30–11:30 A.M., lunch and dinner 11:30 A.M.–8:30 P.M., brunch Sat.–Sun. 9 A.M.–3 P.M., $10–20), set in a renovated barbershop at Rutledge and Cannon near the Medical University of South Carolina. Primarily revered for his Sunday brunch, Chef Robert Stehling has fun, almost mischievously so, breathing new life into American and Southern classics. Because this is largely a locals' place, you can impress your friends back home by saying you had the rare pleasure of the Hominy's sautéed shad roe with bacon and mushrooms—when the shad are running, that is.

Italian

The newest rave of Charleston foodies is the Tuscan-inspired fare of Chef Ken Vedrinski at **❰ Trattoria Lucca** (41 Bogard St., 843/973-3323, www.trattorialuccadining.com, Tues.–Thurs. 6–10 P.M., Fri.–Sat. 6–11 P.M., Sun. 5–8 P.M., $20–23). The menu is simple but perfectly focused, featuring handmade pasta and signature items like the pork chop or the fresh cheese plate. You'll be surprised at how much food your money gets you here. Sunday evenings see a family-style, prix fixe communal dinner.

WEST ASHLEY
American

The kitchen at **Gene's Haufbrau** (17 Savannah Hwy., 843/225-4363, www.geneshaufbrau.com, daily 11:30 A.M.–1 A.M., $6–10) complements its fairly typical bar-food menu with some good wraps. Start with the "Drunken Trio" (beer-battered cheesesticks, mushrooms, and onion rings) and follow with a portobello wrap or a good old-fashioned crawfish po' boy. One of the best meals for the money in town is Gene's rotating $6.95 blue plate special, offered Monday–Friday 11:30 A.M.–4:30 P.M. The late-night kitchen hours, until 1 A.M., are a big plus.

Barbecue

For connoisseurs, **Bessinger's** (1602 Savannah Hwy., 843/556-1354, www.bessingersbbq.com, prices and hours vary) is worth the trip over to West Ashley for its Carolina-style mustard-based wizardry. There are two scenes at Bessinger's, the sit-down Southern buffet (Thurs. 5–8 P.M., Fri.–Sat. 5–9 P.M., Sun. noon–8 P.M., $11.50 adults, $5.95 children)—Friday is fried catfish night—and the Sandwich Shop (Mon.–Sat. 10:30 A.M.–9:30 P.M., $6.35 for a "Big Joe" basket) for quick takeout. In old-school tradition, Bessinger's is a dry joint that doesn't sell alcohol.

(To clarify: Bessinger's in Charleston was founded by the brother of Maurice Bessinger, who started the Columbia-based "Maurice's Gourmet BBQ" chain, famous for its ultra–right-wing, neo-Confederate sensibilities. You may safely patronize Bessinger's in Charleston without worrying that you are supporting anything you may have objections to.)

However, another West Ashley joint, **❰ Fiery Ron's Home Team BBQ** (1205 Ashley River Rd., 843/225-7427, www.hometeambbq.com, Mon.–Sat. 11 A.M.–9 P.M., Sun. 11:30 A.M.–9 P.M., $7–20) is even better than Bessinger's. I cannot say enough about both the pulled pork and the ribs, which rank with the best I've had anywhere in the country. Even the sides are amazing here, including perfect collards and tasty mac-and-cheese. Chef Madison Ruckel provides an array of tableside sauces, from hot to indigenous South Carolina mustard to his own "Alabama white," a light and delicious mayonnaise-based sauce.

As if that weren't enough, the owners' close ties to the regional jam-band community

Make sure you try Fiery Ron's ribs and pulled pork.

means there's great live blues and indie rock after 10 P.M. most nights (Thursday is bluegrass night) to spice up the bar action, which goes until 2 A.M.

Classic Southern

Tucked away on the grounds of the Middleton Place Plantation is the romantic **Middleton Place Restaurant** (843/556-6020, www .middletonplace.org, lunch daily 11 A.M.–3 P.M., dinner Tues.–Thurs. 6–8 P.M., Fri.–Sat. 6–9 P.M., Sun. 6–8 P.M., $15–25). Theirs is a respectful take on traditional plantation fare like hoppin' John, gumbo, she-crab soup, and collards. The special annual Thanksgiving buffet is a real treat.

Reservations are required for dinner. A nice plus is being able to wander the gorgeous landscaped gardens before dusk if you arrive at 5:30 P.M. or later with a dinner reservation.

Mediterranean

Anything on this Northern Italian–themed menu is good, but the risotto—legacy of original chef John Marshall—is the specialty

dish at **Al Di La** (25 Magnolia Rd., 843/571-2321, Tues.–Sat. 6–10 P.M.), West Ashley's most popular fine dining spot. Reservations recommended.

MOUNT PLEASANT

Most restaurant action in Mount Pleasant centers on the picturesque shrimping village of Shem Creek, which is dotted on both banks with bars and restaurants, most dealing in fresh local seafood. As with Murrells Inlet up the coast, some spots on Shem Creek border on tourist traps. Don't be afraid to go where the lines aren't.

Mediterranean

Tasty Greek cuisine is the order of the day at the relatively new **Samos Taverna** (819 Coleman Blvd., 843/856-5055, Mon.–Thurs. 5:30–10 P.M., Fri.–Sat. 5:30–11 P.M., $15), named after the Aegean island from whence one of the partners came. The decor is upscale, if the prices aren't. Best thing to do here is sample several of the *mezethes,* or small plates. Don't forget the octopus!

Seafood

A well-regarded spot on Shem Creek is **Water's Edge** (1407 Shrimp Boat Lane, 843/884-4074, daily 11 A.M.–11 P.M., $20–30), which consistently takes home a Wine Spectator Award of Excellence for its great selection of vintages. Native Charlestonian Jimmy Purcell concentrates on fresh seafood with a slightly more upscale flair than many Shem Creek places.

Right down the road from Water's Edge is another popular spot, especially for a younger crowd: **Vickery's Shem Creek Bar and Grill** (1313 Shrimp Boat Lane, 843/884-4440, daily 11:30 A.M.–1 A.M., $11–16). With a similar menu to its partner location on the peninsula, this Vickery's has the pleasant added bonus of a beautiful view overlooking the Creek. You'll get more of the Vickery's Cuban flair here, with a great black bean soup and an awesome Cuban sandwich.

If you find yourself thirsty and hungry in Mount Pleasant after dark, you might want to stop in the **Reddrum Gastropub** (803 Coleman Blvd., 843/849-0313, www.reddrum pub.com, Mon. and Tues. 5:30–9 P.M., Wed.–Sat. 5:30–10 P.M.), so named because here the food is just as important as the drink. While you're likely to need reservations for the dining room, where you can enjoy Lowcountry/Tex-Mex fusion-style cuisine with a typically Mount Pleasant–like emphasis on seafood, the bar scene is very hopping and fun, with live music every Wednesday and Thursday night.

Vegetarian

For a vegetarian-friendly change of pace from seafood, go to the **Mustard Seed** (1026 Chuck Dawley Blvd., 843/849-0050, Mon.–Sat. 11 A.M.–2:30 P.M. and 5–9:30 P.M., $14–18). The pad thai is probably the best thing on New York–trained Chef Sal Parco's creative and dynamic menu, but you might also get a kick out of the sweet potato ravioli.

For a *real* change of pace, try **The Sprout Cafe** (629 Johnnie Dodds Blvd., 843/849-8554, www .thehealthysprout.com, Mon.–Fri. 6 A.M.–8 P.M., Sat. 9 A.M.–3 P.M., Sun. 11 A.M.–3 P.M., $3–10) on U.S. 17. Dealing totally in raw foods, the obvious emphasis here is on health and freshness of ingredients. You might be surprised at the inventiveness of their breakfast-through-dinner, seasonal menu—memorably described by the staff as "grab and go"—which might include a tasty crepe topped with a pear-and-nut puree and maple syrup, or a raw squash and zucchini "pasta" dish topped with walnut "meatballs."

SULLIVAN'S ISLAND

A new location of **Fiery Ron's Home Team** (2209 Middle St., 843/883-3131, www .hometeambbq.com, kitchen open Mon.–Sat. 11 A.M.–11 P.M., Sun. 11:30 A.M.–11 P.M., $8–14) provides the same incredible, melt-in-your-mouth pork and ribs made famous by the original West Ashley location.

For a friendly bite and an adult beverage or two, go straight to **Poe's Tavern** (2210 Middle St., 843/883-0083, daily 11 A.M.–2 A.M., kitchen closes 10 P.M.), a nod to Edgar Allan Poe's stint at nearby Fort Moultrie.

Atlanticville (2063 Middle St., 843/883-9452, www.atlanticville.net, daily 5:30–10 P.M., Sunday brunch 10 A.M.–2 P.M., $25) is where to go for classic fine dining on Sullivan's.

If you just want to pick up some healthy goodies for picnicking on the beach, head to the little **Green Heron Grocery** (2019 Middle St., 843/883-0751).

FOLLY BEACH

Breakfast and Brunch

The closest thing to a taste of old Folly is the **Lost Dog Café** (106 W. Huron St., 843/588-9669, daily 6:30 A.M.–3 P.M., $5–7), so named for its bulletin board stacked with alerts about lost pets, pets for adoption, and newborns for sale or giveaway. They open early, the better to offer a tasty, healthy breakfast to the surfing crowd. It's a great place to pick up a quick, inexpensive, and tasty meal while you're near the beach.

Mexican

Taco Boy (15 Center St., 843/588-9761, Sun.–Thurs. 11 A.M.–10 P.M., Fri.–Sat. 11 A.M.–11 P.M., $5–15) is a fun place to get a fish taco, have a margarita, and take a walk on the nearby beach afterward. Though no one is under any illusions that this is an authentic Mexican restaurant, the fresh guacamole is particularly rave-worthy, and there's a good selection of tequilas and beers *hecho en Mexico*, with the bar staying open until 2 A.M. on weekends.

Seafood

Fans of the legendary (**Bowens Island Restaurant** (1870 Bowens Island Rd., 843/795-2757, Tues.–Sat. 5–10 P.M., $5–15, cash only), on James Island just before you get to Folly, went into mourning when it burned to the ground in 2006. But you can't keep a good oysterman down, and owner Robert Barber rebuilt. Regulars insist that this institution, which began in the 1940s as a fishing camp, remains as old-school as ever.

A universe removed from the Lexus-and-khaki scene downtown, Bowens Island isn't the place for the uptight. This is the place to go when you want shovels of oysters literally thrown onto your table, freshly steamed and delicious and all-you-can-eat. The fried shrimp, flounder, and hush puppies are incredible too. The understated setting—a nondescript building, little to no signage—only adds to the authenticity of the whole experience.

To get there from the peninsula, take Calhoun Street west onto the James Island Connector/Highway 30. Take exit 3 onto Highway 171 South and look for Bowens Island Road on your right. The restaurant will be on your left in a short while, after passing by several ritzy McMansions that in no way resemble the restaurant you're about to experience.

Set within the renovated Holiday Inn Folly Beach Oceanfront, the spacious **Blu Restaurant and Bar** (1 Center St., 843/588-6658, www.blufollybeach.com, daily 7 A.M.–11 P.M., $10–20) specializes in sustainable local seafood like the pan-fried grouper and signature cocktails like the Tru Blu Martini.

NORTH CHARLESTON

If you have a hankering for pizza in North Charleston, don't miss **EVO Pizzeria** (1075 E. Montague Ave., 843/225-1796, www.evopizza .com, lunch Tues.–Fri. 11 A.M.–2:30 P.M., dinner 5–10 P.M., Sat. 6–10 P.M., $10–15) in the Olde North Charleston area at Park Circle. They specialize in a small but rich menu of unusual gourmet pizza toppings, like pistachio pesto.

COFFEE, TEA, AND SWEETS

By common consensus, the best java joint in Charleston is **Kudu Coffee** (4 Vanderhorst Ave., 843/853-7186, Mon.–Sat. 6:30 A.M.–7 P.M., Sun. 9 A.M.–6 P.M.) in the Upper King area. A kudu is an African antelope, and the Africa theme extends to the beans, which all have an African pedigree. Poetry readings and occasional live music add to the mix. A lot of green-friendly, left-of-center community activism goes on here as well; a recent discussion group was titled "How to Survive the Bible Belt but Still Find God." The adjacent African art store is owned by the coffeehouse.

If you find yourself needing a quick pick-me-up while shopping on King Street, avoid the lines at the two Starbucks on the avenue and instead turn east on Market and duck inside **City Lights Coffeehouse** (141 Market St., 843/853-7067, Mon.–Thurs. 7 A.M.–9 P.M., Fri.–Sat. 7 A.M.–10 P.M., Sun. 8 A.M.–6 P.M.). The sweet goodies are delectable in this cozy little Euro-style place, and the Counter Culture organic coffee is to die for. If you're really lucky they'll have some of their Ethiopian Sidamo brewed.

Though technically a retail location of a national chain rather than a traditional tea room per se, you can get an outstanding fresh cup of herbal tea or maté at **Teavana** (340 King St., 843/723-0600, www.teavana.com, Mon.–Thurs. 10 A.M.–6 P.M., Fri.–Sat. 10 A.M.–9 P.M., Sun. noon–6 P.M.). Take the time to enjoy it in the little courtyard out back. Stored in big cans along the back wall, all the tea here is loose, fresh, and of extremely high quality. The friendly and knowledgeable staff will let you do sniff tests until you find the aroma that appeals to you most.

A unique Charleston phenomenon on Upper King by Marion Square is the aptly named **Cupcake** (433 King St., 843/853-

8181, www.freshcupcakes.com, Mon.–Sat. 10 A.M.–7 P.M.). Their eponymous specialty compels Charlestonians to form lines onto the sidewalk, waiting to enjoy one or more of the 30 flavors of little cakes.

Routinely voted as having the best desserts in the city, **Kaminsky's** (78 N. Market St., 843/853-8270, daily noon–2 A.M.) cakes alone are worth the trip to the City Market area. The fresh fruit torte, the red velvet, and the "Mountain of Chocolate" are the three best sellers. There's a Mount Pleasant location, too (1028 Johnnie Dodds Blvd., 843/971-7437).

Some key **Starbucks** locations in Charleston are 239 King Street, 387 King Street, 168 Calhoun Street, and 475 East Bay Street.

MARKETS AND GROCERIES

A fun and favorite local fixture from April through mid-December, the **Charleston Farmers Market** (843/724-7309, www .charlestoncity.info, every Sat. 8 A.M.–2 P.M.) rings beautiful Marion Square with stalls of local produce, street eats, local arts and crafts, and kids activities. Running April through October, East Cooper has its own version in the

Mount Pleasant Farmers Market (843/884-8517, http://townofmountpleasant.com, every Tues. 3 P.M. until dark) at the Moultrie Middle School on Coleman Boulevard.

For organic groceries and/or a quick, healthy bite while you're in Mount Pleasant, check out **Whole Foods** (923 Houston Northcutt Blvd., 843/971-7240, daily 8 A.M.–9 P.M.). The biggest and best supermarket near the downtown tourist area is the regional chain **Harris Teeter** (290 E. Bay St., 843/722-6821, daily 24 hours). There are other Harris Teeter stores in Mount Pleasant (920 Houston Northcutt Blvd. and 620 Long Point Rd., 843/881-4448) and Folly Beach (675 Folly Rd., 843/406-8977).

For a charming grocery shopping experience, try **King Street Grocery** (435 King St., 843/958-8004, daily 8 A.M.–midnight) on Upper King. If you're down closer to the Battery, go to the delightful **Queen Street Grocery** (133 Queen St., 843/723-4121, Mon.–Sat. 8 A.M.–8:30 P.M., kitchen Mon.–Sat. 10 A.M.–5 P.M., Sun. 11 A.M.–3 P.M.).

Need groceries at 4 A.M. on Folly Beach? Go to **Bert's Market** (202 E. Ashley Ave., 843/588-9449), open 24 hours.

Information and Services

VISITORS CENTERS

I highly recommend a stop at the **Charleston Visitor Reception and Transportation Center** (375 Meeting St., 800/774-0006, www.charles toncvb.com, Mon.–Fri. 8:30 A.M.–5 P.M.). Housed in a modern building with an inviting, open design, the Center has several high-tech, interactive exhibits, including an amazing model of the city under glass. Wall after wall of well-stocked, well-organized brochures will keep you informed on everything a tourist would ever want to know about or see in the city. A particularly welcoming touch is the inclusion of the work of local artists all around the Center.

I recommend using the attached parking garage not only for your stop at the Center but also anytime you want to see the many

sights this part of town has to offer, such as the Charleston Museum, the Manigault and Aiken-Rhett Houses, and the Children's Museum. The big selling point at the Center is the friendliness of the smiling and courteous staff, who welcome you in true Charleston fashion and are there to book rooms and tours and find tickets for shows and attractions.

If for no other reason, you should go to the Center to take advantage of the great deal offered by the **Charleston Heritage Passport** (www.heritagefederation.org), which gives you 40 percent off admission to all of Charleston's key historic homes, the Charleston Museum, and the two awesome plantation sites on the Ashley River: Drayton Hall and Middleton Place. You can get the Heritage Passport *only* at the Charleston Visitor Reception and Transportation Center on Meeting Street.

Other area visitors centers include the **Mt. Pleasant-Isle of Palms Visitor Center** (Johnnie Dodds Blvd., 843/853-8000, daily 9 A.M.–5 P.M.) and the new **North Charleston Visitor Center** (4975-B Centre Pointe Dr., 843/853-8000, Mon.–Sat. 10 A.M.–5 P.M.).

HOSPITALS
If there's a silver lining in getting sick or injured in Charleston, it's that there are plenty of high-quality medical facilities available. The premier institution is the **Medical University of South Carolina** (171 Ashley Ave., 843/792-2300, www.muschealth.com) in the northwest part of the peninsula.

Two notable facilities are near each other downtown: **Roper Hospital** (316 Calhoun St., 843/402-2273, www.roperhospital.com) and **Charleston Memorial Hospital** (326 Calhoun St., 843/792-2300).

In Mount Pleasant there's **East Cooper Regional Medical Center** (1200 Johnnie Dodds Blvd., www.eastcoopermedctr.com). In West Ashley there's **Bon Secours St. Francis Hospital** (2095 Henry Tecklenburg Ave., 843/402-2273, www.ropersaintfrancis.com).

POLICE
For non-emergencies in Charleston, West Ashley, and James Island, contact the **Charleston Police Department** (843/577-7434, www.charlestoncity.info). You can also contact the police department in Mount Pleasant (843/884-4176). North Charleston is a separate municipality with its own police department (843/308-4718, www.northcharleston.org).

Of course, for emergencies always call **911.**

MEDIA
Newspapers
The daily newspaper of record is the *Post and Courier* (www.charleston.net). Its entertainment insert, *Preview,* comes out on Thursdays.

The free alt-weekly is the *Charleston City Paper* (www.charlestoncitypaper.com), which comes out on Wednesdays and is the best place to find local music and arts listings.

A particularly well-done and lively metro glossy is *Charleston Magazine* (www.charlestonmag.com), which comes out once a month.

Radio and Television
The National Public Radio affiliate is the South Carolina ETV radio station WSCI 89.3 FM.

South Carolina ETV is on television at WITV. The local NBC affiliate is WCBD, the CBS affiliate is WCSC, the ABC affiliate is WCIV, and the Fox affiliate is WTAT.

LIBRARIES
The main branch of the **Charleston County Public Library** (68 Calhoun St., 843/805-6801, www.ccpl.org, Mon.–Thurs. 9 A.M.–9 P.M., Fri.–Sat. 9 A.M.–6 P.M., Sun. 2–5 P.M.) has been on its current site since 1998. Named for Sullivan's Island's most famous visitor, the **Edgar Allan Poe** (1921 I'On Ave., 843/883-3914, www.ccpl.org, Mon. and Fri. 2–6 P.M., Tues., Thurs., and Sat. 10 A.M.–2 P.M.) has been housed in Battery Gadsden, a former Spanish-American War gun emplacement, since 1977.

The College of Charleston's main library is the **Marlene and Nathan Addlestone Library** (205 Calhoun St., 843/953-5530, www.cofc.edu), home to special collections, the Center for Student Learning, the main computer lab, the media collection, and even a café. The college's **Avery Research Center for African American History and Culture** (125 Bull St., 843/953-7609, www.cofc.edu/avery, Mon.–Fri. 10 A.M.–5 P.M., Sat. noon–5 P.M.) houses documents relating to the history and culture of African Americans in the Lowcountry.

For other historical research on the area, check out the collections of the **South Carolina Historical Society** (100 Meeting St., 843/723-3225, www.southcarolinahistoricalsociety.org, Mon.–Fri. 9 A.M.–4 P.M., Sat. 9 A.M.–2 P.M.). There's a $5 research fee for non-members.

GAY AND LESBIAN RESOURCES

Contrary to many media portrayals of the region, Charleston is quite open to gays and lesbians, who play a major role in arts, culture, and business. As with any other place in the South, however, it's generally expected that people—straights as well—will keep personal preferences and politics to themselves in public settings.

A key local advocacy group is the **Alliance for Full Acceptance** (29 Leinbach Dr., Ste. D-3, 843/883-0343, www.affa-sc.org). The **Lowcountry Gay and Lesbian Alliance** (843/720-8088) holds a potluck the last Sunday of each month. For the most up-to-date happenings, try the Gay Charleston blog (http:///gaycharleston.ccpblogs.com), part of the *Charleston City Paper.*

Getting There and Around

BY AIR

Way up in North Charleston is **Charleston International Airport** (5500 International Blvd., 843/767-1100, airport code CHS, www.chs-airport .com), served by AirTran (www.airtran.com), American Airlines (www.aa.com), Continental Airlines (www.continental.com), Delta (www .delta.com), United Airlines (www.ual.com), and US Airways (www.usairways.com).

As in most cities, taxi service from the airport is regulated. The fare from the airport is $2.15 per mile, with a $12 fee for each passenger over two (no additional charge up to two people). For example, this translates to about $27 for two people from the airport to Charleston Place downtown. For the airport vicinity there's a fixed rate of $9 per person.

BY CAR

There are two main routes into Charleston, I-26 from the west-northwest (which dead-ends downtown) and U.S. 17 from the west (called Savannah Highway when it gets close to Charleston proper), which continues on over the Ravenel Bridge into Mount Pleasant and beyond.

There's a fairly new perimeter highway, I-526 (Mark Clark Expressway), which loops around the city from West Ashley to North Charleston to Daniel Island and into Mount Pleasant. It's accessible both from I-26 and U.S. 17.

Keep in mind that I-95, while certainly a gateway to the region, is actually a good ways out of Charleston, about 30 miles west of the city.

Car Rentals

Charleston International Airport has rental kiosks for **Avis** (843/767-7031), **Budget** (843/767-7051), **Dollar** (843/767-1130), **Enterprise** (843/767-1109), **Hertz** (843/767-4550), **National** (843/767-3078), and **Thrifty** (843/647-4389).

There are a couple of rental locations downtown: **Budget** (390 Meeting St., 843/577-5195) and **Enterprise** (398 Meeting St., 843/723-6215). **Hertz** has a location in West Ashley (3025 Ashley Town Center Dr., 843/573-2147), as does **Enterprise** (2004 Savannah Hwy., 843/556-7889).

BY BUS

Public transportation by **Charleston Area Regional Transit Authority** (843/724-7420, www.ridecarta.com), or CARTA, is a convenient and inexpensive way to enjoy Charleston without the more structured nature of an organized tour. There's a wide variety of routes, but most visitors will limit their acquaintance to the tidy, trolley-like **DASH** (Downtown Area Shuttle) buses run by CARTA primarily for tourists. Each ride is $1.25 per person (seniors are $0.60). The best deal is the $4 one-day pass, which you get at the Charleston Visitor Center (375 Meeting St.). Keep in mind that DASH only stops at designated places.

DASH has three routes: the 210, which runs a northerly circuit from the Aquarium to the College of Charleston; the 211, running up and down the parallel Meeting and King Streets from Marion Square down to the Battery; and the 212 Market/Waterfront shuttle from the Aquarium area down to Waterfront Park.

BY TAXI

The South is generally not big on taxis, and Charleston is no exception. The best bet is simply to call, rather than try to flag one down. Charleston's most fun service is **Charleston Black Cabs** (843/216-2627, www.charlestonblackcabcompany.com), using Americanized versions of the classic British taxi. A one-way ride anywhere on the peninsula below the bridges is a flat $10 per person, and rates go up from there. They're very popular, so call as far ahead as you can or try to get one at their stand at Charleston Place. Two other good services are **Safety Cab** (843/722-4066) and **Yellow Cab** (843/577-6565).

You can also try a human-powered taxi service from **Charleston Rickshaw** (843/723-5685). A cheerful (and energetic) young cyclist will pull you and a friend to most points on the lower peninsula for about $10–15. Call 'em or find one by City Market. They work late on Friday and Saturday nights, too.

PARKING

As you'll quickly see, parking is at a premium in downtown Charleston. An exception seems to be the large number of free spaces all along the Battery, but unless you're an exceptionally strong walker, that's too far south to use as a reliable base from which to explore the whole peninsula.

Most metered parking downtown is on and around Calhoun Street, Meeting Street, King Street, Market Street, and East Bay Street. That may not sound like a lot, but it constitutes the bulk of the area that most tourists visit. Most meters have three-hour limits but you'll come across some as short as 30 minutes. Technically you're not supposed to "feed the meter" in Charleston, as city personnel put little chalk marks on your tires to make sure people aren't overstaying their welcome. Metered parking is free 6 P.M.–6 A.M. and all day on Sunday. On Saturdays, expect to pay.

The city has several conveniently located and comparatively inexpensive parking garages. I strongly suggest that you make use of them. They're located at: The Aquarium, Camden and Exchange Streets, Charleston Place, Concord and Cumberland Streets, East Bay and Prioleau Streets, Marion Square, Gaillard Auditorium, Liberty and St. Philip Streets, Majestic Square, the Charleston Visitor Reception and Transportation Center, and Wentworth Street. There are several private parking garages as well, primarily clustered in the City Market area. They're convenient, but many have parking spaces that are often too small for some vehicles.

The city's website (www.charlestoncity.info) has a good interactive map of parking.

Greater Charleston

Though one could easily spend a lifetime enjoying the history and attractions of Charleston itself, there are many unique experiences to be had in the less-developed areas surrounding the city. Generally there are two types of vibes: isolated close-knit communities with little overt development (though that's changing), or private, resort-style communities amid stunning natural beauty.

SUMMERVILLE AND VICINITY

The Dorchester County town of Summerville, population 30,000, is gaining a reputation as a friendly, scenic, and upscale suburb north of Charleston. That's funny, since that's basically what Summerville has always been.

Founded as Pineland Village in 1785, Summerville made its reputation as a place for plantation owners and their families to escape the insects and heat of the swampier areas of the Lowcountry. While the plantation system disintegrated with the South's loss in the Civil War, Summerville got a second wind at the turn of the 20th century, when it was recommended by doctors all over the world as a great place to recover from tuberculosis (supposedly all the turpentine fumes in the air from the pine trees were a big help).

Summerville's about 30 minutes from downtown Charleston. Take I-26 north.

Sights

Due to its longstanding popularity as a getaway for wealthy planters and then as a spa town, Summerville boasts a whopping 700 buildings on the National Register of Historic Places. For a walking tour of the historic district, download the map at www.visitsummerville.com or pick up a hard copy at the **Summerville Visitors Center** (402 N. Main St., 843/873-8535). (Alas, the grand old Pine Forest Inn, perhaps the greatest of all Summerville landmarks, Winter White House for presidents William Taft and Theodore Roosevelt, was torn down after World War II, a victim of the Florida vacation craze.)

Much visitor activity in Summerville centers on **Azalea Park** (South Main St. and W. 5th St. South, daily dusk–dawn, free), rather obviously named for its most scenic inhabitants. Several fun yearly events take place here, most notably the **Flowertown Festival** (www.flowertownfestival.com, free) each April, a three-day affair heralding the coming of spring and the blooming of the flowers. One of the biggest festivals in South Carolina, a quarter-million people usually attend. Another event, **Sculpture in the South** (www.sculptureinthesouth.com) in May, takes advantage of the extensive public sculpture in the park.

To learn more about Summerville's interesting history, go just off Main Street to the **Summerville-Dorchester Museum** (100 E. Doty Ave., 843/875-9666, www.summervilledorchestermuseum.org, Mon.–Sat. 9 A.M.–2 P.M.). Located in the former town

police station, the museum has a wealth of good exhibits and boasts a new curator, Chris Ohm, with wide local experience, including at Middleton Place and with the CSS *Hunley* project in North Charleston.

Just south of Summerville on the way back to Charleston is **Colonial Dorchester State Historic Site** (300 State Park Rd., 843/873-1740, www.southcarolinaparks.com, daily 9 A.M.–6 P.M., $2 adults, 15 and under free), marking the remains of the dead town of Dorchester. With a pedigree going back to 1697, Dorchester was fortified by colonists during the Revolution and commanded briefly for a time by the Swamp Fox himself, Francis Marion. The encampment was reclaimed by the surrounding forest, with research not beginning until the 1960s. Today you can view the poignant remains of the 1719 church bell tower and a circa-1750 tabby fort from the French and Indian War, as well as enjoying interpretive trails.

Accommodations and Food

The renowned **Woodlands Resort & Inn** (125 Parsons Rd., 843/875-2600, $325–650) is one of a handful of inns in America with a five-star rating both for lodging and dining. Its 18 rooms within the 1906 great house are decorated in a mix of old-fashioned plantation high-style and contemporary designer aesthetics, with modern, luxurious baths. There's also a freestanding guest cottage ($850) which seeks to replicate a hunting-lodge type of vibe.

As you'd expect, there's a full day spa on premises; an hour massage, the most basic offering, will run you $110. The pool is outside, but heated for all-year enjoyment, at least theoretically. Woodlands is making a big play for the growing pet-friendly market, and eagerly pampers your dog or cat while you stay. You might not want to leave the grounds, but you should take advantage of their complimentary bikes to tour around historic Summerville.

Within Woodlands is its award-winning, world-class restaurant, simply called **The Dining Room** (Mon.–Sat. 11 A.M.–2 P.M. and

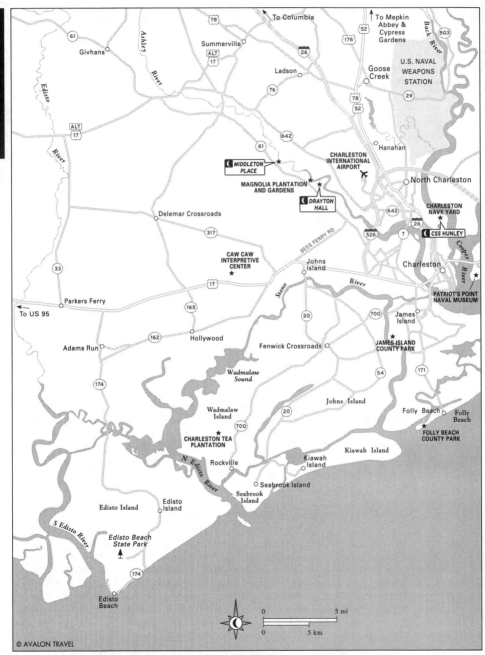

© AVALON TRAVEL

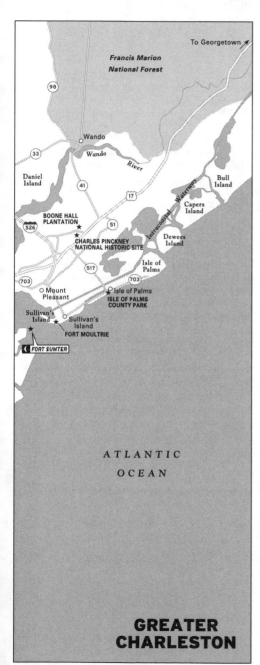

ATLANTIC

OCEAN

GREATER CHARLESTON

6–9 P.M., brunch Sun. 11:30 A.M.–2 P.M., $25–40). New executive chef Nate Whiting, once the *sous chef* here, mixes the love of the fresh ingredients of his Italian heritage with the boldness of his French training. His signature dishes include a linguini with wild burgundy escargot and sweet chili threads. It will come as no surprise to find out that the 900-entry wine list and sommelier are collectively awesome, as are the desserts of pastry chef Sheree McDowell. Jackets required, and reservations are highly advisable.

In Summerville proper, try **Mustard Seed** (101 N. Main St., 843/821-7101, lunch Mon.–Sat. 11 A.M.–2:30 P.M., dinner Mon.–Thurs. 5–9 P.M. and Fri.–Sat. 5–10 P.M., $8–10), a health food restaurant that doesn't skimp on the taste. For a more down-home-style pancakes-and-sandwich place that's popular with the locals at all hours of the day, try **Flowertown Restaurant** (120 E. 5th North St., 843/871-3202, daily 24 hours, $8).

Another popular local landmark is **Guerin's Pharmacy** (140 S. Main St., 843/873-2531, Mon.–Fri. 9 A.M.–6 P.M., Sat. 9 A.M.–5 P.M.), which claims to be the State's oldest pharmacy. Complete with old-fashioned soda fountain, they offer malted milkshakes and lemonade.

Moncks Corner
MEPKIN ABBEY
The little Berkeley County burg of Moncks Corner is actually named for a person, not a vocation. But nonetheless that's where you'll find a fully active, practicing Trappist monastery, Mepkin Abbey (1098 Mepkin Abbey Rd., Moncks Corner, 843/761-8509, www.mepkinabbey.org, Tues.–Fri. 9 A.M.–4:30 P.M., Sat. 9 A.M.–4 P.M., Sun. 1–4 P.M., free), notable for the fact that it's not only open to visitors, but welcomes them.

The beautiful Abbey and grounds on the Cooper River are on what was once the plantation of the great Carolina statesman Henry Laurens (whose ashes are buried here), and later the home of famous publisher Henry Luce and his wife Clare Boothe Luce. The focal point of natural beauty is the Luce-commissioned

Mepkin Abbey Botanical Garden (closed Mon.), a 3,200-acre tract with a camellia garden designed by noted landscape architect Loutrel Briggs, a native New Yorker who made Charleston his adopted home.

When they're not in prayer, the monks generally observe silence. In accordance with the emphasis the order puts on the spiritual value of manual labor, farming is the main physical occupation, with the monks' efforts producing eggs, honey, preserves, soap, and even compost from the gardens, all of which you can purchase in the Abbey gift shop in the reception center, which will always be your first stop. Tours of the Abbey itself are usually given at 11:30 A.M. and 3 P.M. most days.

The majority of visitors to the Abbey are casual day visitors, eager to enjoy the relaxing quiet, the kiss of the river's breeze, and the humming of the honeybees. But for those wanting a contemplative, quiet retreat of a distinctly Christian nature, the Abbey lets you stay up to

---

THE MONKS OF MONCKS CORNER

Near Moncks Corner, South Carolina, the old Mepkin Plantation is now the home of the monks of Mepkin Abbey. How and why a monastery came to be in this semi-rural corner of the Deep South is worth a closer look.

Originally the plantation of the great South Carolina statesman and Revolutionary War hero Henry Laurens, by 1936 the grounds had come into the hands of famed *Time* magazine publisher Henry Luce. In 1949, Henry and his wife Clare Boothe – a renowned congresswoman and playwright herself – donated a large portion of Mepkin to the Roman Catholic Church to be used as a monastery. In response, 29 monks from the Abbey of Gethsemane in Kentucky answered the call and moved to the Lowcountry to begin Mepkin Abbey. (Though it does contain actual monks, the little town of Moncks Corner north of Charleston was actually named for Thomas Monk, a merchant in the area.)

Mepkin Abbey's monks are of the Order of Cistercians of the Strict Observance, more commonly known simply as Trappists. With the credo "pray and work," the Trappists believe manual labor provides worshippers with the best opportunity to share and experience creation and restoration. They also view manual labor as following in the footsteps of the "Poor Christ" – since their work enriches and provides for the surrounding community, especially the disadvantaged.

Much of the monks' labor centers on various farm activities. Until recently the harvesting of chicken eggs – almost 10 million annually – was the main source of revenue to maintain the Abbey. In the wake of a controversy surrounding those eggs – which began when a member of the animal rights group PETA masqueraded as a retreat guest and secretly filmed the Abbey's chicken coops – the Abbey has decided to phase out egg production and sale and turn to other products to raise money.

As part of their vows, Mepkin Abbey's monks remain silent during the early and late parts of the day. Their daily schedule is very strict, as follows:

- 3 A.M.: Rise

- 3:20 A.M.: Vigils followed by half an hour of meditation, then a reading or private prayer

- 5:30 A.M.: Lauds followed by breakfast

- 7:30 A.M.: Eucharist followed by 15 minutes thanksgiving and Terce

- 8:30-11:30 A.M.: Silence ends and morning work period begins

- Noon: Midday prayer followed by dinner

- 1-1:40 P.M.: "Siesta" (optional)

- 1:45-3:30 P.M.: Afternoon work period

- 5 P.M.: Supper

- 6 P.M.: Vespers

- 7:35 P.M.: Compline

- Silence begins as monks retire for the day.

the church at Mepkin Abbey

six nights in one of their guesthouses (married couples can also take advantage of this).

As you'd imagine, the accommodations are Spartan—a bed, desk, and reading chair, with a private bathroom. Linens, towels, and soap are provided, but other than access to the library there's no other modern stimulation. Retreatants eat together with the monks at the same time, enjoying the same strict vegetarian diet and the same strict mealtime silence (though at lunch a single monk reads aloud from a book). Monks will assist retreat guests in the protocols of the Abbey's prayer schedule.

CYPRESS GARDENS
Nature lovers can also enjoy Cypress Gardens (3030 Cypress Gardens Rd., Moncks Corner, 843/553-0515, www.cypressgardens.info, daily 9 A.M.–5 P.M., last admission 4 P.M., $10 adults, $5 children 6–12), which carries with it a lot of the same quiet, meditative nature of the Abbey, though it's entirely secular. One of the first nature preserves in the Lowcountry, Cypress

Garden is the life's work of Benjamin R. Kittredge and his son Benjamin, Jr. Together they brought back the former glory of the old Dean Hall plantation, which the elder Kittredge, a New Yorker married into a wealthy Charleston family, had bought in 1909.

Only instead of rice, the main crop was to be flowers. *Millions* of flowers, from azaleas to daffodils to camellias to wisteria to dogwoods to roses to lotus and then some. The old paddy system was made navigable for small boats—today they're glass-bottomed—to meander among the tall cypress trees. The city of Charleston acquired the tract from the family, and later Berkeley County would come into possession of it.

The current 170-acre park was heavily damaged during Hurricane Hugo in 1989, but has made quite a comeback, and its inspiring and calming natural beauty remains true to the vision of the Kittredges. The founders would certainly approve of a particularly modern addition, the "Butterfly House," a 2,500-square-foot building packed full of butterflies,

Cypress Gardens

caterpillars, turtles, and birds. Just go in quietly, remain as quiet as you can, and the butterflies will find you, an unforgettable experience for child and adult alike.

You can also walk two nature trails and enjoy the flora and fauna of this area untouched by modern development. There's a new "Crocodile Isle" exhibit with several rare species of the reptile. A freshwater Aquarium has 30 species of fish as well as about 20 species of reptiles and amphibians. Out on the water, you can enjoy one of those glass-bottomed boat rides on the blackwater or—and this is what I recommend—paddle yourself in a canoe (included in the admission price) amongst the gorgeous cypress trees.

AWENDAW AND POINTS NORTH

This area just north of Charleston along Highway 17—named for the Sewee Indian village originally located here, and known to the world chiefly as the place where Hurricane Hugo made landfall—is seeing some new

growth, but still hews to its primarily rural, nature-loving roots.

Sewee Visitor and Environmental Education Center

Twenty miles north of Charleston you'll find the Sewee Visitor and Environmental Education Center (5821 Hwy. 17, 843/928-3368, www.fws.gov/seweecenter, Tues.–Sat. 9 A.M.–5 P.M., free). Besides being a gateway of sorts for the almost entirely aquatic Cape Romain National Wildlife Refuge, Sewee is primarily known for its population of rare red wolves, who were part of a unique release program on nearby Bull Island begun in the late 1970s.

Cape Romain National Wildlife Refuge

One of the best natural experiences in the area is north of Charleston at Cape Romain National Wildlife Refuge (5801 Hwy. 17 N., 843/928-3264, www.fws.gov/caperomain, sunrise–sunset year-round). Essentially comprising

CHARLESTON

four barrier islands, the 66,000-acre refuge—almost all of which is marsh—provides a lot of great paddling opportunities, chief among them **Bull Island** (no overnight camping). A fairly lengthy trek from where you put in lies famous Boneyard Beach, where hundreds of downed trees lie on the sand, bleached by sun and salt.

Slightly to the south within the refuge, **Capers Island Heritage Preserve** (843/953-9300, www.dnr.sc.gov, daily dawn–dusk, free) is still a popular camping locale, despite heavy damage from Hurricane Hugo. Get permits in advance by calling the South Carolina Department of Natural Resources. You can kayak to the refuge yourself or take the only approved ferry service from **Coastal Expeditions** (654 Serotina Ct., 843/881-4582, www.coastalexpeditions.com). **Barrier Island Eco Tours** (50 41st Ave., 843/886-5000, www.nature-tours.com) on Isle of Palms also runs trips to the area.

I'on Swamp Trail

Once part of a rice plantation, the I'on Swamp Trail (843/928-3368, www.fs.fed.us, daily dawn–dusk, free) is one of the premier bird-watching sites in South Carolina, particularly during spring and fall migrations. The rare Bachman's warbler, commonly considered one of the most elusive birds in North America, has been seen here. To get here head about 15 miles north of Mount Pleasant and take a left onto I'on Swamp Road (Forest Service 228). The parking area is 2.5 miles ahead on the left.

Food

A must-stop roadside diner in the Awendaw area is **☾ See Wee Restaurant** (4808 U.S. Hwy. 17 N, 843/928-3609, Mon.–Thurs. 11 a.m.–8:30 p.m., Fri.–Sat. 11 a.m.–9:30 p.m., Sun. 11 a.m.–8 p.m., $10–23), located about a 20-minute drive north of Charleston in a humble former general store on the west side of Highway 17 (the bathrooms are still outside). Folks come from Charleston and as far away as Myrtle Beach to enjoy signature menu items like the grouper and the unreal she-crab soup,

considered by some epicures to be the best in the world; you can't miss with any of their seafood entrées. Occasionally the crowds can get thick, but rest assured it's worth any wait.

POINTS WEST AND SOUTHWEST

Caw Caw Interpretive Center

Just west of town on U.S. 17, you'll find the unique Caw Caw Interpretive Center (5200 Savannah Hwy., Ravenel, 843/889-8898, www.ccprc.com, Wed.–Sun. 9 a.m.–5 p.m., $1), a treasure trove for history buffs and naturalists wanting to learn more about the old rice culture of the South. With a particular emphasis on the expertise of those who worked on the rice plantations using techniques they brought with them from Africa, the county-run facility comprises 650 acres of land (on an actual former rice plantation built on former cypress swamp), eight miles of interpretive trails, an educational center with exhibits, and a wildlife sanctuary with seven different habitats. Most Wednesday and Saturday mornings, guided bird walks are held at 8:30 a.m. ($5 per person). You can put in your own canoe for $10 on Saturdays and Sundays October–April. Bikes and dogs aren't allowed on the grounds.

Johns Island

The outlying community of Johns Island is where you'll find **Angel Oak Park** (3688 Angel Oak Rd., Mon.–Sat. 9 a.m.–5 p.m., Sun. 1–5 p.m.) home of a massive live oak, 65 feet in circumference, that's well over 1,000 years old and commonly considered the oldest tree east of the Mississippi River. The tree and the park are owned by the city of Charleston, and the grounds are often used for weddings and special events. Get here from Charleston by taking U.S. 17 over the Ashley River, then Highway 171 to Maybank Highway. Take a left onto Bohicket Road near the Piggly Wiggly, and then look for signs on your right.

Here is also where you'll find **Legare Farms** (2620 Hanscombe Point Rd., 843/559-0763, www.legarefarms.com), open to the public for various activities, like its annual pumpkin patch in October, its "sweet corn" festival in June, and bird walks each Saturday morning in autumn (8:30 A.M., $6 adults, $3 children).

If you find your tummy growling on Johns Island, don't miss **Ⓒ Fat Hen** (3140 Maybank Hwy., Johns Island, 843/559-9090, Tues.– Sat. 11:30 A.M.–3 P.M. and 5:30–10 P.M., Sun. 10 A.M.–3 P.M., $15–20), a self-styled "country French bistro" begun by a couple of old Charleston restaurant hands. The fried oysters are a particular specialty. There's also a bar menu for late-night hours (10 P.M.–2 A.M.).

If barbecue's more your thing, head straight to **Ⓒ JB's Smokeshack** (3406 Maybank Hwy., 843/557-0426, www.jbssmokeshack .com, Wed.–Sat. 11 A.M.–8:30 P.M., $8), one of the best 'cue joints in the Lowcountry. They offer a buffet for $8.88 per person ($4.95 for kids 10 and under), or you can opt for a barbecue plate, including hash, rice, and two sides. In a nice twist, the plates include a three-meat option: pork, chicken, ribs, or brisket.

Wadmalaw Island

Like Johns Island, Wadmalaw Island is one of those lazy, scenic areas gradually becoming subsumed within Charleston's growth. That said, there's plenty of meandering, laid-back beauty to enjoy, and a couple of interesting sights.

Currently owned by the R.C. Bigelow Tea corporation, the **Charleston Tea Plantation** (6617 Maybank Hwy., 843/559-0383, www .bigelowtea.com, Mon.–Sat. 10 A.M.–4 P.M., Sun. noon–4 P.M., free) is no cute living history exhibit: It's a big, working tea plantation—the only one in the U.S.—with acre after acre of *Camilla sinensis* being worked by modern farm machinery. Visitors get to see a sample of how the tea is made, "from the field to the cup," as they put it here, first by a trolley tour of the "Back 40" ($10) and then at a viewing gallery of the processing machines at work. And of course there's a gift shop where you can sample and buy all types of teas and tea-related products.

Unlike many agricultural sites in the area, the 127-acre Charleston Tea Plantation was never actually a plantation. It was first planted at the relatively late date of 1960, when the Lipton tea company moved some plants from Summerville, South Carolina, to its research facility on Wadmalaw Island. Lipton decided the climate and high labor costs of the American South weren't conducive to making money, so they sold the land to two employees, Mack Fleming and Bill Hall, in 1987. The two held onto the plantation until 2003, when R.C. Bigelow won it at auction for $1.28 million.

Growing season is from April through October. The tea bushes, direct descendants of plants brought over in the 1800s from India and China, "flush up" 2–3 inches every few weeks during growing season.

To get here from Charleston, take the Ashley River Bridge, stay left to Folly Road (Highway 171), turn right onto Maybank Highway for 18 miles, and look for the sign on your left.

The muscadine grape is the only varietal that dependably grows in South Carolina. That said, the state has several good wineries, among them Wadmalaw's own **Irvin House Vineyard** (6775 Bears Bluff Rd., 843/559-6867, www.charlestonwine.com, Thurs.–Sat. 10 A.M.–5 P.M.), the Charleston area's only vineyard. Jim Irvin, a Kentucky boy, and his wife Anne, a Johns Island native, make several varieties of muscadine wine here, with tastings and a gift shop. They also give free tours of the fifty-acre grounds every Saturday at 2 P.M. There's a Grape-Stomping Festival at the end of each August ($5 per car). To get here from town, go west on Maybank Highway about ten miles to Bears Bluff Road, veering right. The vineyard entrance is on your left after about eight miles.

Also on the Irvin vineyard grounds you'll find **Firefly Distillery** (6775 Bears Bluff Rd., 843/559-6867, www.fireflyvodka.com), home of their signature Firefly Sweet Tea Vodka. They offer tastings at the distillery ($6 per tasting) Wednesday–Saturday 11 A.M.–5 P.M. (closed Jan.).

Kiawah Island

Only one facility for the general public exists on beautiful Kiawah Island, the **Kiawah**

Island Beachwalker Park (843/768-2395, www.ccprc.com, weekends only 10 A.M.–6 P.M. Mar.–Apr. and Oct., 9 A.M.–7 P.M. during summer, 10 A.M.–6 P.M. Sept., closed Nov.–Feb., $7 per vehicle, free for pedestrians and cyclists). Get there from downtown by taking Lockwood Avenue onto the Highway 30 Connector bridge over the Ashley River. Turn right onto Folly Road, then a left onto Maybank Highway. After about 20 minutes you'll take a left onto Bohicket Road, which leads you to Kiawah in 14 miles. Turn left from Bohicket onto the Kiawah Island Parkway. Just before the security gate, turn right on Beachwalker Drive and follow the signs to the park.

The island's other main attraction is the **Kiawah Island Golf Resort** (12 Kiawah Beach Dr., 800/654-2924, www.kiawahgolf.com), which is a key location for PGA tournaments. Several smaller private, family-friendly resorts exist on Kiawah, with fully furnished homes and villas and every amenity you could ask for and then some, giving you full access to the island's 10 miles of beautiful beach. Go to www .explorekiawah.com for a full range of options or call 800/877-0837.

Through the efforts of the **Kiawah Island Conservancy** (23 Beachwalker Dr., 843/768-2029, www.kiawahconservancy.org), over 300 acres of the island have been kept as undeveloped nature preserve. The island's famous bobcat population has made quite a comeback, with somewhere between 24 and 36 animals currently active. The bobcats are vital to the island ecosystem, since as top predator they help cull what would otherwise become untenably large populations of deer and rabbit. As a side note, while you're enjoying the beautiful scenery of the islands on the Carolina coast, it's always important to remember that most, including Kiawah, were logged and/or farmed extensively in the past. While they're certainly gorgeous now, it would be incorrect to call them "pristine."

Seabrook Island

Like its neighbor Kiawah, Seabrook Island is also a private resort-dominated island. In addition to offering miles of beautiful beaches, on its 2,200 acres are a wide variety of golfing, tennis, equestrian, and swimming facilities, as well as extensive dining and shopping options. There are also a lot of kids' activities as well. For information on lodging options and packages, go to www.seabrook.com or call 866/249-9934.

BEAUFORT AND THE LOWCOUNTRY

For many people around the world, the Lowcountry is the first image that comes to mind when they think of the American South. For the people that live here the Lowcountry is altogether unique, but it does embody many of the region's most noteworthy qualities: an emphasis on manners, a constant look back into the past, and a slow and leisurely pace (embodied in the joking but largely accurate nickname "Slowcountry").

History hangs in the humid air where first the Spanish came to interrupt the native tribes' ancient reverie, then the French, followed by the English. Though time, erosion, and development have erased most traces of these multicultural occupants, you can almost hear their ghosts in the rustle of the branches in a sudden sea breeze, or in the piercing call of a heron over the marsh.

Artists and arts lovers the world over are drawn here to paint, photograph, or otherwise be inspired by some of the most gorgeous wetlands in the United States, so vast that human habitation appears fleeting and intermittent. Sprawling between Beaufort and Charleston is the huge ACE (Ashley, Combahee, Edisto) Basin, a beautiful and important estuary and a national model for good conservation practices.

In all, the defining characteristic of the Lowcountry is its liquid nature—not only literally, in the creeks and waterway that dominate every vista and the seafood cooked in all manner of ways, but figuratively, too, in the slow but deep quality of life here. Once outside what passes for urban areas here, you'll find yourself taking a look back through the decades to a time of roadside produce stands, shade tree mechanics, and men fishing and crabbing on tidal creeks—not for sport but for the family dinner.

Indeed, not so very long ago, before the influx

© JIM MOREKIS

HIGHLIGHTS

¶ Henry C. Chambers Waterfront Park:
Walk the dog or while away the time on a porch swing at this clean and inviting gathering place on the serene Beaufort River (page 122).

¶ St. Helena's Episcopal Church:
To walk through this Beaufort sanctuary and its walled graveyard is to walk through Lowcountry history (page 124).

¶ Penn Center: Not only the center of modern Gullah culture and education, this is a key site in civil rights history as well (page 135).

¶ Hunting Island State Park: One of the most peaceful natural getaways on the East Coast, but only minutes away from the more civilized temptations of Beaufort (page 141).

¶ ACE Basin: It can take a lifetime to learn your way around this massive, marshy estuary – or just a few hours soaking in its lush beauty (page 142).

¶ Edisto Beach State Park: Relax at this quiet, friendly, and relatively undeveloped Sea Island, a mecca for shell collectors (page 146).

¶ Pinckney Island National Wildlife Refuge: This well-maintained sanctuary is a major birding location and a great getaway from nearby Hilton Head (page 152).

¶ Old Bluffton: Gossipy and gorgeous by turns, this charming village on the May River centers on a thriving artist colony (page 165).

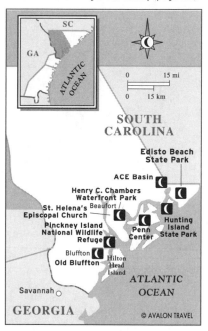

LOOK FOR **¶** TO FIND RECOMMENDED SIGHTS, ACTIVITIES, DINING, AND LODGING.

of resort development, retirement subdivisions, and tourism, much of the Lowcountry was like a flatter, more humid Appalachia—poverty-stricken and desperately underserved. While the archetypal South has been marketed in any number of ways to the rest of the world, here you get a sense that this is the real thing—timeless, endlessly alluring, but somehow very familiar.

South of Beaufort is the historically significant Port Royal area and the East Coast Marine Recruit Depot of Parris Island. East of Beaufort is the center of Gullah culture, St. Helena Island, and the scenic gem of Hunting Island. To the south is the scenic but entirely

developed golf and tennis mecca, Hilton Head Island, and Hilton Head's close neighbor but diametrical opposite in every other way, Daufuskie Island, another important Gullah center. Nestled in between is the close-knit and gossipy little village of Bluffton on the gossamer May River.

PLANNING YOUR TIME

The small-scale and comparative lack of traffic in most of the Lowcountry are its more charming aspects. Don't let that fool you into thinking you can knock everything out in a day, though. That would defeat the purpose, which

BEAUFORT

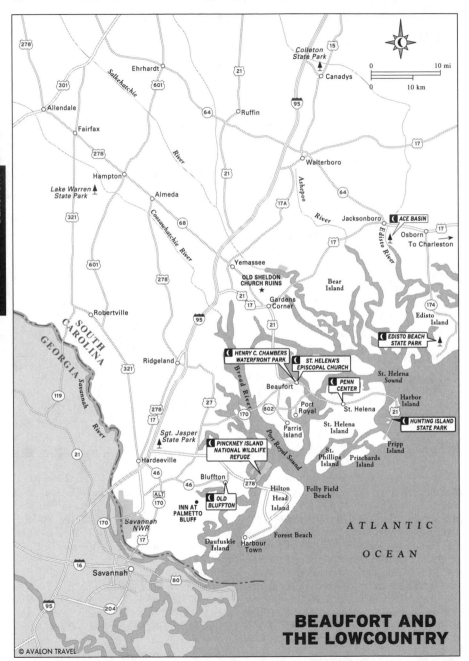

© AVALON TRAVEL

BEAUFORT AND THE LOWCOUNTRY

is not only to see the sights but to fully enjoy its laid-back, slow, and leisurely pace. A common-sense game plan is to use the centrally located Beaufort as a home base. Take at least a half-day of leisure to walk all over Beaufort. Another full day should go to St. Helena's Penn Center and on to Hunting Island. If you're in the mood for a road trip, dedicate a full day to tour the surrounding area to the north and northeast, with perhaps a jaunt to the ACE Basin National Wildlife Refuge, and a stop at the Old Sheldon Church Ruins in the late afternoon on your way back to Beaufort. If you have extra time, split it between Port Royal and a tour of the historic and military sites of interest on Parris Island.

While the New York accents fly fast and furious on Hilton Head Island, that's no reason for you to rush. Certainly a casual visitor can do Hilton Head in a day but its natural attractions beg for a more considered sort of enjoyment. Plan on at least a half-day just to enjoy the fine, broad beaches alone. I recommend another half-day to tour the island itself, maybe including a stop in Sea Pines for a late lunch or dinner.

While most of the marketing materials make scant mention of it, nature-lovers shouldn't miss the Pinckney Island National Wildlife Refuge, gorgeous enough to be a must-see, but small and convenient enough to fully enjoy in a few hours.

Beaufort

Sandwiched halfway between the prouder, louder cities of Charleston and Savannah, Beaufort is in many ways a more authentic slice of life from the past than either of those two. Long a staple of movie crews seeking to portray some archetypal aspect of the old South (*The Prince of Tides, The Great Santini, Forrest Gump*) or just to film beautiful scenery for its own sake (*Jungle Book, Last Dance*), Beaufort—pronounced "Byoofert," by the way, not "Bo-fort"—features many well-preserved examples of Southern architecture, most all of them in idyllic, family-friendly neighborhoods.

The pace in Beaufort is languid, slower even than the waving Spanish moss in the massive old live oak trees. The line between business and pleasure is a blurry one here. As you can tell from the signs you see on storefront doors saying things like "Back in an hour or so," time is an entirely negotiable commodity.

The architecture combines the relaxed Caribbean flavor of Charleston with the Anglophilic dignity of Savannah. In fact, plenty of people prefer the individualistic old homes of Beaufort, seemingly tailor-made for the exact spot on which they sit, to the historic

districts of either Charleston or Savannah in terms of sheer architectural delight.

While you'll run into plenty of charming and gracious locals during your time here, you might be surprised at the amount of transplanted Northerners. That's due not only to the high volume of retirees who've moved to the area, but the active presence of three major U.S. Navy facilities: the Marine Corps Air Station Beaufort, the Marine Corps Recruit Depot on nearby Parris Island, and the Beaufort Naval Hospital. Many's the time a former sailor or Marine has decided to put down roots in the area after being stationed here, the most famous example being author Pat Conroy's father, a.k.a. "The Great Santini."

HISTORY
Though little known to most Americans, the Port Royal Sound area is not only one of the largest natural harbors on the East Coast, it's one of the nation's most historic places. It's a fact made all the more maddening in how little of that history remains.

This was the site of the second landing by the Spanish on the North American continent, the expedition of Captain Pedro de Salazar in

1514. (Ponce de Leon's more famous landing at St. Augustine was but a year earlier.) A Spanish slaver named Francisco Cordillo (sometimes spelled Gordillo) made a brief stop in 1521, long enough to name the area Santa Elena—one of the oldest European place names in America.

Port Royal Sound didn't get its modern name until the first serious attempt at a permanent settlement, Jean Ribault's exploration in 1562. Though ultimately disastrous, Ribault's base of Charlesfort was the first French settlement in America. Ribault returned to France for reinforcements to find his country in an all-out religious civil war. He sought safety in England only to be clapped in the Tower of London.

Meanwhile his soldiers at Charlesfort became restive and revolted against their absentee commander, with most moving to the French settlement Fort Caroline near present-day Jacksonville, Florida. In a twist straight out of Hollywood, in 1565 Fort Caroline bought food and a ship to return to France from a passing vessel, which turned out to be commanded by the infamous English privateer John Hawkins. While the French waited for a favorable wind for the trip home, who should arrive but none other than Jean Ribault himself, fresh out of prison and at the head of 600 French soldiers and settlers sent to rescue his colony!

In yet another unlikely development, a Spanish fleet soon appeared, intent on driving the French out for good. Ribault went on the offensive, intending to mount a preemptive attack on the Spanish base at St. Augustine. However, a storm wrecked the French ships and Ribault was washed ashore near St. Augustine and killed by waiting Spanish troops.

As if the whole story couldn't get any stranger, back at Charlesfort things had become so desperate for the 27 original colonists who stayed behind that they decided to build a ship to sail back home to France—technically the first ship built in America for a transatlantic crossing. The vessel made it across the Atlantic, but not without price; running out of food, the French soldiers began eating shoe leather before moving on, so the accounts say,

to eating each other. Twenty survivors were rescued in the English Channel.

After the French faded from the scene, Spaniards came to garrison Santa Elena. But steady Indian attacks and Francis Drake's attack on St. Augustine forced the Spanish to abandon the area in 1587. Within the next generation British indigo planters had established a firm presence in the Port Royal area, chief among them John "Tuscarora Jack" Barnwell of Port Royal Island and Thomas Nairn of St. Helena. These men would go on to found the town of Beaufort, named for Henry Somerset, Duke of Beaufort, and it was chartered in 1711 as part of the original Carolina colony.

In 1776, Beaufort planter Thomas Heyward Jr. signed the Declaration of Independence. After independence was gained, Lowcountry planters turned to cotton as the main cash crop, since England had been their prime customer for indigo. The gambit paid off, and Beaufort soon became one of the wealthiest towns in the new nation.

The so-called "Golden Age" of Sea Island cotton saw storm clouds gather on the horizon as the Lowcountry became the hotbed of secession, with the very first Ordinance of Secession being drawn up in Beaufort's Milton Maxey House. Only seven months after secessionists fired on Fort Sumter in nearby Charleston in 1861, a huge Union fleet sailed into Port Royal and occupied Hilton Head, Beaufort, and the rest of the Lowcountry for the duration of the war—a relatively uneventful occupation that ensured that many of the classic homes would survive.

Gradually developing their own distinct dialect and culture, much of it linked to their West African roots, isolated Lowcountry African Americans became known as the Gullah. Evolving from an effort by abolitionist missionaries early in the Civil War, in 1864 the Penn School was formed on St. Helena Island specifically to teach the children of the Gullah communities. Now known as the Penn Center, the facility has been a beacon for the study of this aspect of African American culture ever since.

The 20th century ushered in a time of increased dependence on military spending, with the opening of a training facility on Parris Island in the 1880s (the Marines didn't begin training recruits there until 1915). The Lowcountry got a further boost from wartime spending in the '40s. Parris Island, already thriving as a Marine hub, was joined by the Marine Corps Naval Air Station in nearby Beaufort in 1942. In 1949, the Naval Hospital opened.

Today, the tourism industry has joined the military as a major economic driver in the Lowcountry. Hollywood discovered its charms as well, in a series of critical and box-office hits like *The Big Chill, The Prince of Tides,* and *Forrest Gump.*

ORIENTATION

Don't be discouraged by the big-box sprawl that assaults you on the approaches to Beaufort on Boundary Street, lined with the usual discount megastores, fast food outlets, and budget motels. This is a popular area for relocation as well as for tourists, and when you add to the mix the presence of several bustling military facilities, you have a recipe for gridlock and architectural ugliness.

But after you make the big ninety-degree bend where Boundary turns into Carteret Street—known locally as the "Bellamy Curve"—it's like entering a whole new world of slow-paced, Spanish moss–lined avenues, friendly people, gentle breezes, and inviting storefronts. While you can make your way to downtown by taking Carteret all the way to Bay Street—don't continue over the big bridge unless you want to go straight to Lady's Island and St. Helena Island—I suggest availing yourself of one of the "Downtown Access" signs before you get that far. Because Carteret Street is the only way to that bridge, it can get backed up at rush hour. By taking a quick right and then a left all the way to Bay Street,

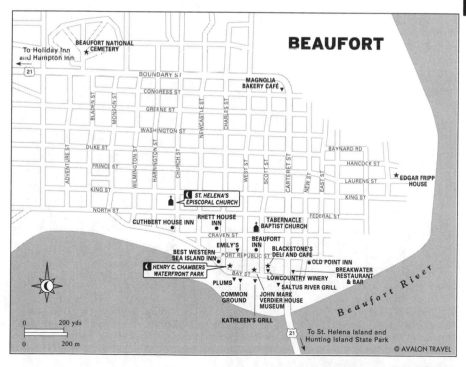

BEAUFORT

you can come into town from the other, quieter end, with your first glimpse of downtown proper being its timelessly beguiling views of the Beaufort River.

Once there, try to park your car slightly outside the town center and simply walk everywhere you want to go. Conversely you can park in the long-term metered spaces at the marina. Unlike Charleston or Savannah, any visitor in reasonably good shape can walk the entire length and breadth of Beaufort's 300-acre downtown with little trouble. In fact, that's by far the best way to experience it.

SIGHTS
◖ Henry C. Chambers Waterfront Park

Before you get busy shopping and dining and admiring Beaufort's fine old homes, go straight to the town's pride and joy since 1980, the Henry C. Chambers Waterfront Park (843/525-7054, www.cityofbeaufort.org, daily 24 hours), stretching for hundreds of feet directly on the Beaufort River. A tastefully designed and user-friendly mix of walkways, bandstands, and patios, Waterfront Park is a favorite gathering place for locals and visitors alike, beckoning one and all with its open greenspace and wonderful marsh-front views. My favorite part is the long row of swinging benches on which to peacefully sit and while away the time looking out over the marsh.

Kids will especially enjoy the park not only because there's so much room to run around, but for the charming playground at the east end near the bridge, complete with a jungle gym in the form of a Victorian home. The clean, well-appointed public restrooms are a particularly welcome feature here.

John Mark Verdier House Museum

A smallish but stately Federalist building on the busiest downtown corner, the Verdier House Museum (801 Bay St., 843/379-6335, www.historicbeaufort.org, Mon.–Sat. 10 A.M.–4 P.M., $5) is the only historic Beaufort home open to regular tours. Built in 1805 for the wealthy planter John Mark Verdier, its main claim to fame was acting as the Union headquarters during the long occupation of Beaufort during the Civil War.

However, perhaps its most intriguing link

Henry C. Chambers Waterfront Park

© JIM MOREKIS

PAT CONROY'S LOWCOUNTRY

I was always your best subject, son. Your career took a nose dive after The Great Santini *came out.*

– Colonel Donald Conroy to his son Pat

Though born in Georgia, no other person is as closely associated with the South Carolina Lowcountry as author Pat Conroy. After moving around as a child in a military family, he began high school in Beaufort.

His painful teen years there formed the basis of his first novel, a brutal portrait of his domineering Marine pilot father, Colonel Donald Conroy, a.k.a., Colonel Bull Meecham of *The Great Santini* (1976). Many scenes from the 1979 film adaptation were filmed at the famous "Tidalholm," or Edgar Fripp House (1 Laurens St.) in Beaufort. (The house was also front and center in *The Big Chill*.)

Conroy's pattern of thinly veiled autobiography actually began with his first book, the self-published *The Boo*, a tribute to a teacher at The Citadel in Charleston while Conroy was still a student there.

His second work, *The Water is Wide* (1972), is a chronicle of his experiences teaching in a one-room African American school on Daufuskie Island. Though ostensibly a straightforward, first-person journalistic effort, Conroy changed the location to the fictional Yamacraw Island, supposedly to protect Daufuskie's fragile culture from curious outsiders. The 1974 film adaptation starring Jon Voight was titled *Conrack* after the way his students mispronounced his name. You can visit that same two-room school today on Daufuskie. Known as the Mary Field School, the building is now a local community center.

Conroy also wrote the foreword to the cookbook *Gullah Home Cooking the Daufuskie Way: Smokin' Joe Butter Beans, Ol' 'Fuskie Fried Crab Rice, Sticky-Bush Blackberry Dumpling, and Other Sea Island Favorites*, by Daufuskie native and current Savannah resident Sallie Ann Robinson.

Conroy would go on in 1980 to publish *The Lords of Discipline*, a reading of his real-life experience with the often-savage environment faced by cadets at The Citadel – though Conroy would change the name, calling it the Carolina Military Institute. Still, when it came time to make a film adaptation in 1983, The Citadel refused to allow it to be shot there. So the "Carolina Military Institute" was filmed in England instead!

Conroy's latest novel, *South of Broad*, is also based in Charleston. There's a new walking tour based on the book, **Pat Conroy South of Broad Tour** (843/568-0473, www.southofbroadwalkingtour.com, Tues.-Sat. 11 A.M., $25), leaving from the Mills House hotel at 115 Meeting Street downtown.

For many of his fans, Conroy's *The Prince of Tides* is his ultimate homage to the Lowcountry. Surely, the 1991 film version starring Barbra Streisand and Nick Nolte – shot on location and awash in gorgeous shots of the Beaufort River marsh – did much to implant an idyllic image of the area to audiences around the world. According to local legend, Streisand originally didn't intend to make the film in Beaufort, but a behind-the-scenes lobbying effort allegedly coordinated by Conroy himself, and including a stay at the Rhett House Inn, convinced her.

The Bay Street Inn (601 Bay St.) in Beaufort was seen in the film, as was the football field at the old Beaufort High School. The beach scenes were shot on nearby Fripp Island. Interestingly, some scenes set in a Manhattan apartment were actually shot within the old Beaufort Arsenal (713 Craven St.), now a museum. Similarly, the Beaufort Naval Hospital doubled as New York's Bellevue.

Despite the many personal tribulations he faced in the area, Conroy has never given up on the Lowcountry and still makes his home there with his family on Fripp Island. As for the "Great Santini" himself, you can visit the final resting place of Colonel Conroy in the Beaufort National Cemetery – Section 62, Grave 182.

to history—a link it shares with Savannah's Owens-Thomas House—is its connection to the Revolutionary War hero the Marquis de Lafayette, who stayed at the Verdier House on the Beaufort leg of his 1825 U.S. tour. Despite the late hour of his arrival, a crowd gathered at the corner of Bay and Scott Streets, and Lafayette finally had to come to the entrance-way to satisfy their desire for a speech.

When the Verdier House was faced with demolition in the 1940s, the Historic Beaufort Foundation purchased the house and renovated it to its current state, reflective of the early 1800s.

Beaufort Arsenal & Visitors Center

The imposing yellow-gray tabby facade of the 1852 Beaufort Arsenal (713 Craven St.) once housed the Beaufort Museum, which sadly closed due to financial issues. The historic building currently houses the relocated offices of the Beaufort Chamber of Commerce and Convention and Visitors Bureau (843/986-5400, www.beaufortsc.org, daily 9 A.M.–5:30 P.M.).

◖ St. Helena's Episcopal Church

Nestled within the confines of a low brick wall surrounding this historic church and cemetery, St. Helena's Episcopal Church (505 Church St., 843/522-1712, Tues.–Fri. 10 A.M.–4 P.M., Sat. 10 A.M.–1 P.M.) has witnessed some of Beaufort's most compelling tales. Built in 1724, this was the parish church of Thomas Heyward, one of South Carolina's signers of the Declaration of Independence. John "Tuscarora Jack" Barnwell, early Indian fighter and one of Beaufort's founders, is buried on the grounds.

The balcony upstairs in the sanctuary was intended for black parishioners; as was typical throughout the region before the Civil War, both races attended the same church services. After the entire congregation fled with the Union occupation, Federal troops decked over the second floor and used St. Helena's as a hospital—with surgeons using tombstones as operating tables. The wooden altar was carved

by the crew of the USS *New Hampshire* while the warship was docked in the harbor during Reconstruction.

While the cemetery and sanctuary interior are likely to be your focus, take a close look at the church exterior—many of the bricks are actually ship ballast stones. Also be aware that you're not looking at the church's original footprint; the building has been expanded several times since its construction (a hurricane in 1896 destroyed the entire east end). A nearly $3 million restoration, mostly for structural repairs, was completed in 2000.

Tabernacle Baptist Church

Built in 1845, this handsome sanctuary (911 Craven St., 843/524-0376) had a congregation of over 3,000 before the Civil War. Slaves made up most of the congregation, though the vast majority of slaves generally worshipped separately on plantation ground. During the war, freed slaves purchased the church for their own use. A congregant was the war hero Robert Smalls, who kidnapped the Confederate steamer he was forced to serve on and delivered

tribute to Robert Smalls at Tabernacle Baptist Church

© JIM MOREKIS

BEAUFORT

it to Union forces. He is buried in the church cemetery and has a nice memorial dedicated to him there, proudly facing the street.

Beaufort National Cemetery

It's not nearly as poignantly ornate as Savannah's Victorian cemeteries, but Beaufort National Cemetery (1601 Boundary St., daily 8 A.M.–sunset) is worth a stop, as you enter or leave Beaufort, for its history. Begun by order of Abraham Lincoln in 1863, this is one of the few cemeteries containing the graves of both Union and Confederate troops, mostly the former. National Cemetery is where 19 soldiers of the all-black Massachusetts 54th and 55th Infantries were re-interred with full military honors after being found on Folly Island near Charleston.

Sergeant Joseph Simmons, "Buffalo Soldier" and veteran of both World Wars, is buried here, as is none other than "The Great Santini" himself, novelist Pat Conroy's father, Donald.

Tours

Colorful character Jon Sharp runs the popular **Jon Sharp's Walking History Tour** (843/575-5775, www.jonswalkinghistory.com, Tues.–Sat. 11 A.M., $20), taking a break during the summer months. The two-hour jaunt begins and ends at the Downtown Marina and takes you all through the downtown area.

The Spirit of Old Beaufort (103 West St. Extension, 843/525-0459, www.thespiritof oldbeaufort.com, Mon.–Sat. 10:30 A.M., 2 P.M., and 7 P.M., $13 adults, $8 children) runs a series of good, year-round walking tours, roughly two hours long, with guides usually in period dress. If you don't want to walk, you can hire one of their guides to join you in your own vehicle for a $50 minimum.

As you might expect, few things could be more Lowcountry than an easy-going carriage ride through the historic neighborhoods. **Southurn Rose Buggy Tours** (843/524-2900, www.southurnrose.com, daily 10 A.M.–5 P.M., $18 adults, $7 children)—yes, that's how they spell it—offers 50-minute narrated carriage rides of the entire Old Point, including

movie locations, embarking and disembarking near the Downtown Marina about every 40 minutes.

An important specialty bus tour in the area is **Gullah-N-Geechie Man Tours** (843/838-7516, www.gullahngeechietours.net, $20 adults, $18 children), focusing on the rich Gullah history and culture of the St. Helena Island area, including the historic Penn Center. Call for pickup information.

ENTERTAINMENT AND EVENTS
Nightlife

Those looking for a rowdy time will be happier seeking it in the notorious party towns of Charleston or Savannah. However, a few notable places in downtown Beaufort do double duty as dining havens and neighborhood watering holes.

Sadly, the well-regarded restaurant within the Beaufort Inn on Port Republic Street closed for good in 2007. But several establishments tucked together on Bay Street, all with café seating out back facing the waterfront, can also show you a good time.

The convivial **Kathleen's Grill** (822 Bay St., 843/524-2500, daily 11 A.M.–2 A.M.) features live music by a variety of regional artists. Weekend tunes crank up about 10 P.M.

Plum's (904½ Bay St., 843/525-1946, daily 5 P.M.–2 A.M.) offers not only a tasty menu but some fun at 10 P.M. when the kitchen closes down and the focus turns to its great beer selection. Close by is **Luther's Rare & Well Done** (910 Bay St., 843/521-1888, 5 P.M.–midnight, $15), which offers a late-night appetizer menu to go with its rock-oriented live music on weekends.

Performing Arts

Beaufort's fine arts scene is small but professional in outlook. Most performances are based in the nice new Performing Arts Center on the oak-lined campus of the University of South Carolina Beaufort (801 Carteret St., 843/521-4100).

A prime mover of the local performing arts

A WALKING TOUR OF BEAUFORT HOMES

One of the unique aspects of the Lowcountry is the large amount of historic homes in totally private hands. When buyers purchase one of these fine old homes, they generally know what's in store: a historical marker of some sort will be nearby, organized tours will periodically swing by their home, and production companies will sometimes approach them about using the home as a film set. It's a trade-off most homeowners are only too glad to accept.

Here's a walking tour of some of Beaufort's fine historic homes in private hands. You won't be taking any tours of the interior, but these homes are part of the legacy of the area and are locally valued as such. Be sure to respect the privacy of the inhabitants by keeping the noise level down and not trespassing on private property to take photos.

· **Thomas Fuller House:** Begin at the corner of Harrington and Bay, and view this 1796 home (1211 Bay St.), one of the oldest in existence in Beaufort and even more unique in that much of the building material is tabby (hence the home's other name, the Tabby Manse).

· **Milton Maxcy House:** Walk east on Bay Street one block and take a left on Church Street; walk up to the corner of Church and Craven Streets. Otherwise known as the Secession House (113 Craven St.), this 1813 home was built on a tabby foundation dating from 1743. In 1860, when it was the residence of attorney Edmund Rhett, the very first Ordinance of Secession was signed here and the rest, as they say, was history.

· **Lewis Reeve Sams House:** Pick up the walking tour on the other side of the historic district, at the foot of the bridge. This gorgeous house (602 Bay St.) at the corner of Bay and New Streets, with its double-decker veranda, dates from 1852 and served as a Union hospital during the Civil War.

· **Berners Barnwell Sams House:** Continue up New Street where you'll find this 1818 home (310 New St.), which served as the African American hospital during the Union occupation. Harriet Tubman of Underground Railroad fame worked here for a time as a nurse.

· **Joseph Johnson House:** Continue up New Street and take a right on Craven Street. Cross East Street to find this 1850 home, nicknamed "The Castle" (411 Craven St.), with the massive live oak in the front yard. Legend has it that when the Yankees occupied Hilton Head, Mr. Johnson buried his valuables under an outhouse. After the war he returned to find his home for sale due to unpaid back taxes. He dug up his valuables, paid the taxes, and resumed living in the home. You might recognize the home from the film *Forces of Nature*.

· **Marshlands:** Backtrack to East Street and walk north to Federal Street. Then take a right and go to the end of the street. Built by James R. Verdier, Marshlands (501 Pinckney St.) was used as a hospital during the Civil War, as many Beaufort homes were, and is now a National Historic Landmark. It was the setting of Francis Griswold's 1931 novel *A Sea Island Lady*.

· **The Oaks:** Walk up to King Street, take a right, and go to the corner of King and Short Streets. The Oaks (100 Laurens St.) at this intersection was owned by the Hamilton family, who lost a son who served with General Wade Hampton's cavalry in the Civil War. After the conflict, the family couldn't afford the back taxes, and neighbors paid the debts and returned the deed to the Hamiltons.

- **Edgar Fripp House:** Walk east on Laurens toward the water to find this handsome Lowcountry mansion, sometimes called Tidalholm (1 Laurens St.). Built in 1856 by the wealthy planter for whom nearby Fripp Island is named, this house was a key setting in *The Big Chill* and *The Great Santini*.

- **Francis Hext House:** Go back to Short Street, walk north to Hancock Street and take a left. This palatial estate, known as Riverview (207 Hancock St.), is one of the oldest structures in Beaufort; it was built in 1720.

- **Robert Smalls House:** Continue west on Hancock Street, take a short left on East Street, and a quick right on Prince Street. This 1834 home (511 Prince St.) was the birthplace of Robert Smalls, a former slave and Beaufort native who stole the Confederate ship *Planter* from Charleston Harbor while serving as its helmsman and delivered it to Union troops in Hilton Head. Smalls and a few compatriots commandeered the ship while the officers were at a party at Fort Sumter, taking it right past Confederate pickets. Smalls used the bounty he received for the act of bravery to buy his boyhood home for his own. After the war, Smalls was a longtime U.S. congressman.

© JIM MOREKIS

Lewis Reeve Sams House in Beaufort

scene is **Beaufort Performing Arts, Inc.** (www.uscb.edu), formed by a mayoral task force in 2003 specifically to encourage arts and cultural development within the area. The most recent season, with performances at USCB's Performing Arts Center, included performances by Celtic fiddler Natalie MacMaster, the Claremont Trio, and the Bee Gees. Ticket prices typically range $12–40.

Perhaps surprisingly for such a small place, Beaufort boasts its own full orchestra, the **Beaufort Orchestra** (1106 Carteret Street, 843/986-5400, www.beaufortorchestra.org), which plays in the Performing Arts Center. A recent season included Paganini's Violin Concerto in D, Tchaikovsky's "Pathetique" Symphony No. 6, and "Beaufort Goes to Broadway."

Cinema

One of only two functional drive-ins in the state, the **Highway 21 Drive In** (55 Parker Dr., 843/846-4500, www.hwy21drivein.com) has two screens, great sound, and awesome concessions including Angus beef hamburgers. All you need to provide is the car and the company. The best multiplex in the area is the cool **Sea Turtle Cinemas** (106 Buckwalter Pkwy., 843/706-2888, www.seaturtlecinemas.com) in the Berkeley Place shopping center.

Festivals and Events

Surprisingly for a town so prominent in so many films, Beaufort didn't have its own film festival until 2007. The **Beaufort Film Festival** (843/986-5400, www.beaufortfilmfestival.com) is held in late winter. It's small in scale—the inaugural festival was only two days, at a now-defunct theater—but boasts a diverse range of high-quality, cutting-edge entries, including shorts and animation.

Foodies will also enjoy **A Taste of Beaufort** (www.downtownbeaufort.com), usually held the first Saturday in May, which features the offerings of two dozen or so local restaurants with live music, all along historic Bay Street.

Now over 20 years old, the **Gullah Festival of South Carolina** celebrates Gullah history and culture on Memorial Day weekend at various locations throughout town, mostly focusing on Waterfront Park.

By far the biggest single event on the local festival calendar is the over 50-year-old **Beaufort Water Festival** (www.bftwaterfestival.com), held over two weeks in June or July each year, centering on the Waterfront Park area. One of the most eclectic and idiosyncratic events of its kind in a region already known for quirky, hyper-local festivals, the Beaufort Water Festival features events as diverse as a raft race, badminton, bocce, billiards, croquet and golf tournaments, a children's toad fishing tournament, a ski show, a bed race, a street dance, and all sorts of live music and local art exhibits. The signature events are the Saturday morning two-hour Grand Parade and a blessing and parade of the shrimp fleet on the closing Sunday.

Fall in the Lowcountry means shrimping season, and early October brings the **Beaufort Shrimp Festival** (www.beaufortsc.org). Highlights include an evening concert with specially lighted shrimpboats docked along the river, a 5K run over the Woods Memorial Bridge, and a more laid-back 5K walk through the historic district. Various cooking competitions are held, obviously centering around the versatile crustaceans that are the raison d'etre of the shrimp fleet.

St. Helena Island hosts the three-day **Penn Center Heritage Days** (www.penncenter.com) each November, without a doubt the Beaufort area's second-biggest celebration after the Water Festival. Focusing on Gullah culture, history, and delicious food, Heritage Days does a great job of combining fun with education. The event culminates in a colorful Saturday morning parade, featuring lots of traditional Gullah garb, from St. Helena Elementary School to the Penn Center Historic District.

SHOPPING

The Beaufort area's shopping allure comes from the rich variety of independently owned shops, most of which keep a pretty high standard and don't deal too much in touristy schlock. The main drag in town, Bay Street, is also the shopping hub. Note that in Beaufort's shops as well as most everything else in town, hours of operation are loose guidelines and not rigidly observed.

My favorite shop in Beaufort is **The Bay Street Trading Company** (808 Bay St., 843/524-2000, www.baystreettrading.com, Mon.–Fri. 10 A.M.–5:30 P.M., Sat. 10 A.M.–5 P.M., Sun. noon–5 P.M.), sometimes known simply as "The Book Shop," which has a very friendly staff and the best collection of Lowcountry-themed books I've seen in one place.

Across the street, the recently renovated, so-bright-red-you-can't-miss-it Old Bay Marketplace houses a few very cute shops, most notably the stylish **Lulu Burgess** (917 Bay St., 843/524-5858, Mon.–Sat. 10 A.M.–6 P.M., Sun. noon–5 P.M.), an eclectic store that brings a rich, quirky sense of humor to its otherwise tasteful assortment of gift items for the whole family.

A unique gift item, as well as something you can enjoy on your own travels, can be found at **Lowcountry Winery** (705 Bay St., 843/379-3010, Mon.–Sat. 10 A.M.–5 P.M.). Not only can you purchase bottles of their various red and white offerings, they host tastings daily in their tasting room (because of state law they must charge a fee for the tasting, but it's only a buck per person).

One of the more unusual shops in town is **Cravings by the Bay** (928 Bay St., 843/522-3000, Mon.–Sat. 10 A.M.–5 P.M., Sun. noon–4 P.M.), primarily known for its collection of gift baskets incorporating regional gourmet goodies like She-Crab Soup, Praline Mustard Glaze, and Benne Wafers, any of which you can purchase separately, of course.

Just off the Waterfront Park and right across the walk from Common Grounds coffeeshop is the delightful **Lollipop Shop** (103 West Street Extension, 843/379-POPS, www.thelollipopshop.net, Mon.–Thurs. 10 A.M.–5 P.M., Fri.–Sat. 10 A.M.–9 P.M., Sun. 1–5 P.M.). Part of a regional franchise chain, the Lollipop Shop offers a wide range of treats from jelly beans to M&Ms in custom colors, as well as wind-up toys and stuff-them-yourself teddy bears.

Art Galleries

As you'd expect in such a visually stirring locale, there's a plethora of great art galleries in the Beaufort-St. Helena area. While most are clustered on Bay Street, there are gems scattered all over. Almost all are worth a look, but here are a few highlights.

My favorite gallery in town is the simply named **The Gallery** (802 Bay St., 843/470-9994, www.thegallery-beaufort.com, Mon.–Sat. 11 A.M.–5 P.M.). Deanna Bowdish brings in the most cutting-edge regional contemporary artists in a large, friendly, loft-like space.

The **Beaufort Art Association Gallery** (1001 Bay St., 843/379-2222, www.beaufortartassociation.com, Mon.–Sat. 10 A.M.–5 P.M.) hosts rotating exhibits by member artists in the stately and historic Elliott House.

A complete art experience blending the traditional with the cutting-edge is at the **I. Pinckney Simons Art Gallery** (711 Bay St., 843/379-4774, www.ipinckneysimonsgallery.com, Tues.–Fri. 11 A.M.–5 P.M., Sat. 11 A.M.–3 P.M.), which is pronounced "Simmons" despite the spelling. There you will find not only paintings, but compelling photography, sculpture, and jewelry as well, all by local and regional artists of renown.

There aren't many local artists featured at **Four Winds Gallery** (709 Bay St., 843/379-5660, www.fourwindstraders.com, Mon.–Wed. and Sat. 10:30 A.M.–5:30 P.M., Thurs. 10:30 A.M.–7 P.M., Sun. 11 A.M.–4 P.M.), but it's a great place to find religious folk art from around the world, from wooden African tribal votives to Orthodox icons from Greece.

A few blocks from Bay Street is a fun local favorite, the **Longo Gallery** (103 Charles St., 843/522-8933, Mon.–Sat. 11 A.M.–5 P.M.). Owners Suzanne and Eric Longo provide a whimsical assortment of less traditional art than you might find in the more touristy waterfront area. Take Charles Street as it works its way toward the waterfront, and the gallery

© JIM MOREKIS

Red Piano Too on St. Helena Island features handmade Gullah art.

is right behind a storefront on the corner of Charles and Bay Streets.

You'll find perhaps the area's best-known gallery over the bridge on St. Helena Island. Known regionally as one of the best places to find Gullah folk art, **Red Piano Too** (870 Sea Island Parkway, 843/838-2241, www.redpiano too.com, Mon.–Sat. 10 A.M.–5 P.M.) is on the corner before you turn onto the road to the historic Penn Center. Over 150 artists from a diverse range of traditions and styles are represented in this charming little 1940 building with the red tin awning, historically significant in its own right because it once hosted a produce cooperative that was the first store in the area to pay African Americans with cash rather than barter for goods.

SPORTS AND RECREATION

Beaufort County comprises over 60 islands, so it's no surprise that nearly all recreation in the area revolves around the water, which dominates so many aspects of life in the Lowcountry. The closer to the ocean you get, the more it's a salt marsh environment. But as you explore more inland, in the sprawling ACE Basin, you'll encounter primarily blackwater.

Kayaking

The Lowcountry is tailor-made for kayaking. An option in downtown Beaufort is to put in at the public ramp at the **Downtown Marina** (1006 Bay St., 843/524-4422) and paddle along the peaceful Intracoastal Waterway, either north up the Beaufort River or south into the Sound.

The catch here, as with all the Lowcountry, is to know your way around if you choose to leave the main waterways. It's easy to get lost because of the sheer number of creeks, and they all seem to look the same once you get into them a good ways. If you don't feel comfortable with your navigation skills, it's a good idea to contact Kim and David at **Beaufort Kayak Tours** (843/525-0810, www.beaufortkayaktours.com), who rent kayaks and can guide you on a number of excellent tours of all three key areas. They charge about $40 for adults and $30 for children for a two-hour trip. A tour with Beaufort Kayak Tours is also the best (and nearly the only) way to access the historically significant ruins of the early British tabby Fort Frederick, now located on the grounds of the Beaufort Naval Hospital and inaccessible by car.

Fishing and Boating

Key public marinas in the area are the Downtown Marina in Beaufort, the **Lady's Island Marina** (73 Sea Island Pkwy., 843/522-0430), and the **Port Royal Landing Marina** (1 Port Royal Landing Dr., 843/525-6664). Hunting Island has a popular thousand-foot fishing pier at the south end. A good local fishing charter service is Captain Josh Utsey's **Lowcountry Guide Service** (843/812-4919, www.beaufortsc fishing.com). Captain Ed Hardee (843/441-6880) offers good inshore charters.

The ACE Basin is a very popular fishing, crabbing, and shrimping area. It has about two dozen public boat ramps, with colorful names like Cuckold's Creek and Steamboat Landing. There's a useful map of them all at www.ace basin.net, or look for the brown signs along the highway.

Hiking and Biking

Despite the Lowcountry's, well, lowness, biking opportunities abound. It might not get your heart rate up like a ride in the Rockies, but the area lends itself to laid-back two-wheeled enjoyment.

Many local B&Bs provide bikes free for guests, and you can rent your own just across the river from Beaufort in Lady's Island at **Lowcountry Bikes** (102 Sea Island Pkwy., 843/524-9585, Mon.–Tues. and Thurs.–Fri. 10 A.M.–6 P.M., Wed. 10 A.M.–1 P.M., Sat. 10 A.M.–3 P.M., about $5/hr.). They can also hook you up with some good routes around the area.

Bicycling around Beaufort is a delight for its paucity of traffic as well as its beauty. Port Royal is close enough that you can easily make a circuit to that little town. To get to Port Royal from Beaufort, take Bay Street west to Ribault Road (U.S. 21) and veer left onto Paris Avenue into downtown Port Royal, where the biking is easy, breezy, and fun.

For a visually delightful ride, the bridge over the Beaufort River also features a pedestrian/bike lane with some awesome views. You can either turn back at the base of the bridge and go back into Beaufort or push on to Lady's Island and St. Helena Island, though the traffic on U.S. 21 can get daunting.

ACCOMMODATIONS

Beaufort's historic district is blessed with an abundance of high-quality accommodations that blend well with their surroundings. There are plenty of budget-minded chain places, some of them acceptable, in the sprawl of Boundary Street outside of downtown, but here are some suggestions within bicycle distance of the Historic District. (That's not a hypothetical, as most inns offer free bicycles to use as you please during your stay.)

Under $150

The aptly named **Old Point Inn** (212 New St., 843/524-3177, www.oldpointinn.com, $115–175) is not only a great value, but also the only historic inn in Beaufort with full views of the river and marsh. Tucked between the historic Lewis Reeve Sams House and the circa-1717 Thomas Hepworth House, the oldest building in town, the Old Point Inn combines Southern style with a delightful lack of pretension. There's a hammock on the upstairs veranda and a small garden patio. Owners Paul and Julie Michau have furnished each themed suite with their own eclectic collection of international furniture and objets d'art.

The **Best Western Sea Island Inn** (1015 Bay St., 843/522-2090, www.bestwestern .com, $135–170) is a good value for those for whom the B&B experience is not paramount. Anchoring the southern end of the historic district in a low, tasteful brick building, the Best Western offers decent service, basic amenities, and surprisingly attractive rates for the location on Beaufort's busiest street.

$150-300

Any list of upscale Beaufort lodging must highlight the ◖ **Beaufort Inn** (809 Port Republic

St., 843/379-4667, www.beaufortinn.com, $152–425), consistently voted one of the best B&Bs in the nation. It's sort of a hybrid in that it comprises not only the 1897 historic central home, but a cluster of freestanding historical cottages, each with a charming little porch and rocking chairs. With everything connected by gardens and pathways, you could almost call it a campus. Still, for its sprawling nature-44 rooms in total—the Beaufort Inn experience is intimate, with attentive service and top-flight amenities such as wet bars, large baths, and sumptuous king beds. Within or without the main building, each suite has a character all its own, whether it's the 1,500-square-foot Loft Apartment (complete with guest bedroom and full kitchen) or one of the cozier (and more affordable) Choice Rooms with a queen-sized bed.

The 18-room, circa-1820 **Rhett House Inn** (1009 Craven St., 843/524-9030, www.rhetthouseinn.com, $175–320) is the local vacation getaway for the stars. Such arts and entertainment luminaries as Robert Redford, Julia Roberts, Ben Affleck, Barbra Streisand, Dennis Quaid, and Demi Moore have all stayed here at one time or another. Owner Steve Harrison is also a local realtor and no doubt has helped many a guest relocate to town after they've fallen in love with it while staying at his inn. As if Beaufort's great restaurants weren't caloric enough, you can put on a few pounds just staying at the Rhett House. Of course you get the requisite full Southern breakfast, but you'll also be treated to afternoon tea and pastries, more munchies at cocktail hour, and homemade late-night desserts.

There's nothing like enjoying the view of the Beaufort River from the expansive porches of the **C** **Cuthbert House Inn** (1203 Bay St., 843/521-1315, www.cuthberthouseinn.com, $205–250), possibly the most romantic place to stay in Beaufort. This grand old circa-1790 Federal mansion was once the home of the wealthy Cuthbert family of rice and indigo planters and is now on the National Register of Historic Places. General Sherman himself spent a night here in 1865. Some of the king rooms have fireplaces and claw-foot tubs. Of course

you get a full Southern breakfast, in addition to sunset hors d'oeuvres on the veranda.

FOOD
Breakfast and Brunch
One of the best breakfasts I've had anywhere was a humble two-egg plate for five bucks at Beaufort's most popular morning hangout, **C** **Blackstone's Café** (205 Scott St., 843/524-4330, Mon.–Sat. 7:30 A.M.–2:30 P.M., Sun. 7:30 A.M.–2 P.M., under $10), complete with tasty hash browns, a comparative rarity in this part of the country where grits rule as the breakfast starch of choice. Many come from miles around just for Blackstone's large-portion shrimp and grits entrée and "shrimpburger" specials.

Tucked on a side street just off busy Bay Street, Blackstone's roomy but inviting interior—festooned with various collegiate, nautical, and military motifs and a checkerboard floor—has more than enough room for you to spread out and relax before continuing on with your travels (there's even free Wi-Fi). The friendly, chipper waitstaff are on a first-name basis with the many regulars, but don't worry—in true Lowcountry fashion, they'll treat you like a regular, too.

Burgers and Sandwiches
Another longtime lunch favorite is **Magnolia Bakery Café** (703 Congress St., 843/524-1961, Mon.–Sat. 9 A.M.–5 P.M., under $10). It's a little ways north of the usual tourist area, but well worth going out of your way for (Beaufort's pretty small, after all). Lump crab cakes are a particular specialty item, but you can't go wrong with any of the lunch sandwiches. They even offer a serviceable crepe. Veggie diners are particularly well taken care of with a large selection of black bean burger plates. As the name indicates, the range of desserts here is tantalizing, to say the least, with the added bonus of a serious espresso bar.

Coffeehouses
The charming and popular **Common Ground** (102 West St., 843/524-2326, daily

LOWCOUNTRY BOIL

What we now know as "Lowcountry Boil" was originally called Frogmore Stew – not because of any amphibian presence, but for the tiny township on St. Helena Island, South Carolina where the first pot was made, supposedly by Mr. Richard Gay of the Gay Fish Company. Old-timers still call it Frogmore Stew, however.

As with any vernacular dish, dozens of local and family variants abound. The key ingredient that makes Lowcountry Boil what it is – a well-blended mélange with a character all its own rather than just a bunch of stuff thrown together in a pot of boiling water – is some type of crab boil seasoning. You'll find Zatarain's seasoning suggested on a lot of websites, but Old Bay is far more common in the eponymous Lowcountry where the dish originated.

In any case, here's a simple six-serving Lowcountry Boil recipe to get you started. The only downside is that it's pretty much impossible to make it for just a few people. The dish is intended for large gatherings, whether a football tailgating party on a Saturday or a family afternoon after church on Sunday. Note the typical ratio of one ear of corn per person and half a pound each of meat and shrimp.

- 6 ears fresh corn on the cob, cut into three-inch sections

- 3 pounds smoked pork sausage, cut into three-inch sections

- 3 pounds fresh shrimp, shells on

- 5 pounds new potatoes

- 6 ounces Old Bay Seasoning

Put the sausage and potato pieces, along with half of the Old Bay, in two gallons of boiling water. When the potatoes are about halfway done, about 15 minutes in, add the corn and boil for about half that time, seven minutes. Add the shrimp and boil for another three minutes, until they just turn pink. *Do not overcook the shrimp.* Take the pot off the heat and drain; serve immediately. If you cook the shrimp just right, the oil from the sausage will cause those shells to slip right off.

This is but one of countless recipes. Some cooks add some lemon juice and beer in the water as it's coming to a boil; others add onion, garlic, and/or green peppers.

7:30 A.M.–10 P.M.) coffeehouse in the Waterfront Park area is not only a great place for a light sandwich or sweet treat: the java is a cut above most such places, featuring a wide selection of excellent fair trade "Dancing Goat" brews.

New Southern

Probably the most buzzworthy local spot these days is the stylishly appointed **Wren** (210 Carteret St., 843/524-9463, $15–25), renowned for any of its chicken dishes. As seems to be typical of Beaufort, the lunches are as good as the dinners.

Seafood

The hottest dinner table in town is at the ◖ **Saltus River Grill** (802 Bay St., 843/379-3474, Sun.–Thurs. 5–9 P.M., Fri.–Sat. 5–10 P.M., $10–39). Executive chef Jim

Spratling has made this fairly new restaurant, housed in a historic tabby building on the waterfront, famous throughout the state for its raw bar menu featuring oysters from Nova Scotia to the Chesapeake Bay to Oregon and British Columbia. Sushi lovers can also get a fix here, whether it's a basic California roll or great sashimi. Other specialties include she-crab bisque, lump crab cakes, flounder fillet, and of course the ubiquitous shrimp and grits. The Saltus River Grill is more upscale in feel and in price than most Lowcountry places, with a very see-and-be-seen type of attitude and a hopping bar. Reservations recommended.

Sharing an owner with the Saltus River Grill is **Plum's** (904½ Bay St., 843/525-1946, lunch daily 11 A.M.–4 P.M., dinner daily 5–10 P.M., $15–25). The short and focused menu keys in on entrées highlighting local ingredients, such as the shrimp penne *al'amatriciana* and fresh black mussel pasta. Because of the outstanding microbrew selection, Plum's is a big nightlife hangout as well; be aware that after 10 P.M., when food service ends but the bar remains open until 2 P.M., it's no longer smoke-free, though there's a friendly porch where you can get some fresh air and feed the resident cat.

An up-and-comer downtown is **Breakwater Restaurant & Bar** (203 Carteret St., 843/379-0052, www.breakwater-restaurant.com, dinner Thurs.–Sat. 6–9:30 P.M., bar until 2 A.M., $10–20). The concise menu makes up in good taste what it lacks in comprehensiveness, with an emphasis on seafood, of course. An especially enticing marine-oriented tapas plate is the diver scallops in a vanilla cognac sauce. (This restaurant recently moved from a West Street location.)

Steaks

Luther's Rare & Well Done (910 Bay St., 843/521-1888, daily 10 A.M.–midnight) on the waterfront is the kind of meat-lover's place where even the French onion soup has a morsel of rib eye in it. While the patented succulent, rubbed steaks are a no-brainer here, the hand-crafted specialty pizzas are also quite popular. Housed in a historic pharmacy building, Luther's is also a great place for late eats after many other places in this quiet town have rolled up the sidewalk. A limited menu of appetizers and bar food is available after 10 P.M.

Tapas

Right around the corner from Breakwater is **Emily's** (906 Port Republic St., 843/522-1866, www.emilysrestaurantandtapasbar.com, dinner Mon.–Sat. 4–10 P.M., bar until 2 A.M., $10–20), a very popular fine dining spot that specializes in a more traditional brand of rich, tasty tapas (available 4–5 P.M.) and is known for its active bar scene.

INFORMATION AND SERVICES

The **Beaufort Visitors Information Center** (713 Craven St., 843/986-5400, www .beaufortsc.org, daily 9 A.M.–5:30 P.M.), the headquarters of the Beaufort Chamber of Commerce and Convention and Visitors Bureau, has relocated from its old Carteret Street location and can now be found within the Beaufort Arsenal, once home to the now-closed Beaufort Museum.

The U.S. Postal Service has a **post office** (501 Charles St., 843/525-9085) in downtown Beaufort.

The daily newspaper of record in Beaufort is the *Beaufort Gazette* (www.beaufortgazette .com). An alternative weekly focusing mostly on the arts is *Lowcountry Weekly* (www .lcweekly.com), published every Wednesday.

GETTING THERE AND AROUND

While the Marines can fly their F-18s directly into Beaufort Naval Air Station, you won't have that luxury. The closest major airport to Beaufort is the **Savannah/Hilton Head International Airport** (400 Airways Ave., 912/964-0514, www.savannahairport.com, airport code SAV) off I-95 outside Savannah. If you're not going into Savannah for any reason, the easiest route to the Beaufort area from the airport is to take exit 8 off I-95, and from there to take U.S. 278 east to U.S. 170.

Conversely, you could fly into the **Charleston International Airport** (5500 International Blvd., www.chs-airport.com, airport code CHS), but because that facility is on the far north side of Charleston it actually might take you longer to get to Beaufort. From the Charleston Airport the best route south to Beaufort is U.S. 17 south, exiting at U.S. 21 at Gardens Corner and then into Beaufort.

If you're coming into the region by car, I-95 will be your likely primary route, with your main point of entry being exit 8 off I-95 connecting to U.S. 278.

There's no public transportation to speak of in Beaufort, but that's OK—the historic section is quite small and can be traversed in an afternoon. A favorite mode of transport is by bicycle, often provided complimentary to bed-and-breakfast guests. Rent one at **Lowcountry Bikes** (102 Sea Island Pkwy., 843/524-9585,

Mon.–Tues. and Thurs.–Fri. 10 A.M.–6 P.M., Wed. 10 A.M.–1 P.M., Sat. 10 A.M.–3 P.M., about $5/hr.) in Lady's Island just over the bridge.

OUTSIDE BEAUFORT

The areas outside tourist-traveled Beaufort can take you even further back into sepia-toned Americana, into a time of sharecropper homesteads, sturdy oystermen, and an altogether variable and subjective sense of time.

Lady's Island

Directly across the Beaufort River is Lady's Island, now a predominantly residential area with a bigger variety of national shopping and grocery outlets than you'll find in Beaufort proper.

Cuisine options include the casual **Steamer Oyster and Steak House** (168 Sea Island Pkwy., 843/522-0210, daily 11 A.M.–9:30 P.M., $15–20). The big hit here is the Frogmore stew, a.k.a. Lowcountry Boil. For vegan/vegetarian soups, salads, and sandwiches, try **It's Only Natural** (45 Factory Creek Ct., 843/986-9595, Mon.–Fri. 8 A.M.–6 P.M., Sat. 9 A.M.–4:30 P.M.,

$5), which also offers a range of health food items and produce. It's visible right off the main road, the Sea Island Parkway (U.S. 21).

◖ Penn Center

By going across the Richard V. Woods Memorial Bridge over the Beaufort River on the Sea Island Parkway (which turns into U.S. 21), you'll pass through Lady's Island and reach St. Helena Island. Known to old-timers as Frogmore, the area took back its old, Spanish-derived place name in the 1980s.

Today St. Helena Island is most famous for the Penn Center (16 Martin Luther King Jr. Dr., 843/838-2474, www.penncenter.com, Mon.–Sat. 11 A.M.–4 P.M., $4 adults, $2 seniors and children), the spiritual home of Gullah culture and history. When you visit here among the live oaks and humble but well-preserved buildings, you'll instantly see why Dr. Martin Luther King Jr. chose this as one of his major retreat and planning sites during the civil rights era.

The dream began as early as 1862, when a group of abolitionist Quakers from

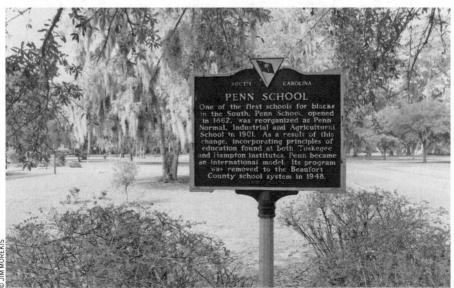

© JIM MOREKIS

the Penn Center on St. Helena Island

THE LOST ART OF TABBY

Let's clear up a couple of misconceptions about tabby, that unique construction technique combining oyster shells, lime, water, and sand found all along the South Carolina and Georgia coast.

First, it did not originate with Native Americans. The confusion is due to the fact that the native population left behind many middens, or enormous trash heaps, of oyster shells. While these middens indeed provided the bulk of the shells for tabby buildings to come, Native Americans had little else to do with it.

Secondly, though the Spanish were responsible for the first use of tabby in the Americas,

© JIM MOREKIS

St. Helena Island's Chapel of Ease is a great example of tabby construction.

Philadelphia came during the Union occupation with the goal of teaching recently freed slave children. They were soon joined by African American educator Charlotte Forten. After Reconstruction, the Penn School continued its mission by offering teaching and agricultural/industrial trade curricula.

The migration of blacks out of the South during World War II took a toll on the school, however, which became a community improvement center after classes ceased in 1948. In the late 1960s, the Southern Christian Leadership Conference used the school as a retreat and planning site, with both the Peace Corps and the Conscientious Objector Programs training here.

In addition to its role as an education hub for the study of Gullah culture, the Penn Center continues to serve an important civil rights role by providing legal counsel to African American homeowners in St. Helena. Because clear title is difficult to acquire in the area due to the fact that so much of the land has stayed in the families of former slaves, developers are constantly making shady offers so that ancestral land can be opened up to upscale development.

The beautiful 50-acre campus of the Penn Center is part of the Penn School Historic

contrary to lore almost all remaining tabby in the area dates from later English settlement. The British first fell in love with tabby after the siege of Spanish-held St. Augustine, Florida and quickly began building with it in their colonies to the north.

Scholars are divided as to whether tabby was invented by West Africans, or its use spread to Africa from Spain and Portugal, circuitously coming to America through the knowledge of imported slaves. The origin of the word itself is also unclear, as similar words exist in Spanish, Portuguese, Gullah, and Arabic to describe various types of wall.

We do know for sure how tabby is made: The primary technique was to burn alternating layers of oyster shells and logs in a deep hole in the ground, thus creating lime. The lime was then mixed with oyster shells, sand, and freshwater and poured into wooden molds, or "forms," to dry and then be used as building blocks, much like large bricks. The walls were usually plastered with stucco. Tabby is remarkably strong and resilient, able to easily survive the hurricanes that often batter the area. It stays cool in the summer and is insect-resistant, two enormous plusses down here.

Following are the best examples of true tabby you can see today on the South Carolina and Georgia coasts, from north to south:

- **Dorchester State Historic Site** (300 State Park Rd., Summerville), north of Charleston, contains a well-preserved tabby fort.

- Several younger tabby buildings still exist in downtown Beaufort: the **Barnwell-Gough House** (705 Washington St.); the magnificent Thomas Fuller House, or **"Tabby Manse"** (1211 Bay St.); and the **Saltus House** (on the 800 block of Bay St.), perhaps the tallest surviving tabby structure.

- The **Chapel of Ease** (off Land's End Rd.) on St. Helena Island dates from the 1740s. If someone tells you Sherman burned it down, don't believe them; the culprit was a forest fire long after the war.

- The **Stoney-Baynard Ruins** (Plantation Dr.) in Sea Pines Plantation on Hilton Head are all that's left of the home of the old Braddock's Point Plantation. Foundations of a slave quarters are nearby.

- **Wormsloe Plantation** near Savannah has the remains of Noble Jones's fortification of the Skidaway Narrows.

- The remarkably intact walls of the **Horton-DuBignon House** on Jekyll Island, Georgia, date from 1738, and the house was occupied into the 1850s.

BEAUFORT

District, a National Historic Landmark comprising 19 buildings, most of key historical significance, including Darrah Hall, the oldest building on the campus; the old "Brick Church" right across MLK Jr. Drive; and Gantt Cottage, where Dr. King himself stayed periodically in the 1963–1967 period. Another building, the Retreat House, was intended for Dr. King to continue his strategy meetings, but he was assassinated before being able to stay there. The museum and bookshop are housed in the Cope Building, now called the York W. Bailey Museum, situated right along MLK Jr. Drive. A self-guided nature trail takes you all around the campus.

The key public event here happens each November with the Penn Center Heritage Days, in which the entire St. Helena community comes together to celebrate and enjoy entertainment such as the world-famous, locally based Hallelujah Singers.

To get to the Penn Center from Beaufort, proceed over the bridge until you get to St. Helena Island. Take a right onto MLK Jr. Drive when you see the Red Piano Too Art Gallery. The Penn Center is a few hundred yards down on your right.

If you drive past the Penn Center and continue a few hundred yards down MLK Jr.

Drive, look for the ancient tabby ruins on the left side of the road. This is the **Chapel of Ease,** the remnant of a 1740 church destroyed by forest fire in the late 1800s.

If you get hungry, just before you take a right to get to the Penn Center on St. Helena Island is **Gullah Grub** (877 Sea Island Pkwy., 843/838-3841, Mon.–Thurs. 11:30 A.M.–7 P.M., under $20), an unpretentious, one-room lunch spot focusing on down-home Southern specialties with a Lowcountry touch, such as hushpuppies, collard greens, and shrimp-'n'-shark.

Old Sheldon Church Ruins

A short ways north of Beaufort are the poignantly desolate ruins of the once-magnificent Old Sheldon Church (Old Sheldon Church Rd. off U.S. 17 just past Gardens Corner, daily dawn–dusk, free). Set a couple of miles off the highway on a narrow road, the serene, oak-lined grounds containing this massive, empty edifice give little hint of the violence so intrinsic to its history.

One of the first Greek Revival structures in the United States, the house of worship held its first service in 1757 as Prince William's Parish Church. The sanctuary was first burned by the British in 1779, mainly because of reports that the Patriots were using it to store gunpowder captured from a British ship. After being rebuilt in 1826, the sanctuary survived until General Sherman's arrival in 1865, whereupon Union troops razed it once more. Nothing remains now but these towering walls and columns, made of red brick instead of the tabby often seen in similar ruins on the coast.

It's now owned by the nearby St. Helena's Episcopal Church in Beaufort, which holds outdoor services here the second Sunday after Easter. In all, it's an almost painfully compelling bit of history set amid stunning natural beauty, and well worth the short drive.

Oyotunji Village

By continuing north of the Sheldon Church a short ways, the more adventurous can find a quirky Lowcountry attraction, Oyotunji Village (56 Bryant Ln., 843/846-8900, hours vary). Built in 1970 by self-proclaimed "King" Ofuntola Oseijeman Adelabu Adefunmi I, a former used car dealer with an interesting past, Oyotunji claims to be North America's only

Old Sheldon Church ruins

© JIM MOREKIS

authentic African village, with 5–10 families residing on its 30 acres. It also claims to be a separate kingdom and not a part of the United States—though I'm sure the State Department begs to differ.

With a mission to preserve the religious and cultural aspects of the Yoruba Orisa culture of West Africa, each spring the village hosts an annual Warrior's Festival, celebrating traditional male rites of passage. Truth is, there's not much to see here but a few poorly built "monuments." But connoisseurs of roadside Americana will be pleased.

Yemassee

Going still further north on U.S. 17 you'll come to the small, friendly town of Yemassee. Its main claim to fame is nearby **Auldbrass,** designed by Frank Lloyd Wright in 1939. The home is privately owned by Hollywood producer Joel Silver, but rare, much-sought-after tours happen every other year in November through the auspices of the Beaufort County Open Land Trust. To find out about the next tour and to get on the list, email your mailing address to bcolt2@islc.net or call 843/521-2175 to receive ticket information the summer prior.

The busy but somewhat dilapidated Amtrak train depot in downtown Yemassee actually has an important historic vintage as one of the oldest continuously used train stations in the region. From 1914-1964 it was the point of embarkation for Marine recruits headed for boot camp at Parris Island. Under the auspices of the Yemassee Revitalization Corporation, plans are afoot to restore the historic depot to a nostalgic 1940s ambience.

Port Royal

This sleepy hamlet between Beaufort and Parris Island touts itself as a leader in "small town New Urbanism," with an emphasis on livability, retro-themed shopping areas, and relaxing walking trails. However, Port Royal is still pretty sleepy—but not without very real charms, not the least of which is the fact that everything is within easy walking distance of everything else.

The highlight of the year is the annual Soft Shell Crab Festival, held each April to mark the short-lived harvesting season for that favorite crustacean.

While much of the tiny historic district has a scrubbed, tidy feel, the main historic structure is the charming little **Union Church** (11th St., 843/524-4333, Mon.–Fri. 10 A.M.–4 P.M.), one of the oldest buildings in town, with guided docent tours.

Don't miss the new boardwalk and observation tower at **The Sands** municipal beach and boat ramp. The 50-foot-tall structure provides a commanding view of Battery Creek. To get to The Sands, go to 7th Street and then turn onto Sands Beach Road.

Another environmentally oriented point of pride is the **Lowcountry Estuarium** (1402 Paris Ave., 843/524-6600, www.lowcountry estuarium.org, Wed.–Sat. 10 A.M.–5 P.M., feedings at 11:30 A.M. and 3 P.M., $5 adults, $3 children). The point of the facility is to give hands-on opportunities to learn more about the flora and fauna of the various ecosystems of the Lowcountry, such as salt marshes, beaches, and estuaries.

If you get hungry in Port Royal, try the waterfront seafood haven **11th Street Dockside** (1699 11th St., 843/524-7433, daily 4:30–10 P.M., $17–27). The Dockside Dinner is a great sampler plate with lobster tail, scallops, crab legs, and shrimp. The views of the waterfront and the adjoining shrimp-boat docks are relaxing and beautiful.

Parris Island

Though more commonly known as the home of the legendary **Marine Corps Recruit Depot Parris Island** (283 Blvd. de France, 843/228-3650, www.mcrdpi.usmc.mil, free), the island is also of historic significance as the site of some of the earliest European presence in America. The U.S. Marine Corps began its association with Parris Island in 1891, though the island's naval roots actually go back to its use as a coaling station during the long Union occupation.

By the outbreak of World War I, a full-blown

BEAUFORT

© JIM MOREKIS

You don't have to be a U.S. Marine to get something out of a trip to Parris Island.

military town had sprung up, now with its own presence on the National Register of Historic Places. In November 1915, Parris Island went into business as a recruit depot, and today it's where all female Marine recruits and all male recruits east of the Mississippi River go through the grueling 13-week boot camp.

Almost every Friday during the year marks the graduation of a company of newly minted Marines. That's why you might notice an influx of visitors to the area each Thursday, a.k.a. "Family Day," with the requisite amount of celebration on Fridays after that morning's ceremony.

Unlike many military facilities in the post-9/11 era, Parris Island still hosts plenty of visitors, about 120,000 a year. It's easy to get onto the Depot. Just check in with the friendly sentry at the gate and show your valid driver's license, registration, and proof of insurance. Rental car drivers must show a copy of the rental agreement.

On your way to the Depot proper, there are a couple of beautiful picnic areas. Because this is a military base and therefore immune to the rampant residential development that has come to the Lowcountry, you will see some ancient, incredible live oak trees in this part of the facility.

Once inside, stop first at the **Douglas Visitor Center** (Bldg. 283, Blvd. de France, 843/228-3650, Mon. 7:30 A.M.–noon, Tues. and Wed. 7:30 A.M.–4:30 P.M., Thurs. 6:30 A.M.–7 P.M., Fri. 7:30 A.M.–3 P.M.), a great place to find maps and touring information.

As you go by the big parade ground, or "deck," be sure to check out the beautiful sculpture recreating the famous photo of Marines raising the flag on Iwo Jima.

A short ways ahead is the **Parris Island Museum** (Bldg. 111, 111 Panama St., 843/228-2951, daily 8:30 A.M.–4:30 P.M.) a little ways in from the museum, which not only lovingly details the entire U.S. military experience in the area, but also features a good exhibit on the area's earliest colonial history. Be sure to check out the second floor for a particularly detailed and well-done series of exhibits on Marine campaigns through the centuries.

The Spanish built Santa Elena directly

on top of the original French settlement, Charlesfort. They then built two other settlements, San Felipe and San Marcos. The Santa Elena/Charlesfort site (http://santaelena.us), now on the circa-1950s depot golf course, is now a National Historic Landmark. Many artifacts are viewable at the nearby **clubhouse/ interpretive center** (daily 7 A.M.–5 P.M.). You can take a self-guided tour; to get to the site from the museum, continue on Panama Street and take a right on Cuba Street. Follow the signs to the golf course and continue through the main parking lot of the course.

Do not use your cell phone while driving. While Parris Island kindly welcomes visitors, be aware that all traffic rules within the camp are strictly enforced, and your vehicle is subject to inspection at any time.

❰ Hunting Island State Park

Rumored to be a hideaway for Blackbeard himself, the aptly named Hunting Island was indeed for many years a notable hunting preserve, and its abundance of wildlife holds true to this day. The island is one of the East Coast's best birding spots and also hosts dolphins, loggerheads, alligators, and deer. However, thanks to preservation efforts by President Franklin Roosevelt and the Civilian Conservation Corps, the island is no longer for hunting but for sheer enjoyment. And enjoy it people do, to the tune of a million visitors a year.

A true family-friendly outdoor adventure spot, Hunting Island State Park (2555 Sea Island Pkwy., 866/345-7275, www.hunting island.com, daily 6 A.M.–6 P.M., until 9 P.M. DST, $4 adults, $1.50 children) has something for everyone—kids, parents, and newlyweds. Yet it still retains a certain sense of lush wildness—so much so that it doubled as Vietnam in *Forrest Gump.*

At the north end past the campground is the island's main landmark, the historic **Hunting Island Light,** which dates from 1875. Though the lighthouse ceased operations in 1933, a rotating light—not strong enough to serve as an actual navigational aid—is turned on at night. While the 167-step trek to the top ($2 donation per person) is quite strenuous, the view from the little observation area at the top of the

© JIM MOREKIS

the view from the top of the Hunting Island Light

lighthouse is stunning, a complete panorama of Hunting Island and much of the Lowcountry coast.

At the south end of the island is a marsh walk, nature trail, and a fishing pier complete with a cute little nature center. Hunting Island's three miles of beautiful beaches also serve as a major center of loggerhead turtle nesting and hatching, a process that begins around June as the mothers lay their eggs and culminates in late summer and early fall, when the hatchlings make their daring dash to the sea. At all phases the turtles are strictly protected, and while there are organized events to witness the hatching of the eggs, it is strictly forbidden to touch or otherwise disturb the turtles or their nests. Contact the park ranger for more detailed information.

The tropical-looking inlet running through the park is a great place to kayak or canoe.

Getting to Hunting Island couldn't be easier—just take the Sea Island Parkway (U.S. 21) about 20 minutes beyond Beaufort and you'll run right into it.

Fripp Island

If you keep driving past Hunting Island you'll reach Fripp Island, one of South Carolina's private, developed barrier islands. Unlike its more egalitarian neighbor, Fripp only welcomes visitors who are guests of the **Fripp Island Golf and Beach Resort** (800/845-4100, www .frippislandresort.com), which offers a range of lodging from oceanfront homes to villas to golf cottages. Family-friendly recreation abounds, not only in 36 holes of high-caliber golf, but in over three miles of uncrowded beach. A major allure is Camp Fripp, providing activities for kids.

◖ ACE Basin

Occupying pretty much the entire area between Beaufort and Charleston, the ACE Basin—the acronym signifies its role as the collective estuary of the Ashepoo, Combahee, and Edisto Rivers—is one of the most enriching natural experiences America has to offer. The Basin's three core rivers, the Edisto being the largest,

are the framework for a matrix of waterways crisscrossing its approximately 350,000 acres of salt marsh.

It's this intimate relationship with the tides that makes the area so enjoyable, and also what attracted so many plantations throughout its history (canals and dikes from the old rice paddies are still visible throughout). Other uses have included tobacco, corn, and lumbering. While the ACE Basin can in no way be called "pristine," it's a testament to the power of nature that after 6,000 years of human presence and often intense cultivation the Basin manages to retain much of its untamed feel.

The ACE Basin is so big that it is actually broken up into several parts for management purposes under the umbrella of the ACE Basin Project (www.acebasin.net), a task force begun in 1988 by the state of South Carolina, the U.S. Fish and Wildlife Service, and various private firms and conservation groups. The Project is now considered a model for responsible watershed preservation techniques in a time of often rampant coastal development. A host of species, both common and endangered, thrive in the area, including wood storks, alligators, sturgeon, loggerheads, teals, and bald eagles.

About 12,000 acres of the ACE Basin Project comprise the **Ernest F. Hollings ACE Basin National Wildlife Refuge** (8675 Willtown Rd., 843/889-3084, www.fws.gov/acebasin, grounds open daylight–dark year-round, office open weekdays 7:30 A.M.–4 P.M., free), run by the U.S. Fish and Wildlife Service. The historic 1828 **Grove Plantation House** is in this portion of the Basin and in fact houses the refuge's headquarters. Sometimes featured on local tours of homes, it's one of only three antebellum homes left in the ACE Basin. Surrounded by lush, ancient oak trees, it's really a sight in and of itself.

This section of the Refuge, the Edisto Unit, is almost entirely composed of impounded rice paddies from the area's role as a plantation before the Civil War. Restored rice trunks—the tidal gates used to manage water flow into the paddies—are still used to maintain the amount of water in the impounded areas, which are

© JIM MOREKIS

the Grove Plantation House at the Ernest F. Hollings ACE Basin National Wildlife Refuge

now rife with birds since the refuge is along the Atlantic Flyway. You may not always see them, but you'll definitely hear their calls echoing over the miles of marsh. (Speaking of miles, there are literally miles of walking and biking trails throughout the Edisto Unit, through both wetland and forest.)

To get to the Edisto Unit of the Hollings/ACE Basin NWR, take U.S. 17 to Highway 174 (going all the way down this route takes you to Edisto Island) and turn right onto Willtown Road. The unpaved entrance road is about two miles ahead on your left. There are restrooms and a few picnic tables, but no other facilities of note.

You can also visit the two parts of the Combahee Unit of the Refuge, which offers a similar scene of trails among impounded wetlands along the Combahee River, with parking. It's further west near Yemassee. Get there by taking a left off U.S. 17 onto Highway 33. The larger portion of the Combahee Unit is very soon after the turnoff, and the smaller, more northerly portion about five miles up the road. About 135,000 acres of the entire ACE

Basin falls under the protection of the South Carolina Department of Natural Resources as part of the **National Estuarine Research Reserve System** (www.nerrs.noaa.gov/ace basin). The South Carolina DNR also runs two Wildlife Management Areas, **Donnelly WMA** (843/844-8957, www.dnr.sc.gov, Mon.–Sat. 8 A.M.–5 P.M. year-round) and **Bear Island WMA** (843/844-8957, www.dnr.sc.gov, Mon.–Sat. dawn–dusk Feb. 1–Oct. 14), both of which provide rich opportunities for birding and wildlife observation.

Over 128,000 acres of the ACE Basin Project are permanently protected through conservation easements, management agreements, and fee title purchases. While traditional uses such as farming, fishing, and hunting do indeed continue in the ACE Basin, the area is off-limits to the gated communities, which are sprouting like mildew all along the Carolina coast. Because it is so well defended, the ACE Basin also functions like a huge outdoor laboratory for the coastal scientific community, with constant research going on in botany, zoology, microbiology, and marine science.

Recreation

KAYAKING

A 10-minute drive away from Beaufort in little Port Royal is **The Sands** public boat ramp into Battery Creek. You can also put in at the ramp at the **Lady's Island Marina** (73 Sea Island Pkwy., 843/522-0430) just across the bridge from Beaufort.

Hunting Island State Park (2555 Sea Island Pkwy., 866/345-7275, www.hunting island.com, daily 6 A.M.–6 P.M., until 9 P.M. DST, $4 adults, $1.50 children) has a wonderful inlet that is very popular with kayakers.

North and northeast of Beaufort lies the ACE Basin region, with about two dozen public ramps indicated by brown signs. Comprising hundreds of miles of creeks and tributaries in addition to its three eponymous rivers, the ACE Basin also features a fun paddling bonus: canals from the old rice plantations.

A good service for rental and knowledgeable guided tours of the Basin is **Outpost Moe's** (843/844-2514, www.geocities.com/outpost moe), where the basic 2.5-hour tour costs $40 per person, and an all-day extravaganza through the Basin is $80. Moe's provides lunch for most of its tours.

Another premier local outfitter for ACE Basin tours is **Carolina Heritage Outfitters** (Hwy. 15 in Canadys, 843/563-5051, www .canoesc.com), who focus on the Edisto River trail. In addition to guided tours ($30) and rentals, you can camp overnight in their cute treehouses along the kayak routes ($125). They load you up with your gear and drive you 22 miles upriver, then you paddle downriver to the treehouse for the evening. The next day you paddle yourself the rest of the way downriver back to home base.

To have a more dry experience of the ACE Basin from the deck of a larger vessel, try **ACE Basin Tours** (One Coosaw River Dr., 843/521-3099, www.acebasintours.com, Wed. and Sat. 10 A.M. Mar.–Nov., $35 adults, $15 children), which will take you on a three-hour tour in the 40-passenger *Dixie Lady.* To get to their dock, take Carteret Street over the bridge to St. Helena Island and then take a left on Highway 802 east (Sam's Point Rd.). Continue until you cross Lucy Point Creek, and the ACE Basin Tours marina is on your immediate left after you cross the bridge.

If you prefer self-guided paddling, keep in mind that you can spend a lifetime learning your way around the ACE Basin. But the state of South Carolina has conveniently gathered some of the best self-guided kayak trips at www.acebasin.net/canoe.html.

BIRD-WATCHING

Because of its abundance of both saltwater and freshwater environments and its relatively low human density, the Lowcountry offers a stunning glimpse into the diversity and majesty of the Southeast's bird population, both regional and migratory.

Serious birders swear by **Hunting Island State Park** (2555 Sea Island Pkwy., 866/345-7275, www.huntingisland.com, daily 6 A.M.–6 P.M., until 9 P.M. DST, $4 adults, $1.50 children), which—thanks to its undeveloped state and its spot on key migratory routes—is a great place to see brown pelicans, loons, herons, falcons, plovers, and egrets of all types. Park naturalists conduct frequent guided walks.

The tall observation tower at Port Royal's The Sands, where Battery Creek joins the Beaufort River, is a convenient vantage point from which to see any number of local bird species. The **ACE Basin** (8675 Willtown Rd., 843/889-3084, www.fws.gov/acebasin, grounds year-round daylight–dark, office Mon.–Fri. 7:30 A.M.–4 P.M.) hosts at least 19 species of waterfowl and 13 species of wading birds. At the northeast corner of the ACE Basin is the **Bear Island Wildlife Management Area** (843/844-8957, www. dnr.sc.gov, Mon.–Sat. dawn–dusk Feb.–Oct.), considered one of the best birding spots in South Carolina. To get there, take U.S. 21 north out of Beaufort to U.S. 17 north. Take a right on Bennett's Point Road and continue south about 13 miles. The entrance is about a mile on your left after crossing the Ashepoo River.

BIKING

Bikes can be rented at **Lowcountry Bikes**

(102 Sea Island Pkwy., 843/524-9585, Mon.–Tues. and Thurs.–Fri. 10 A.M.–6 P.M., Wed. 10 A.M.–1 P.M., Sat. 10 A.M.–3 P.M., about $5/hr.) in Lady's Island.

GOLF

Golf is much bigger in Hilton Head than in the Beaufort area, but here are some local highlights. The best-regarded public course in the area, and indeed one of the best military courses in the world, is **Legends at Parris Island** (Building 299, Parris Island, 843/228-2240, www.mccssc.com, $30). You need to call in advance for a tee time before you can come on Parris Island to golf.

Another popular public course is **South Carolina National Golf Club** (8 Waveland Ave., Cat Island, 843/524-0300, www.scnational.com, $70). Get to secluded Cat Island by taking the Sea Island Parkway onto Lady's Island and continuing south as it turns into Lady's Island Drive. Take Island Causeway and continue.

CAMPING

Hunting Island State Park (2555 Sea Island Pkwy., 866/345-7275, www.huntingisland.com, daily 6 A.M.–6 P.M., until 9 P.M. DST, $4 adults, $1.50 children, $25 campsites, $87–172 cabins) has 200 campsites on the north end of the island, with individual water and electric hookups. Most are available by reservation only, but 20 are available on a first-come, first-served basis.

On the south end the park has 15 two- or three-bedroom cabins for rent, fully heated and air-conditioned and equipped with TVs and kitchens. The cabins sometimes fill up a full year in advance, so book as early as you can. There's a one-week minimum stay during the high season (Mar.–Nov.) and a two-night minimum at other times. Also be aware that checkout time at the cabins is a chipper 10 A.M., which is strictly enforced.

Another neat place to camp is **Tuck in De Wood** (22 Tuc In De Wood Lane, St. Helena, 843/838-2267, $25), a 74-site campground just past the Penn Center on St. Helena Island.

Edisto Island

One of the last truly unspoiled places in the Lowcountry, Edisto Island has been highly regarded as a getaway spot since the Edisto tribe first started coming here for shellfish. (Proof of their patronage is in the huge shell midden, or debris pile, at the state park.) In fact, locals here swear that the island was settled by English-speaking colonists even before Charleston was settled in 1670.

In any case, we do know that the Spanish established a short-lived mission on St. Pierre's Creek. Then in 1674, the island was purchased from the Edistos for a few trinkets by the perhaps appropriately named Earl of Shaftesbury. For most of its modern history, cotton plantations specializing in the top-of-the-line Sea Island strain were Edisto Island's main claim to fame—it was called McConkey's Island for most of that time—though after the Civil War fishing became the primary occupation.

Because of several hurricanes in the mid-20th century, little remains of previous eras.

Now this barrier island, for the moment unthreatened by the encroachment of planned communities and private resorts so endemic to the Carolina coast, is a nice getaway for area residents in addition to just plain being a great—if a little isolated—place to live for its 800 or so full-time residents. The beaches are quiet and beautiful, the shells are plentiful, the walks are romantic, the people are friendly, and the food is good but casual. The residents operate on "Edisto Time," with a *mañana* philosophy (i.e., it'll get done when it gets done) that results in a mellow pace of life out in these parts.

ORIENTATION

Edisto Island is basically halfway between Beaufort and Charleston. There's one main land route here, south on Highway 174 off

© SOPHIA MOREKIS

The beach at Edisto Island is remarkably free of overdevelopment.

U.S. 17. It's a long way down to Edisto, but the 20–30 minute drive is scenic and enjoyable.

Most activity on the island centers on the township of Edisto Beach, which voted to align itself with Colleton County for its lower taxes (the rest of Edisto Island is part of Charleston County).

Once in town, there are two main routes to keep in mind. Palmetto Boulevard runs parallel to the beach and is noteworthy for the lack of high-rise-style development so common in other beach areas of South Carolina. Jungle Road runs parallel to Palmetto Boulevard several blocks inland, and contains the tiny "business district."

◖ EDISTO BEACH STATE PARK

Edisto Beach State Park (8377 State Cabin Rd., 843/869-2156, www.southcarolinaparks .com, daily 8 A.M.–6 P.M. Nov.–mid-Mar., 6 A.M.–10 P.M. mid-Mar.–Oct., $4 adult, $1.50 children, 5 and under free) is one of the world's foremost destinations for shell collectors. Largely because of fresh loads of silt from the adjacent ACE Basin, there are always

new specimens, many of them fossils, washing ashore.

The park stretches almost three miles and features the state's longest system of fully accessible hiking and biking trails, including one leading to the 4,000-year-old shell midden, now much eroded from past millennia. The new and particularly well-done **interpretive center** (Tues.–Sat. 9 A.M.–4 P.M.) has plenty of interesting exhibits about the nature and history of the park as well as the surrounding ACE Basin. Don't let the kids miss it.

Like many state recreational facilities in the South, Edisto Beach State Park was developed by the Civilian Conservation Corps (CCC), one of President Franklin D. Roosevelt's New Deal programs during the Great Depression, which had the doubly beneficial effect of employing large numbers of people while establishing much of the conservation infrastructure we enjoy today.

OTHER SIGHTS

The charming **Edisto Museum** (8123 Chisolm Plantation Rd., 843/869-1954, www.edisto museum.org, Tues.–Sat. 1–4 P.M., adults $4, $2

© JIM MOREKIS

the visitors center at Edisto Beach State Park

children, under 10 free), a project of the Edisto Island Historic Preservation Society, is in the midst of a major expansion that will incorporate a nearby slave cabin. Its well-done exhibits of local lore and history are complemented by a good gift shop. The Edisto Museum is before you get to the main part of the island, off Highway 174.

The **Botany Bay Wildlife Management Area** (www.preserveedisto.org, dawn–dusk Wed.–Mon., closed Tuesdays and on hunt days, free) is a great way to enjoy the unspoiled nature of Edisto Island. On grounds of two former rice and indigo plantations comprising 4,000 acres, Botany Bay features several historic remains of the old plantations and a small, wonderful beach. There are no facilities to speak of, so pack and plan accordingly.

Opened in 1999 by local snake-hunters the Clamp brothers, the **Edisto Island Serpentarium** (1374 Hwy. 174, 843/869-1171, www.edistoserpentarium.com, seasonal hours vary, $12.95 adults, $9.95 ages 6–12, $5.95 ages 4–5, under 3 free) is educational and fun, taking you up-close and personal with a variety of reptilian creatures native to the area.

The Serpentarium is on the main route into Edisto before you get to the beach area. Keep in mind they usually close Labor Day through April 30.

TOURS

Edisto has many beautiful plantation homes, relics of the island's longtime role as host to cotton plantations. While all are in private hands and therefore off limits to the public, an exception is offered through **Edisto Island Tours & T'ings** (843/869-9092, $20 adults, $10 ages 12 and under). You'll take a van tour around Edisto's beautiful churches and old plantations.

The only other way to see the homes is during the annual **Tour of Homes** (843/869-1954, www.edistomuseum.org) the second weekend in October, run by the Edisto Island Historic Preservation Society. Tickets sell out very early.

SHOPPING

Not only a convenient place to pick up odds and ends, the **Edistonian Gift Shop & Gallery** (406 Hwy. 174, 843/869-4466, daily

9 A.M.–7 P.M.) is also an important landmark, as the main supplying point before you get into the main part of town. Think of a really nice convenience store with an attached gift shop and you'll get the picture.

For various ocean gear, try the **Edisto Surf Shop** (145 Jungle Rd., 843/869-9283, daily 9 A.M.–5 P.M.). You can find whimsical Lowcountry-themed art for enjoyment or purchase at **Fish or Cut Bait Gallery** (142 Jungle Rd., 843/869-2511, Tues.–Sat. 10 A.M.–5 P.M., www.fishorcutbaitgallery.com).

If you need some groceries, there's always the **Piggly Wiggly** (104 Jungle Rd., 843/869-0055, Sun.–Thurs. 7 A.M.–9 P.M., Fri.–Sat. 7 A.M.–10 P.M.) grocery store, a.k.a., "The Pig." For fresh seafood, try **Flowers Seafood Company** (1914 Hwy. 174, 843/869-0033, Mon.–Sat. 9 A.M.–7 P.M., Sun. 9 A.M.–5 P.M.).

SPORTS AND RECREATION

As the largest river of the ACE (Ashepoo, Combahee, Edisto) Basin complex, the Edisto River figures large in the lifestyle of residents and visitors. A good public landing is at Steamboat Creek off Highway 174 on the way down to the island. Take Steamboat Landing Road (Hwy. 968) off Highway 174 near the James Edwards School. Live Oak Landing is farther up Big Bay Creek near the Interpretive Center at the State Park. The **Edisto Marina** (3702 Docksite Rd., 843/869-3504) is on the far west side of the island.

Captain Ron Elliott of **Edisto Island Tours** (843/869-1937) offers various ecotours and fishing trips, as well as canoe and kayak rentals for about $25 a day. A typical kayak tour runs about $35 per person for a one-and-a-half to two-hour trip, though he offers a "beachcombing" trip for $15 per person. **Ugly Ducklin'** (843/869-1580) offers creek and inshore fishing charters.

You can get gear as well as book boat and kayak tours of the entire area, including into the ACE Basin, at **Edisto Watersports & Tackle** (3731 Docksite Rd., 843/869-0663, www.edistowatersports.com). Their guided tours run about $30 per person, with a two-hour rental running about $20.

Riding a bike on Edisto Beach and all around the island is a great, relaxing way to get some exercise and enjoy its scenic, laid-back beauty. The best place to rent a bike—or a kayak or canoe, for that matter—is **Island Bikes and Outfitters** (140 Jungle Rd., 843/869-4444, Mon.–Sat. 9–4 P.M.). Bike rentals run about $16 a day; single kayaks are about $60 a day.

There's one golf course on the island, the 18-hole **Plantation Course at Edisto** (21 Fairway Dr., 843/869-1111, $60), finished in 2006.

ACCOMMODATIONS

A great thing about Edisto Island is the total absence of ugly chain lodging or beachfront condo development. My recommended option is staying at the **Edisto Beach State Park** (843/869-2156, www.southcarolinaparks.com, $75–100 cabins, $25 tent sites) itself, either at a campsite on the Atlantic side or in a marsh-front cabin on the northern edge. During high season (Apr.–Nov.), there's a minimum week-long stay in the cabins; during the off-season, the minimum stay is two days. You can book cabins up to 11 months in advance, and I highly recommend doing so as they go very quickly.

If you want something a little more plush, there are rental homes galore on Edisto Island. Because of the aforementioned lack of hotels, this is the most popular option for most vacationers here—indeed, just about the only option. Contact **Edisto Sales and Rentals Realty** (1405 Palmetto Blvd., 800/868-5398, www.edistorealty.com).

FOOD

One of the all-time great barbecue places in South Carolina is on Edisto, 【 **Po Pigs Bo-B-Q** (2410 Hwy. 174, 843/869-9003, Wed.–Sat. 11:30 A.M.–9 P.M., $4–10) on the way into town. This is the real thing, the full pig cooked in all its many ways: white meat, dark meat, cracklin's, and hash, served in the local style of "all you care to eat." Unlike many BBQ spots, they do serve beer and wine.

Another popular joint on the island is **Whaley's** (2801 Myrtle St., 843/869-2161,

Tues.–Sat. 11:30 A.M.–2 P.M. and 5–9 P.M., bar daily 5 P.M.–2 A.M., $5–15), a down-home place in an old gas station a few blocks off the beach. This is a good place for casual seafood like boiled shrimp, washed down with a lot of beer. The bar is open seven days a week.

Though it was closed from 2005-2009, the legendary **(** **Old Post Office** (1442 Hwy. 174, 843/869-2339, www.theoldpostoffice restaurant.com, Tues.–Sun. 5:30–10 P.M., $20), a fine dining Lowcountry-style spot, kept a devoted clientele for 20 years. It recently reopened with a bang and thankfully kept its old school mystique intact. Specialties include fine crab cakes drizzled with Mousseline sauce, the pecan-encrusted Veal Edistonian, and a Carolina Ribeye topped with a pimiento cheese sauce, something of a state culinary tradition.

McConkey's Jungle Shack (108 Jungle Rd., 843/869-0097, Mon.–Fri. 11 A.M.–8 P.M., Sat.–Sun. 8 A.M.–8 P.M., $4–10) on the eastern end of the beach is known for its fish-and-chips basket and great burgers.

Hilton Head Island

Literally the prototype of the modern planned resort community, Hilton Head Island is also a case study in how utterly a landscape can change when enough money is introduced. Once consisting almost entirely of African Americans with deep historic roots in the area, in the mid-1950s Hilton Head began its transformation into an almost all-white, upscale golf, tennis, and shopping mecca populated largely by northern transplants and retirees. As you can imagine, the flavor here is now quite different from surrounding areas of the Lowcountry, to say the least, with an emphasis on material excellence, top prices, get-it-done-yesterday punctuality, and the attendant aggressive traffic.

Giving credit where it's due, however, Hilton Head knows what its target audience is and delivers the goods in a thoroughly professional manner. While it's easy to dismiss it as a sort of Disney World for the elite—a disjointed collection of gated communities comprising 70 percent of its area—the truth is that millions of visitors, not all of them elite by any stretch, not only enjoy what Hilton Head has to offer, they swear by it. The attraction is quality, whether in the stunning beaches, outstanding cultural offerings, plush accommodations, attentive service, or copious merchandise. You won't see any litter and you're unlikely to experience any crime. Certainly that's to Hilton Head's credit and no small reason for its continued success.

One of the unsung positive aspects of modern Hilton Head is its dedication to sustainable living. With the support of voters, the town routinely buys large tracts of land to preserve as open space. Hilton Head was the first municipality in the country to mandate the burying of all power lines, and one of the first to regularly use covenants and deed restrictions. All new development must conform to rigid guidelines on setbacks and tree canopy. It has one of the most comprehensive signage ordinances in the country as well, which means no garish commercial displays will disrupt your views of the night sky.

If those are "elite" values, then certainly we might do well in making them more mainstream.

HISTORY

The second-largest barrier island on the East Coast, Hilton Head Island was inhabited by Native Americans at least 10,000 years ago. The first European to sight the island was Spain's Francisco Cordillo in 1521, but it didn't enter mainstream consciousness until the 1663 sighting by Sir William Hilton, who thoughtfully named the island—with its notable headland or "Head"—after himself. Hilton, who like many of Charleston's original settlers was from the British colony of Barbados, was purposely trying to drum up interest in the island

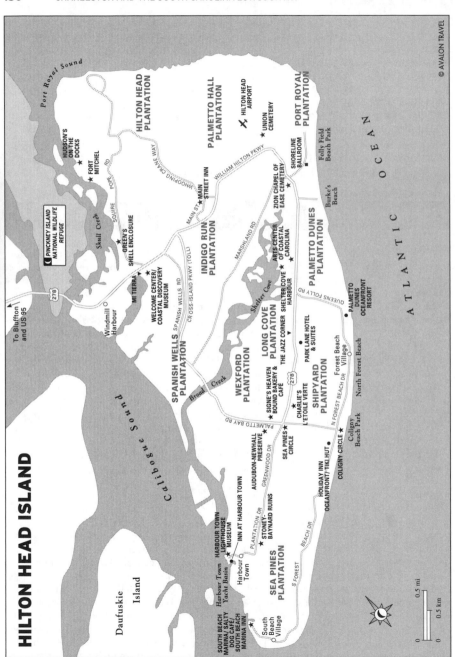

HILTON HEAD ISLAND

Daufuskie Island

Port Royal Sound

© AVALON TRAVEL

BEAUFORT

Calibogue Sound

ATLANTIC OCEAN

HILTON HEAD PLANTATION

PALMETTO HALL PLANTATION

HILTON HEAD AIRPORT

PORT ROYAL PLANTATION

UNION CEMETERY

SHORELINE BALLROOM

Folly Field Beach Park

HUDSON'S ON THE DOCKS

FORT MITCHEL

WHOOPING CRANE WAY

POPE RD

SQUIRE POPE

Skull Creek

GREEN'S SHELL ENCLOSURE

PINCKNEY ISLAND NATIONAL WILDLIFE REFUGE

278

To Bluffton and US 95

MI TIERRA

Windmill Harbour

WELCOME CENTER/ COASTAL DISCOVERY MUSEUM

SPANISH WELLS RD

SPANISH WELLS PLANTATION

MAIN ST

MAIN STREET INN

WILLIAM HILTON PKWY

INDIGO RUN PLANTATION

CROSS-ISLAND PKWY (TOLL)

MARSHLAND RD

Shelter Cove

ZION CHAPEL OF EASE CEMETERY

ARTS CENTER OF COASTAL CAROLINA

SHELTER COVE HARBOUR

PALMETTO DUNES PLANTATION

Burke's Beach

QUEENS FOLLY RD

PALMETTO DUNES OCEANFRONT RESORT

WEXFORD PLANTATION

LONG COVE PLANTATION

THE JAZZ CORNER

PARK LANE HOTEL & SUITES

Forest Beach Village

Broad Creek

SIGNE'S HEAVEN BOUND BAKERY & CAFE

CHARLIE'S L'ETOILE VERTE

SHIPYARD PLANTATION

PALMETTO BAY RD

278

N FOREST BEACH DR

North Forest Beach

AUDUBON-NEWHALL PRESERVE

GREENWOOD DR

SEA PINES CIRCLE

HOLIDAY INN OCEANFRONT/ TIKI HUT

COLIGNY CIRCLE

Coligny Beach Park

STONEY BAYNARD RUINS

PLANTATION DR

INN AT HARBOUR TOWN

HARBOUR TOWN LIGHTHOUSE MUSEUM

Harbour Town

Harbour Town Yacht Basin

BEACH DR

SEA PINES PLANTATION

S FOREST

SOUTH BEACH MARINA/ SALTY DOG CAFE/ SOUTH BEACH MARINA INN

South Beach Village

0   0.5 mi

0   0.5 km

as a commercial venture, famously describing his new namesake as having "sweet water" and "clear sweet air."

Though Hilton Head wasn't the first foothold of English colonization in Carolina, it did acquire commercial status first as the home of rice and indigo plantations. Later it gained fame as the first location of the legendary "Sea Island Cotton," a long-grain variety which, following its introduction in 1790 by William Elliott II of the Myrtle Bank Plantation, would soon be the dominant version of the cash crop.

Hilton Head planters were outspoken in the cause of American independence. The chief pattern in the Lowcountry during that conflict involved the British raiding Hilton Head and surrounding areas from their stronghold on Daufuskie Island, burning plantations and capturing slaves to be resold in Caribbean colonies. As a reminder of the savage guerrilla nature of the conflict in the South, British hit-and-run raids on Hilton Head continued for weeks after Cornwallis surrendered.

Nearby Bluffton was settled by planters from Hilton Head Island and the surrounding area in the early 1800s as a summer retreat. Though Charleston likes to claim the label today, Bluffton was actually the genuine "cradle of secession." Indeed, locals still joke that the town motto is "Divided We Stand."

Fort Walker, a Confederate installation on the site of the modern Port Royal Plantation development on Hilton Head, was the target of the largest fleet ever assembled in North America at the time, when a massive Union force sailed into Port Royal Sound in October 1861. A month later, the Fort—and effectively the entire area—had fallen, though by that time most white residents had long since fled. During the Civil War, Bluffton was also evacuated and, like Hilton Head, escaped serious action. However, in June 1863, Union troops destroyed most of the town except for about a dozen homes and two churches.

Though it seems unlikely given the island's modern demographics, Hilton Head was almost entirely African American through much of the 20th century. When Union troops occupied the island at the outbreak of the Civil War, freed and escaped slaves flocked to the island, and most of the dwindling number of African Americans on the island today are descendants of this original Gullah population.

For the first half of the 20th century, logging was Hilton Head's main commercial pursuit. Things didn't take their modern shape until the 1950s, when the Fraser family bought 19,000 of the island's 25,000 acres with the intent to continue forestry on them. But in 1956—not at all coincidentally the same year the first bridge to the island was built—Charles Fraser convinced his father to sell him the southern tip of Hilton Head Island. Fraser's brainchild and decades-long labor of love—some said his obsession—Sea Pines Plantation was the prototype of the golf-oriented resort community so common today on both U.S. coasts.

Though Fraser himself was killed in a boating accident in 2002, he survived to see Sea Pines encompass much of Hilton Head's economic activity, including Harbour Town, and to see the Town of Hilton Head incorporated in 1983. Fraser is buried under the famous Liberty Oak in Harbour Town, which he personally made sure wasn't harmed during the development of the area.

ORIENTATION

Hilton Head Islanders have long referred to their island as the "shoe" (and speak of driving to the toe, going to the heel, etc.). If you take a look at a map, you'll see why. Hilton Head bears an uncanny resemblance to a running shoe in action pointed toward the southeast, with the aptly named Broad Creek forming a near facsimile of the Nike "swoosh" symbol.

Running the length and circumference of the shoe is the undisputed main drag, U.S. 278 Business (William Hilton Parkway), which crosses onto Hilton Head right at the "tongue" of the shoe, a relatively undeveloped area where there are still a few old African American communities. The new Cross Island Parkway toll route (U.S. 278), beginning up toward the ankle as you first get on the island, is a quicker, more convenient route straight to the toe near Sea Pines.

BEAUFORT

While it is technically the business spur, when locals say "278" they're talking about the William Hilton Parkway. It takes you the entire sole of the shoe, including the beaches, and on down to the toe, where you'll find a confusing, crazy British-style roundabout called Sea Pines Circle. It's also the site of the Harbour Town Marina and the island's oldest planned development, Sea Pines Plantation.

There's no "town center" per se, but activity here tends to revolve around just a few places: the Shelter Cove mall and residential development near the entrance to the island; Coligny Plaza, an older, more casual shopping center near the main beach entrance; Sea Pines Circle, a center of nightlife; and two spots within Sea Pines itself, Harbour Town and South Beach—the former a blend of upscale and family attractions, and the latter catering a bit more to the beach crowd.

While precious little history is left on Hilton Head, place names reverberate with the names of key figures long-gone: Cordillo Parkway, named for the first Spaniard to come to the area; Coligny Plaza, named for the admiral who sent the first French expedition to the

area; and Ribault Road, named for the leader of that expedition. In any case, while making your way around the island always keep in mind that the bulk of it consists of private developments, and local law enforcement frowns on people who aimlessly wander among the condos and villas.

SIGHTS

Contrary to what many think, there are actually quite a few things to do on Hilton Head that don't involve swinging a club at a little white ball or shopping for designer labels, but instead celebrate the area's rich history and natural setting. The following are some of those attractions, arranged in geographical order from where you first access the island.

◖ Pinckney Island National Wildlife Refuge

Though actually consisting of many islands and hammocks, Pinckney Island NWR (912/652-4415, daily dawn–dusk, free) is the only part of this small but very well-managed 4,000-acre refuge that's open to the public. Almost 70 percent of the former rice plantation is salt marsh

© JIM MOREKIS

Pinckney Island National Wildlife Refuge

and tidal creeks, making it a perfect microcosm for the Lowcountry as a whole, as well as a great place to kayak or canoe.

Native Americans liked the area as well, with a 10,000-year presence and over 100 archaeological sites being identified to date. Like many coastal refuges, it was a private game preserve for much of the 20th century. Some of the state's richest birding opportunities abound here, with observers able to spot gorgeous white ibis, rare wood storks, herons, egrets, eagles, and ospreys with little trouble from its miles of trails.

Getting there is easy: On U.S. 278 east to Hilton Head, the refuge entrance is right between the two bridges onto the island.

Coastal Discovery Museum

Surprisingly in an area as awash in money as Hilton Head, the island abounds with small, underfunded, but worthwhile endeavors such as the Coastal Discovery Museum (100 William Hilton Pkwy., 843/689-6767, www.coastaldiscovery.org, Mon.–Sat. 9 A.M.–4:30 P.M., Sun. 11 A.M.–3 P.M., free) just as you get onto Hilton Head. Exhibits here are small-scale but heartfelt, like the excellent little dioramas of traditional island life. The Museum hosts a variety of specialty guided tours, such as a Native Americans on the Sea Islands tour, a Pinckney Island walking tour, and a Sea Pines Plantation Overview. The cost for most of the tours is $12 for adults and $7 for children.

The Museum is a partner with the state in a sea turtle protection program, which you can learn more about once there. Standing exhibits include a historical timeline of Hilton Head, a Butterfly Garden, and the Sea Island Biodiversity Room, intended for use with local schoolchildren but fully available to the public.

The Museum has a second location at the 68-acre **Honey Horn** greenspace (70 Honey Horn Dr., www.coastaldiscovery.org) at the intersection of Cross Island Parkway and U.S. 278. The parcel contains several historic structures and features several boardwalks overlooking the beautiful marsh. A mile-long oystershell trail takes you by a 1,200-square-foot butterfly enclosure, where you can meet about a dozen species of indigenous butterflies.

Green's Shell Enclosure

Lesser-known than the larger Native American shell ring farther south at Sea Pines, the Green's Shell Enclosure (803/734-3886, daily dawn–dusk) is certainly easier to find and you don't have to pay five bucks to enter the area, as with Sea Pines. This three-acre Heritage Preserve dates back to at least the 1300s.

The heart of the site comprises a low embankment, part of the original fortified village. Don't expect to be wowed—shell rings are a subtle pleasure. As is the case with most shell rings, the shells themselves are underneath a layer of dirt. Please don't disturb them.

To get here, take a left at the intersection of U.S. 278 and Squire Pope Road. Turn left into Greens Park, pass the office on the left, and park. The entrance to the shell enclosure is on the left behind a fence. You'll see a small community cemetery that has nothing to do with the shell ring; veer to your right to get to the short trail entrance. No camping allowed.

Union Cemetery

A modest but key aspect of African American history on Hilton Head is at **Union Cemetery** (Union Cemetery Rd.), a small burial ground featuring several graves of black Union Army troops (you can tell by the designation "U.S.C.I." on the tombstone, or "United States Colored Infantry"). Also of interest are the charming, hand-carved cement tombstones of non-veterans.

To get here, turn north off of William Hilton Parkway onto Union Cemetery Road. The cemetery is a short ways ahead on your left. There is no signage or site interpretation.

Fort Mitchel and Mitchelville

There's not much left of the old Union encampment at Fort Mitchel, nor of the freedmen community, Mitchelville, which grew up alongside it. You can see the earthworks, a couple of cannons, and a historical marker on the grounds of the Hilton Head Plantation, a gated development. Tell the security guard you'd like to see Fort Mitchel. Once inside Hilton Head Plantation, take a left onto Seabrook Drive and then a right onto Skull Creek Drive. Fort Mitchel is a short ways ahead on your left. It's not a well-maintained site, but it's an important part of local history.

At the intersection of Bay Gall and Beach City Roads is a marker for the site of Mitchelville, founded in 1862 as the first freedman settlement in the U.S. Also on Beach City Road is a fenced-in area with what's left of Fort Howell, a Union encampment built by African American troops.

Zion Chapel of Ease Cemetery

More like one of the gloriously desolate scenes common to the rest of the Lowcountry, this little cemetery in full view of the William Hilton Parkway at Folly Field Road is all that remains of one of the "Chapels of Ease," a string of chapels set up in the 1700s. The cemetery (daily dawn–dusk, free) is said to be haunted by the ghost of William Baynard, whose final resting place is in a mausoleum on-site (the remains of his ancestral home are farther south at Sea Pines Plantation).

Audubon-Newhall Preserve

Plant lovers shouldn't miss this small but very well-maintained 50-acre wooded tract in the south-central part of the island on Palmetto Bay Road between the Cross Island Parkway and Sea Pines circle. Almost all plant life, even that in the water, is helpfully marked and identified. But if all you want to do is just enjoy, that's fine too, because the preserve has two miles of nature trails. Unusually, there's a well-preserved bog environment (*pocosin* to the indigenous tribes here). The preserve (dawn–dusk year-round, free) is open to the public, but you can't camp here. For more information, call the Hilton Head Audubon Society (843/842-9246).

Sea Pines Plantation

This private residential resort development at

Audubon-Newhall Preserve

the extreme west end of the island—first on Hilton Head and the prototype of every other such development in the U.S.—hosts several attractions that collectively are well worth the $5 per vehicle "road use" fee, which you pay at the main entrance gate.

HARBOUR TOWN

Okay, it's not that historic and not all that natural, but Harbour Town is still pretty cool. The dominant element is the squat, colorful **Harbour Town Lighthouse Museum** (149 Lighthouse Rd., 843/671-2810, www.harbour townlighthouse.com, 10 A.M.–dusk), which has never really helped a ship navigate its way to the island. The 90-foot structure was built in 1970 purely to give the tourists a little atmosphere, and that it does, as kids especially love climbing the stairs to the top (at $2 per person, that is) and looking out over the island's expanse. This being Hilton Head, of course, there's a gift shop, too. The other attractions here are the boisterous café and shopping scene around the marina and the nearby park area.

© JIM MOREKIS

the scene at Harbour Town in Sea Pines Plantation

STONEY-BAYNARD RUINS

These tabby ruins (Plantation Dr., dawn–dusk, free) in a residential neighborhood are what remains of the circa-1790 central building of the old Braddock's Point Plantation, first owned by Patriot and raconteur Captain "Saucy Jack" Stoney and then the Baynard family. Active during the island's heyday as a cotton center, the plantation was destroyed after the Civil War. Site interpretation here is barebones, but suffice it to say that this is a great remaining example of colonial tabby architecture. Two other foundations are nearby, one for slave quarters and one whose use is still unknown. Note that there is a $5 fee to enter Sea Pines.

SEA PINES FOREST PRESERVE

The Sea Pines Forest Preserve (175 Greenwood Dr., 843/363-4530, free) is set amid the Sea Pines Plantation golf resort development, but you don't need a bag of clubs to enjoy this 600-acre preserve, which is built on the site of an old rice plantation (dikes and logging trails are still visible). Here you can ride a horse,

fish, or just take a walk on the eight miles of trails (open dawn–dusk) and enjoy the natural beauty around you. No bike riding is allowed on the trails, however.

As we've seen, Hilton Head has a Native American shell ring further north off Squire Pope Road. The Sea Pines Forest Preserve also boasts a shell ring set within a canopy of tall pines, forming a natural cathedral of sorts. A combination ceremonial area and communal common space, the shell ring today is actually a series of low rings made of discarded oyster shells covered with earth. The rewards here are contemplative in nature, since the vast bulk of the actual oyster shells are beneath layers of soil. Scientists date the ring itself to about 1450 B.C., though human habitation on the island goes as far back as 8000 B.C.

Tours and Cruises

Almost all guided tours on Hilton Head focus on the water. **Harbour Town Cruises** (843/363-9023, www.vagabondcruise.com) offers several sightseeing tours, as well as excursions to Daufuskie and Savannah. They also offer a tour on a former America's Cup racing yacht.

"Dolphin tours" are extremely popular on Hilton Head and there is no shortage of proprietors. **Dolphin Watch Nature Cruises** (843/785-4558, $25 adults, $10 children) departs from Shelter Cove, as does **Lowcountry Nature Tours** (843/683-0187, www.lowcountry naturetours.com, $40 adult, $35 children, 2 and under free). The **Gypsy** (843/363-2900, www.bitemybait.com, $15 adults, $7 children) sails out of South Beach Marina, taking you all around peaceful Calibogue Sound.

Two dolphin tours are based on Broad Creek, the large body of water which almost bisects the island through the middle. "Captain Jim" runs **Island Explorer Tours** (843/785-2100, www.dolphintourshiltonhead.com, $45 per person for two-hour tour) from a dock behind the old Oyster Factory on Marshland Road. Not to be outdone, "Captain Dave" leads tours at **Dolphin Discoveries** (843/681-1911, $40 adults, $30 ages 12 and under for two-hour tour), leaving out of Simmons Landing next to the Broad Creek Marina on Marshland Road.

Outside Hilton Head (843/686-6996, www.outsidehiltonhead.com) runs a variety of eco/dolphin waterborne tours as well as a guided day-trip excursion to Daufuskie, complete with golf cart rental.

ENTERTAINMENT AND EVENTS
Nightlife

The crowd's on the older side, but the most high-quality live entertainment on the island is at **The Jazz Corner** (1000 William Hilton Pkwy., 843/842-8620, www.thejazzcorner .com, dinner daily 6–9 P.M., late-night menu after 9 P.M.), which brings in the best names in the country—and outstanding regulars like Bob Masteller and Howard Paul—to perform in this space in the somewhat unlikely setting of a boutique mall, the Village at Wexford. The dinners are great, but the attraction here is definitely the music. Reservations are recommended. Live music starts around 7 P.M.

The premier live concert venue in Hilton Head these days is the **Shoreline Ballroom** (40 Folly Field Rd., 843/842-0358, www .shorelineballroom.com), which has an eclectic show calendar of acts ranging from rapper Snoop Dogg to bluegrass legend Ralph Stanley.

For years islanders have jokingly referred to the "Barmuda Triangle," an area named for the preponderance of bars within walking distance of Sea Pines Circle. The longtime heart of the Barmuda Triangle is the **Tiki Hut** (1 S. Forest Beach Dr., 843/785-5126, Sun.–Thurs. 11 A.M.–8 P.M., Fri.–Sat. 11 A.M.–10 P.M., bar until 2 A.M.), actually part of the Holiday Inn Oceanfront Hotel at the entrance to Sea Pines. This popular watering hole is the only beachfront bar on the island, which technically makes it the only place you can legally drink alcohol on a Hilton Head beach.

Another Barmuda Triangle staple is **Hilton Head Brewing Company** (7 Greenwood Dr., 843/785-3900, daily 11 A.M.–2 A.M.), the only brewpub on the island. They offer a wide range of handcrafted brews, from a Blueberry Wheat to a Mocha Porter.

Inside Sea Pines is the **Quarterdeck Lounge and Patio** (843/842-1999, www.seapines.com, Sun.–Thurs. 5:30–10 P.M., Fri.–Sat. 5:30 P.M.–midnight) at the base of the Harbour Town Lighthouse. This is where the party's at after a long day on the fairways during the Verizon Heritage golf tournament.

Within Sea Pines at the South Beach marina is also where you'll find **The Salty Dog Cafe** (232 S. Sea Pines Dr., 843/671-2233, www .saltydog.com, lunch daily 11 A.M.–3 P.M., dinner daily 5–10 P.M., bar daily until 2 A.M.), one of the area's most popular institutions (some might even call it a tourist trap) and something akin to an island empire, with popular T-shirts, a gift shop, books, and an ice cream shop, all overlooking the marina. It's a fun place at night, with live entertainment and a fun-loving, reasonably diverse crowd. Margaritas are great here, but skip the food; if you're hungry, try the affiliated Wreck of the Salty Dog nearby.

Performing Arts

Because so many of its residents migrated here from art-savvy metropolitan areas in the northeast, Hilton Head maintains a very high standard of top-quality entertainment. Much of the activity centers on the multimillion-dollar **Arts Center of Coastal Carolina** (14 Shelter Cove Ln., 843/842-2787, www.artshhi.com), which hosts touring shows, resident companies, musical concerts, dance performances, and visual arts exhibits.

Now over a quarter-century old and under the direction of maestro Mary Woodmansee Green, the **Hilton Head Symphony Orchestra** (843/842-2055, www.hhso.org) performs a year-round season of masterworks and pops programs at various venues. They also take their show on the road with several concerts in Bluffton, and even perform several "Symphony Under the Stars" programs at Shelter Cove.

Chamber Music Hilton Head (www.cmhh .org) performs throughout the year with selections ranging from Brahms to Smetana at All Saints Episcopal Church (3001 Meeting St.).

The **South Carolina Repertory Company** (136 Beach City Rd., 843/342-2057, www .hiltonheadtheatre.com) performs an eclectic, challenging season, from musicals to cutting-edge drama to the avant-garde.

Cinema

There's an art house on Hilton Head, the charming **Coligny Theatre** (843/686-3500, www.colignytheatre.com) in the Coligny Plaza shopping center before you get to Sea Pines. For years this was the only movie theater for miles around, but it reincarnated as a primarily indie film venue in 2002. Look for the entertaining murals by local artist Ralph Sutton. Daily showtimes are 4 P.M. and 7 P.M. (no 7 P.M. show on Mondays) and Monday, Tuesday, and Friday at 11:30 A.M.

The main multiplex on Hilton Head is **Northridge Cinema 10** (Hwy. 278 and Mathews Dr., 843/342-3800, www.southeast cinemas.com) in the Northridge Plaza shopping center. Off the island is the way-cool new **Sea Turtle Cinemas** (106 Buckwalter Pkwy., 843/706-2888, www.seaturtlecinemas.com) in the Berkeley Place shopping center. To get there take the William Hilton Parkway/U.S. 278 west off Hilton Head about 10 miles. Turn left at Buckwalter Parkway. Sea Turtle Cinemas is a half-mile farther on the right.

the Coligny Theatre in Coligny Plaza

BEAUFORT

BEAUFORT

Festivals and Events

Late February and early March brings the **Hilton Head Wine and Food Festival** (www.hiltonheadhospitality.org), culminating in what they call "The East Coast's Largest Outdoor Public Tasting and Auction," which in 2010 was held at the Coastal Discovery Museum at Honey Horn. Some events charge admission.

Hilton Head's premier event is the **Verizon Heritage Classic Golf Tournament** (843/671-2248, www.verizonheritage.com), held each April at the Harbour Town Golf Links on Sea Pines Plantation. Formerly known as the MCI Heritage Classic, the event is South Carolina's only PGA Tour event and brings thousands of visitors to town yearly.

A fun and fondly anticipated yearly event is the **Kiwanis Club Chili Cookoff** (www.hilton headkiwanis.org), held each October at Honey Horn on the island's south end. A low admission price gets you all the chili you can eat plus free antacids. All funds go to charity, and all excess chili goes to a local food bank.

Every November brings Hilton Head's second-largest event, the world-famous **Hilton Head Concours d'Elegance & Motoring Festival** (www.hhiconcours.com), a multiday event bringing together vintage car clubs from throughout the nation and culminating in a prestigious "Best of Show" competition.

SHOPPING

As you'd expect, Hilton Head is a shopper's delight, with an emphasis on upscale stores and prices to match. Keep in mind that hours may be shortened in the off-season (Nov.–Mar.). Here's a rundown of the main island shopping areas in the order you'll encounter them as you enter the island.

Shelter Cove

Associated with the attached residential community, this shopping area on Broad Creek right off the William Hilton Parkway actually comprises three entities, the larger **Mall at Shelter Cove,** the smaller **Plaza at Shelter Cove,** and the dockside **Shelter Cove Harbour.**

The Mall opens at 10 A.M. Monday–Saturday

and noon on Sunday and features the usual national stores you'd expect, but with a few typically Hilton Head upgrades like **Off 5th/ Saks Fifth Avenue Outlet** (843/341-2088) and **Williams-Sonoma** (843/785-2408). Other neat stores in the Mall are **DeGullah Creations** (843/686-5210), specializing in authentic Gullah wares, and **Blue Parrot** (800/252-6653), with gift lines such as Wee Forest Folk and Swarovski Crystal.

The most interesting store at the Plaza is the flagship location of **Outside Hilton Head** (843/686-6996, www.outsidehilton head.com, Mon.–Sat. 10 A.M.–5:30 P.M., Sun. 11 A.M.–5:30 P.M.), a complete outdoor outfitter with a thoroughly knowledgeable staff (they have a smaller satellite store in Sea Pines). Whatever outdoor gear you need and whatever tour you want to take, they can most likely hook you up.

Shelter Cove Harbour hosts a few cute shops hewing to its overall nautical/vacation theme, such as the clothing stores **Camp Hilton Head** (843/842-3666, Mon.–Sat. 10 A.M.–9 P.M., Sun. noon–5 P.M.) and the marine supplier **Ship's Store** (843/842-7001, Mon.–Sat. 7:30 A.M.–5 P.M., Sun. 7:30 A.M.–4 P.M.).

Village at Wexford

This well-shaded shopping center on William Hilton Parkway hosts plenty of well-tended shops, including the Lily Pulitzer signature women's store **S.M. Bradford Co.** (843/686-6161, Mon.–Sat. 10 A.M.–6 P.M.) and the aromatic **Scents of Hilton Head** (843/842-7866, Mon.–Fri. 10 A.M.–6 P.M., Sat. 10 A.M.–5 P.M.).

Coligny Circle

This is the closest Hilton Head comes to funkier beach towns like Tybee Island or Folly Beach, though it doesn't really come that close. You'll find some delightful and somewhat quirky stores here, many keeping long hours in the summer, like the self-explanatory **Coligny Kite & Flag Co.** (843/785-5483, Mon.–Sat. 10 A.M.–9 P.M., Sun. 11 A.M.–6 P.M.), the hippie-fashion **Loose Lucy's** (843/785-

8093, Mon.–Sat. 10 A.M.–6 P.M., Sun. 11 A.M.–5 P.M.), and the Caribbean-flavored **Jamaican Me Crazy** (843/785-9006, daily 10 A.M.–10 P.M.). Kids will love both **The Shell Shop** (843/785-4900, Mon.–Sat. 10 A.M.–9 P.M., Sun. noon–9 P.M.) and **Black Stone Minerals** (843/785-7090, Mon.–Sat. 10 A.M.–10 P.M., Sun. 11 A.M.–8 P.M.).

Harbour Town

The Shoppes at Harbour Town (www.sea pines.com) are a collection of 20 mostly boutique stores along Lighthouse Road in Sea Pines Plantation. Probably the most interesting is **Match** (843/671-4653, www.match goods.com, daily 10 A.M.–9 P.M.), an upscale vintage store that acquires antiques, designer items, and home goods through a corporate partnership for resale, and also boasts its own walk-in humidor.

At **Planet Hilton Head** (843/363-5177, www.planethiltonhead.com, daily 10 A.M.–9 P.M.) you'll find some cute, eclectic gifts and home goods. Other highlights include the clothier **Knickers Men's Store** (843/671-2291, daily 10 A.M.–9 P.M.), and the **Top of the Lighthouse Shoppe** (843/671-2810, www.harbourtownlighthouse.com, daily 10 A.M.–9 P.M.), where many a climbing tourist has been coaxed to part with some of their disposable income.

South Beach Marina

On South Sea Pines Drive at the Marina you'll find several worthwhile shops, including an "outpost" location of the great local outfitter **Outside Hilton Head** (800/686-6996, www .outsidehiltonhead.com, daily 9 A.M.–6 P.M.) as well as a good ship's store and all-around grocery dealer **South Beach General Store** (843/671-6784, daily 8 A.M.–10 P.M.).

I like to stop in the **Blue Water Bait and Tackle** (843/671-3060, daily 7 A.M.–8 P.M.) and check out the cool nautical stuff. They can also hook you up with a variety of kayak trips and fishing charters. And of course right on the water there's the ever-popular **Salty Dog Café** (843/671-2233, www.saltydog.com, lunch daily 11 A.M.–3 P.M., dinner daily 5–10 P.M.), whose ubiquitous T-shirts seem to adorn every other person on the island.

Thrift Shops

Don't scoff. Every thrift store connoisseur knows the best place to shop second-hand is in an affluent area like Hilton Head, where the locals try hard to stay in style and their castoffs are first-class. Key stops here are **The Bargain Box** (546 William Hilton Pkwy., 843/681-4305, Mon., Wed., and Fri. 1–4 P.M., Sat. 9:15 A.M.–12:15 P.M.) and **St. Francis Thrift Store** (2 Southwood Dr., 843/689-6563, Wed.–Sat. 10 A.M.–3 P.M.) right off the William Hilton Parkway.

Art Galleries

Despite the abundant wealth apparent in some quarters here, there's no free-standing art museum in the area, that role being filled by dozens of independent galleries.

For a more formal approach, go to **Morris & Whiteside Galleries & Sculpture Garden** (807 William Hilton Pkwy., 843/842-4433, www .morris-whiteside.com, daily 10 A.M.–5 P.M.), which features a variety of paintings and sculpture, heavy on landscapes but also showing some fine figurative work.

Not to be confused with the Red Piano Too on St. Helena Island, the **Red Piano Art Gallery** (220 Cordillo Pkwy., 843/785-2318, www.redpianoartgallery.com, daily 10 A.M.–5 P.M.) isn't devoted to Gullah art, but rather concentrates on natural landscapes with an often-whimsical touch.

The nonprofit **Art League of Hilton Head** (Pineland Station, Suite 207, Mon.–Sat. 10 A.M.–6 P.M.) displays work by member artists in all media.

SPORTS AND RECREATION
Beaches

First, the good news: Hilton Head Island has 12 miles of some of the most beautiful, safe beaches you'll find anywhere. The bad news is that there are only a few ways to gain access, generally at locations referred to as "beach parks." Don't just drive into a residential neighborhood and think you'll be able to park and find your way to the beach; for better or worse, Hilton Head is not set up for that kind of casual access. Driessen Beach Park has 207 long-term parking spaces, costing $0.25 for 30 minutes. There's free parking but fewer spaces at the Coligny Beach Park entrance and at Fish Haul Creek Park. Also, there are 22 metered spaces at Alder Lane Beach Access, 51 at Folly Field Beach Park, and 13 at Burkes Beach Road. Most other beach parks are for permit parking only. Clean, well-maintained public restrooms are available at all the beach parks. You can find beach information at 843/342-4580 and www.hiltonheadislandsc.gov. Beach Park hours vary: Coligny Beach Park is open daily 24 hours. All other beach parks are open 6 A.M.–8 P.M. March–September and 6 A.M.–5 P.M. October–February.

Alcohol is strictly prohibited on Hilton Head's beaches. This may cut down on your vacation fun, but the plus side is the ban makes the beaches very friendly for families. There are lifeguards on all the beaches during the summer, but be aware that the worst undertow is on the northern stretches. Also please remember to leave the sand dollars where they are; their population is dwindling due to souvenir hunting.

Kayaking

Kayakers will enjoy Hilton Head Island, which offers several gorgeous routes, including Calibogue Sound to the south and west and Port Royal Sound to the north. For particularly good views of life on the salt marsh, try Broad Creek, which nearly bisects Hilton Head Island, and Skull Creek, which separates Hilton Head from the natural beauty of Pinckney Island. Broad Creek Marina is a good place to put in. There are also two public landings, Haigh Landing and Buckingham Landing, on Mackays Creek at the entrance to the island, one on either side of the bridge.

If you want a guided tour, there are plenty of great kayak tour outfits to choose from in the area. Chief among them is certainly **Outside Hilton Head** (32 Shelter Cove Ln., 800/686-6996, www.outsidehiltonhead.com). They offer a wide range of guided trips, including "The Outback," in which you're first boated to a private island and then taken on a tour of tidal creeks, and five- or seven-hour "Ultimate Lowcountry Day" trips to Daufuskie, Bluffton, or Bull Creek.

Other good places to book a tour or just rent a kayak are **Water-Dog Outfitters** (Broad Creek Marina, 843/686-3554) and **Kayak Hilton Head** (Broad Creek Marina, 843/684-1910). Leaving out of the Harbour Town Yacht Basin is **H2O Sports** (843/671-4386, www.h2osportsonline.com), which offers 90-minute guided kayak tours ($30) and rents kayaks for about $20 per hour.

Within Palmetto Dunes Oceanfront Resort (4 Queens Folly Rd., 800/827-3006, www.palmettodunes.com) is **Palmetto Dunes Outfitters** (843/785-2449, www.pdoutfitters.com, daily 9 A.M.–5 P.M.), which rents kayaks and canoes and offers lessons on the resort's 11-mile lagoon.

Fishing and Boating

As you'd expect, anglers and boaters love the Hilton Head/Bluffton area, which offers all kinds of saltwater, freshwater, and fly-fishing opportunities. Captain Brian Vaughn runs **Off the Hook Charters** (68 Helmsman Way, 843/298-4376, www.offthehookcharters.com), which offers fully licensed trips at $400 for a half-day. **Miss Carolina Sportfishing** (168 Palmetto Bay Rd., 843/298-2628, www.misscarolinafishing.com) offers deep-sea action at a little over $100 an hour. Captain Dave Fleming of **Mighty Mako Sport Fishing Charters** (164 Palmetto Bay Rd., 843/785-6028, www.mightymako.com) can take you saltwater fishing, both backwater and nearshore, on the 25-foot *Mighty Mako* for about $400 for a half-day.

If you're at the South Beach Marina area of Sea Pines Plantation head into **Blue Water Bait and Tackle** (843/671-3060) and see if they can hook you up with a trip.

Public landings in the Hilton Head area include the Marshland Road Boat Landing and the Broad Creek Boat Ramp under the Charles Fraser Bridge.

Hiking and Biking

Though the very flat terrain is not challenging, Hilton Head provides some scenic and relaxing biking opportunities. Thanks to wise planning and foresight, the island has an extensive 40-mile-plus network of biking trails that does a great job of keeping bikers out of traffic. A big plus is the long bike path paralleling the William Hilton Parkway, enabling cyclists to use that key artery without braving its traffic. There is even an underground bike path beneath the Parkway to facilitate crossing that busy road. In addition, there are also routes along Pope Avenue and North and South Forest Beach Drive.

Palmetto Dunes Oceanfront Resort (4 Queens Folly Rd., 800/827-3006, www.palmettodunes.com) has a particularly nice, 25-mile network of bike paths which all link up to the island's larger framework. Within the resort is **Palmetto Dunes Outfitters** (843/785-2449, www.pdoutfitters.com, daily 9 A.M.–5 P.M.), which will rent you any type of bike you might need. Sea Pines Plantation also has an extensive, 17-mile network of bike trails; you can pick up a map at most information kiosks within the plantation.

With the exception of Sea Pines, where five bucks gets you daily access, for biking purposes be aware that on the private residential developments, such as Palmetto Dunes, access technically is limited to residents and you may be challenged and asked where you're residing. Also, please pay attention to the miniature stop signs on the bike paths, ignorance of which can lead to some nasty scrapes or worse.

But the best bike path on Hilton Head is the simplest of all, where no one will ask you where you're staying that night: the beach. For a few hours before and after low tide the beach effectively becomes a 12-mile bike path around most of the island, and a pleasant morning or afternoon ride may well prove to be the highlight of your trip to the island. There's a plethora of bike rental facilities on

Hilton Head with competitive rates. Be sure to ask if they offer free pick-up and delivery. Try **Hilton Head Bicycle Company** (112 Arrow Rd., 843/686-6888, Mon.–Sat. 9 A.M.–5 P.M., Sun. noon–5 P.M.).

Hikers will particularly enjoy Pinckney Island National Wildlife Refuge, which takes you through several key Lowcountry ecosystems, from maritime forest to salt marsh. Other peaceful, if non-challenging, trails are at the Audubon-Newhall Preserve on Hilton Head Island.

Horseback Riding

Within the Sea Pines Forest Preserve is **Lawton Stables** (190 Greenwood Dr., 843/671-2586, www.lawtonstableshhi.com), which features pony rides, a small animal farm, and guided horseback rides through the Preserve. You don't need any riding experience, but you do need reservations.

Bird-Watching

The premier birding locale in the area is the **Pinckney Island National Wildlife Refuge** (U.S. 278 East just before Hilton Head, 912/652-4415, www.fws.gov). You can see bald eagles, ibis, wood storks, painted buntings, and many more species. Birding is best in spring and fall. The refuge has several freshwater ponds that serve as wading bird rookeries. During migratory season, so many beautiful birds abound here making such a ruckus that you'll think you wandered onto an Animal Planet shoot.

Another good bird-watching locale is **Victoria Bluff Heritage Preserve** (803/734-3886, daily dawn–dusk, free), a 1,100-acre pine-and-palmetto habitat. Get here from Hilton Head by taking U.S. 278 off the island. Take a right onto Sawmill Creek Road heading north. The parking area is shortly ahead on your right. Note that there are no facilities available here.

Golf

Hilton Head is one of the world's great golf centers, with no less than 23 courses, and one could easily write a book about nothing but that. This, however, is not that book. Perhaps contrary to what you might think, most courses on the island are public and some are downright affordable. (All courses are 18 holes unless otherwise described; green fees are averages and vary with season and tee time.)

The best-regarded course, with prices to match, is **Harbour Town Golf Links** (Sea Pines Plantation, 843/363-4485, www.seapines.com, $239). It's on the island's south end at Sea Pines and is the home of the annual Verizon Heritage Classic, far and away the island's number-one tourist draw.

There are two Arthur Hills–designed courses on the island, **Arthur Hills at Palmetto Dunes Resort** (843/785-1140, www.palmetto dunes.com, $125) and **Arthur Hills at Palmetto Hall** (Palmetto Hall Plantation, 843/689-4100, www.palmettohallgolf.com, $130), both of which now offer the use of Segway vehicles on the fairways.

The reasonably priced **Barony Course** at Port Royal Plantation (843/686-8801, www .portroyalgolfclub.com, $98) also boasts some of the toughest greens on the island. Another challenging and affordable course is the **George Fazio** at Palmetto Dunes Resort (843/785-1130, www.palmettodunes.com, $105).

Hilton Head National Golf Club (60 Hilton Head National Dr., 843/842-5900, www.golf hiltonheadnational.com), which is actually on the mainland just before you cross the bridge to Hilton Head, not only boasts a total of 27 challenging holes, but is consistently rated among the best golf locales in the world for both condition and service. *Golf Week* has named it one of America's best golf courses. All three courses here are public and green fees at each are below $100.

It's a good idea to book tee times through the **Golf Island Call Center** (888/465-3475, www.golfisland.com), which can also hook you up with good packages.

Tennis

One of the top tennis destinations in the country, Hilton Head has over 20 tennis clubs, some of which offer court time to the public (walk-on rates vary; call for information). They are: **Palmetto Dunes Tennis Center** (Palmetto Dunes Resort, 843/785-1152, www.palmetto dunes.com, $30/hr.), **Port Royal Racquet Club** (Port Royal Plantation, 843/686-8803, www .portroyalgolfclub.com, $25/hr.), **Sea Pines Racquet Club** (Sea Pines Plantation, 843/363-4495, www.seapines.com, $25/hr.), **South Beach Racquet Club** (Sea Pines Plantation, 843/671-2215, www.seapines.com, $25/hr.), and **Shipyard Racquet Club** (Shipyard Plantation, 843/686-8804, $25/hr.).

Free, first-come-first-served play is available at the following public courts maintained by the Island Recreation Association (www.island reccenter.org): **Chaplin Community Park** (Singleton Beach Rd., four courts, lighted), **Cordillo Courts** (Cordillo Pkwy., four courts, lighted), **Fairfield Square** (Adrianna Ln., two courts), **Hilton Head High School** (School Rd., six courts), and **Hilton Head Middle School** (Wilborn Rd., four courts).

ACCOMMODATIONS
Under $150

It won't blow you away, but you can't beat the price at **Park Lane Hotel and Suites** (12 Park Ln., 843/686-5700, www.hiltonheadpark lanehotel.com, $130). This is your basic suite-type hotel (formerly a Residence Inn) with the basic free Continental breakfast. The allure here is the price, hard to find anywhere these days at a resort location. For a non-refundable $50 fee, you can bring your pet. The one drawback, probably reflected in the price, is that the beach is a good ways away. The hotel does offer a free shuttle, however, so it would be wise to take advantage of that and avoid the usual beach parking hassles.

$150-300

By Hilton Head standards, the **Main Street Inn** (2200 Main St., 800/471-3001, www.main streetinn.com, $160–210) can be considered a bargain stay, and with high quality to boot. With its Old World touches, sumptuous appointments, charming atmosphere, and attentive service, this 33-room inn on the grounds of Hilton Head Plantation seems like it would be more at home in Charleston than Hilton Head. They serve a great full breakfast—not Continental—daily 7:30–10:30 A.M. As a bonus, most of the less-expensive rooms have a great view of the formal garden, another part of that old Lowcountry appeal that's hard to come by on the island. If you want to upgrade, there are larger rooms with a fireplace and a smallish private courtyard for not much more. Overall, it's one of Hilton Head's best values.

Another good place for the price is the **South Beach Marina Inn** (232 S. Sea Pines Dr., 843/671-6498, www.sbinn.com, $186) in Sea Pines. Located near the famous Salty Dog Café and outfitted in a similar nautical theme, the inn not only has some pretty large rooms for the price, it offers a great view of the marina and has a very friendly feel, great for families with kids and romantic couples alike (especially with a beach on calm Calibogue Sound only a couple minutes' walk away). As with all Sea Pines accommodations, staying on the plantation means you don't have to wait in line with other visitors to pay the $5 a day "road fee." Sea Pines also offers a free trolley to get around the plantation.

One of Hilton Head's favorite hotels for true beach-lovers is the **Holiday Inn Oceanfront** (1 South Forest Beach Dr., 843/785-5126, www .hihiltonhead.com, $200), home of the famed Tiki Hut bar on the beach. Staff turnover is less frequent here than at other local accommodations, and while it's no Ritz-Carlton and occasionally shows signs of wear, it's a good value on a bustling area of the island. Parking has always been a problem here, but at least there's a free valet service.

One of the better resort-type places for those who prefer the putter and the racquet to the Frisbee and the surfboard is the **Inn at Harbour Town** (7 Lighthouse Ln., 843/363-8100, www.seapines.com, $199) in Sea Pines. The big draw here is the impeccable service, delivered by a staff of "butlers" in kilts, comprising mostly Europeans who take the venerable trade quite seriously. While it's not on the beach, you can take advantage of the free Sea Pines Trolley every 20 minutes.

Recently rated the number-one family resort in the U.S. by *Travel + Leisure,* the well-run **❰ Palmetto Dunes Oceanfront Resort** (4 Queens Folly Rd., 800/827-3006, www.palmettodunes.com, $150–300) offers something for everybody in terms of lodging. There are small, cozy condos by the beach, or larger villas overlooking the golf course, and pretty much everything in between. The prices are perhaps disarmingly affordable considering the relative luxury and copious recreational amenities, which include 25 miles of very well-done bike trails, 11 miles of kayak/canoe trails, and of course three signature links. As with most developments of this type on Hilton Head, most of the condos are privately owned and therefore each has its particular set of guidelines and cleaning schedules.

Vacation Rentals

Many visitors to Hilton Head choose to rent a home or villa for an extended stay. Try **Resort Rentals of Hilton Head** www.hhivacations .com or **Destination Vacation** (www.desti nationvacationhhi.com).

FOOD

You'll have no problem finding good restaurants in and around Hilton Head. Because of the fairly cosmopolitan nature of the population, with so many transplants from the northeastern United States and Europe, you might be surprised by the quality.

Because of another demographic quirk of the area, its large percentage of senior citizens, you can also find some great deals by looking for some of the common "early bird" dinner specials, usually starting around 5 P.M.

Breakfast and Brunch

There are a couple of great diner-style places on the island. Though known more for its hamburgers and Philly cheesesteaks, **Harold's Diner** (641 William Hilton Pkwy., 843/842-9292, Mon.–Sat. 7 A.M.–3 P.M., $4–6) has great pancakes as well as its trademark brand of hilariously sarcastic service. Unpretentious and authentic in a place where those two adjectives are rarely used, Harold's is one of a few must-visit restaurants on Hilton Head. As one patron has said, "The lack of atmosphere *is* the atmosphere."

You'll find another great locally owned breakfast spot at **Skillets** (1 N. Forest Beach Dr., 843/785-3131, www.skilletscafe.com, breakfast daily 7 A.M.–5 P.M., dinner daily 5–9 P.M., $5–23) in Coligny Plaza. Their eponymous stock in trade is a layered breakfast dish of sautéed ingredients served in a porcelain skillet, like the "Kitchen Sink" (pancakes ringed with potatoes, sausage, and bacon, topped with two poached eggs). The lunches are good too, including, believe it or not, an excellent meatloaf. Dinner is surprisingly upscale; try any of the excellent seafood dishes, like the blackened shrimp and scallops with tasso ham and blue cheese.

A great all-day breakfast place with a twist is ❰ **Signe's Heaven Bound Bakery & Café** (93 Arrow Rd., 843/785-9118, www.signes bakery.com, Mon.–Fri. 8 A.M.–4 P.M., Sat. 9 A.M.–2 P.M., $5–10). The breakfast comprises tasty dishes like frittatas and breakfast polenta, while the twist is the extensive artisan bakery, with delicious specialties like the signature key lime pound cake. You'll be surprised at the quality of the food for the low prices. Expect a wait in line at the counter during peak periods.

Mediterranean

For upscale Italian, try **Bistro Mezzaluna** (55 New Orleans Rd., 843/842-5011, daily 5–9:30 P.M.). Known far and wide for its osso bucco as well as its impeccable service, there's also a great little bar for cocktails before or after dinner.

Mexican

There are a couple of excellent and authentic Mexican restaurants on the island. Just off the William Hilton Parkway near the island's entrance is ❰ **Mi Tierra** (160 Fairfield Square, 843/342-3409, lunch daily 11 A.M.–4 P.M., dinner Mon.–Fri. 4–9 P.M., Sat.–Sun. 4–10 P.M., $3–15). You'll find lots of traditional seafood dishes here, like ceviche,

octopus, shrimp, and oysters. Mondays often host a real Mariachi band.

Another great Mexican place—also with a Bluffton location—is **Amigo's Café Y Cantina** (70 Pope Ave., 843/785-8226, Mon.–Sat. 11 A.M.–9 P.M., $8). While its strip-mall locale is not great, the food is fresh, simple, excellent, fast, and inexpensive.

Seafood

Not to be confused with Charley's Crab House next door to Hudson's, seafood lovers will enjoy the experience down near Sea Pines at ❰ **Charlie's L'Etoile Verte** (8 New Orleans Rd., 843/785-9277, www .charliesofhiltonhead.com, lunch Tues.– Sat. 11:30 A.M.–2 P.M., dinner Mon.–Sat. 6–9:30 P.M., $25–40), which is considered by many connoisseurs to be Hilton Head's single best restaurant. The emphasis here is on "French country kitchen" cuisine—think Provence, not Paris. In keeping, each day's menu is concocted from scratch and handwritten. Listen to these recent entrées and feel your mouth water: flounder saute Meuniere, grilled wild coho salmon with a basil pesto, and breast of duck in a raspberry demi-glace. Get the picture? Of course you'll want to start with the escargot and leeks vol-au-vent, the house paté, or even some pan-roasted Bluffton oysters. As you'd expect, the wine selection is celestial. Reservations are essential.

Perhaps the most unique restaurant on Hilton Head is **Red Fish** (8 Archer Rd., 843/686-3388, www.redfishofhiltonhead .com, lunch Mon.–Sat. 11:30 A.M.–2 P.M., dinner daily beginning with early-bird specials at 5 P.M., $20–37). Strongly Caribbean in decor as well as menu, with romanticism and panache to match, this is a great place for couples. The creative but accessible menu by executive chef Sean Walsh incorporates unique spices, fruits, and vegetables for a fresh, zesty palate. The recommended course of action is to pick your own wine from the truly vast, thousand-bottle-plus, award-winning selection in the attached wine shop and cellar to go with your dinner. Highlights include the grilled grouper with mango avocado salsa, the horseradish-encrusted salmon, and the Dominican braised pork. Reservations are essential.

Fresh seafood lovers will enjoy one of Hilton Head's staples, the huge **Hudson's on the Docks** (1 Hudson Rd., 843/681-2772, www.hudsonsonthedocks.com, lunch daily 11 A.M.–4 P.M., opens for dinner at 5 P.M., $14–23) on Skull Creek just off Squire Pope Road on the less-developed north side. Much of the catch—though not all of it by any means—comes directly off the boats you'll see dockside. Built on the old family oyster factory, Hudson's is now owned by transplants from, of all places, Long Island, New York. Try the stuffed shrimp, filled with crabmeat, or just go for a combination platter. Leave room for one of the home-made desserts crafted by Ms. Bessie, a 30-year veteran employee of Hudson's.

INFORMATION AND SERVICES

The best place to get information on Hilton Head, book a room, or secure a tee time is just as you come onto the island at the **Hilton Head Island Chamber of Commerce Welcome Center** (100 William Hilton Pkwy., 843/785-3673, www.hiltonheadisland.org, daily 9 A.M.–6 P.M.). It's in the same building as the Coastal Discovery Museum.

Hilton Head's paper of record is the *Island Packet* (www.islandpacket.com).

Hilton Head's **post office** (13 William Hilton Pwy., 843/893-3490) is in an easy-to-find location.

GETTING THERE AND AROUND

A few years back, the Savannah International Airport added Hilton Head to its name specifi-cally to identify itself with that lucrative mar-ket. It's been a success, and this facility remains the closest large airport to Hilton Head Island and Bluffton. From the airport go north on I-95 into South Carolina, and take exit 8 onto U.S. 278 east.

There is a local regional airport as well, the Hilton Head Island Airport (120 Beach City Rd., 843/689-5400, www.bcgov.net, airport code HXD). While very attractive and con-venient, keep in mind it only hosts propeller-driven commuter planes because of concerns about noise and runway length.

If you're entering the area by car, the best route is exit 8 off of I-95 onto U.S. 278, which takes you by Bluffton and right into Hilton Head. Near Bluffton, U.S. 278 is called Fording Island Road, and on Hilton Head proper it becomes the William Hilton Parkway business route. Technically, U.S. 278 turns into the new Cross Island Parkway, but when most locals say "278" they're almost always referring to the William Hilton Parkway.

Other than taxi services, there is no public transportation to speak of in the Lowcountry, unless you want to count the free shut-tle around Sea Pines Plantation. Taxi ser-vices include **Yellow Cab** (843/686-6666), **Island Taxi** (843/683-6363), and **Ferguson Transportation** (843/842-8088).

Bluffton and Daufuskie Island

Just outside Hilton Head are two of the Lowcountry's true gems, Bluffton and Daufuskie Island. While Bluffton's outskirts have been taken over by the same gated com-munity sprawl spreading throughout the coast, at its core is a delightfully charming little com-munity on the quiet May River, now called Old Bluffton, where you'd swear you just en-tered a time warp.

Daufuskie Island still maintains much of its age-old isolated, timeless personality, and the island—still accessible by boat only—is still one of the spiritual centers of the Gullah culture and lifestyle.

◖ OLD BLUFFTON

Similar to Beaufort, except even quieter and smaller, historic Bluffton is an idyllic village on the banks of the hypnotically serene and well-preserved May River. Bluffton was the original hotbed of secession, with Charleston diarist Mary Chesnut famously referring to the town as "the center spot of the fire eaters."

While its outskirts (so-called "Greater Bluffton") are now a haven for planned communities hoping to mimic some aspect of Bluffton's historic patina, the town center itself remains an authentic look at old South Carolina. Retro cuts both ways, however, and Bluffton has been a notorious speed trap for generations. Always obey the speed limit.

During their Civil War occupation, Union troops repaid the favor of those original Bluffton secessionists, which is why only nine homes in Bluffton are of antebellum vintage; the rest were torched in a search for Confederate guerrillas.

The center of tourist activity focuses on the **Old Bluffton Historic District,** several blocks of 1800s buildings clustered between the parallel Boundary and Calhoun Streets (old-timers sometimes call this the "original square mile"). Many of the buildings are private residences, but most have been converted into art studios and antiques stores. The wares feature a whimsical, folk art quality very much in tune with Bluffton's whole Southern Shangri-la feel. While the artists and shopkeepers are serious about their work, they make it a point to warmly invite everyone in, even when they're busy at work on the latest project.

Heyward House Historic Center

The Heyward House Historic Center (70 Boundary St., 843/757-6293, www.heyward house.org, Mon.–Fri. 10 A.M.–3 P.M., Sat. 11 A.M.–2 P.M., tours $5 adults, $2 students) is not only open to tours but serves as Bluffton's visitors center. Built in 1840 as a summer home for the owner of Moreland Plantation, John Cole, the house was later owned by George Cuthbert Heyward, grandson of Declaration of Independence signer Thomas Heyward. (Remarkably, it stayed in the family until the 1990s.) Of note are the intact slave quarters on the grounds.

The Heyward House also sponsors walking tours of the historic district by appointment only (843/757-6293, $15). Download your own walking tour map at www.heywardhouse.org.

Church of the Cross

Don't fail to go all the way to the end of Calhoun Street as it dead-ends on a high bluff on the May River at the Bluffton Public Dock. Overlooking this peaceful marsh-front vista is the sublimely photogenic Church of the Cross (110 Calhoun St., 843/757-2661, www.thechurchofthecross.net, tours Mon.–Sat. 10 A.M.–2 P.M.).

Though the current sanctuary was built in 1854 and is one of only two local churches not burned in the Civil War, the parish itself began in 1767, with the first services on this spot held in the late 1830s. Standing here on the bluff, with the steady south breeze blowing the bugs away and relieving you of the Lowcountry heat, you can see why affluent South Carolinians began building summer homes here in the 1800s.

While the church looks as if it were made of cypress, interestingly it's actually constructed of heart pine.

© JIM MOREKIS

Church of the Cross

Bluffton Oyster Company

You might want to get a gander at the state's last remaining working oyster house, the Bluffton Oyster Company (63 Wharf St., 843/757-4010, Mon.–Sat. 9 A.M.–5:30 P.M.), and possibly purchase some of their maritime bounty. The adjoining five acres were recently purchased by the Beaufort County Open Land Trust with the intention of evolving the area into a community greenspace celebrating a key aspect of local heritage, the celebrated May River oyster. Meanwhile Larry and Tina Toomer continue to oversee the oyster harvesting-and-shucking family enterprise, which has roots going back to the early 1900s.

Waddell Mariculture Center

While the oysters are growing scarce on the May River, get a close-up look at an interesting state-funded seafood farm on the Colleton River estuary, the Waddell Mariculture Center (Sawmill Creek Rd., 843/837-3795). Free tours are available Monday, Tuesday, Wednesday, and Friday mornings. Shrimp, fish, and shellfish are some of the "product" raised and harvested here. Get to Waddell by taking U.S. 278

east out of Bluffton and then taking a left on Sawmill Creek Road.

SHOPPING

Bluffton's eccentric little art studios, most clustered in a two-block stretch on Calhoun Street, are by far its main shopping draw. Named for the Lowcountry phenomenon you find in the marsh at low tide amongst the fiddler crabs, Bluffton's **Pluff Mudd Art** (27 Calhoun St., 843/757-5551, Mon.–Sat. 10 A.M.–5:30 P.M.) is a cooperative of 16 great young painters and photographers from throughout the area.

The **Guild of Bluffton Artists** (20 Calhoun St., 843/757-5590, Mon.–Sat., 10 A.M.–4:30 P.M.) features works from many local artists, as does the outstanding **Society of Bluffton Artists** (48 Boundary St., 843/757-6586).

For cool, custom handcrafted pottery, try **Preston Pottery and Gallery** (10 Church St., 843/757-3084). Another great Bluffton place is the hard-to-define **eggs'n'tricities** (71 Calhoun St., 843/757-3446). The name pretty much says it all for this fun and eclectic vintage/junk/jewelry/folk art store.

If you want to score some fresh local seafood

© JIM MOREKIS

Old Bluffton features many interesting shops.

BEAUFORT

Bluffton Oyster Company

for your own culinary adventure, the no-brainer choice is the **Bluffton Oyster Company** (63 Wharf St., 843/757-4010), the state's only active oyster facility. They also have shrimp, crab, clams, and fish, nearly all of it from the nearly pristine May River on whose banks it sits.

For a much more commercially intense experience, head just outside of town on U.S. 278 on the way to Hilton Head to find the dual **Tanger Outlet Centers** (1414 Fording Island Rd., 843/837-4339, Mon.–Sat. 10 A.M.–9 P.M., Sun. 11 A.M.–6 P.M.), an outlet-shopper's paradise with virtually every major brand represented, from Nine West to Ralph Lauren to Abercrombie & Fitch and dozens more, including new additions Skechers and the Limited Too. A serious shopper can easily spend most of a day here between its two sprawling malls, Tanger I and Tanger II, so be forewarned!

SPORTS AND RECREATION

A key kayaking outfitter in Bluffton is **Native Guide Kayak Tours** (8 2nd St., 843/757-5411, www.nativeguidetours.com), which features tours of the May and New Rivers led by native Ben Turner. Another good outfit is **Swamp Girls Kayak Tours** (843/784-2249, www.swampgirls.com), the labor of love of Sue Chapman and Linda Etchells.

To put in your own kayak or canoe on the scenic, well-preserved May River, go to the **Alljoy Landing** at the eastern terminus of Alljoy Road along the river. Or try the dock at the end of Calhoun Street near the Church of the Holy Cross. There's also a rough put-in area at the Bluffton Oyster Company (63 Wharf St.), which has a public park adjacent to it. For fishing, public landings include the dock on Calhoun Street, Alljoy Landing, and Bluffton Oyster Company.

For a much more wild hiking and bird-watching experience, go north of Bluffton to **Victoria Bluff Heritage Preserve** (803/734-3886, daily dawn–dusk, free), a 1,100-acre flatwoods habitat notable for featuring all four native species of palmetto tree. There are no facilities, and a lot of hunting goes on in November and December. Get here from Bluffton by taking Burnt Church Road to U.S.

278. Take a right onto U.S. 278 and then a left onto Sawmill Creek Road heading north. The parking area is shortly ahead on your right.

The closest public golf courses to Bluffton are the Arnold Palmer–designed **Crescent Pointe Golf Club** (1 Crescent Pointe Dr., 888/292-7778, www.crescentpointegolf.com, $90) and the nine-hole **Old Carolina Golf Club** (89 Old Carolina Rd., 888/785-7274, www.oldcarolinagolf.com, $26), certainly one of the best golf deals in the region.

ACCOMMODATIONS
Under $150
A quality bargain stay right between Bluffton and Hilton Head is the **Holiday Inn Express Bluffton** (35 Bluffton Rd., 843/757-2002, www.ichotelsgroup.com, $120), on U.S. 278 as you make the run onto Hilton Head proper. It's not close to the beach or to Old Town Bluffton, so you'll definitely be using your car, but its central location will appeal to those who want to keep their options open.

Over $300
For an ultra-upscale spa and golf resort environment near Bluffton, the clear pick is the **Inn at Palmetto Bluff** (476 Mt. Pelia Rd., 843/706-6500, www.palmettobluffresort.com, $650–900) just across the May River. This Auberge property was picked in 2006 as the number-two U.S. resort by *Condé Nast Traveler* magazine. Despite its glitzy pedigree and extremely upper-end prices, it's more Tara than Trump Tower. The main building is modeled after a Lowcountry plantation home, and the idyllic views of the May River are blissful. Lodging is dispersed among a series of cottages and "village home" rentals.

Needless to say, virtually your every need is provided for here, though the nearest off-site restaurant of any quality is quite a drive away. That will likely make little difference to you, however, since there are three top-flight dining options on the grounds: the fine dining **River House Restaurant** (843/706-6542, breakfast daily 7–11 A.M., lunch or "porch" menu daily 11 A.M.–10 P.M., dinner daily 6–10 P.M., $30–40); the **May River Grill** (Tues.–Sat. 11 A.M.–4 P.M., $9–13) at the golf clubhouse; and the casual **Buffalo's** (843/706-6630, Sun.–Tues. 11:30 A.M.–5 P.M., Wed.–Sat. 11:30 A.M.–9 P.M., $10–15).

FOOD
Breakfast and Brunch
No discussion of Bluffton cuisine is complete without the famous **Squat 'n' Gobble** (1231 May River Rd., 843/757-4242, daily 24 hours) a wholly local phenomenon, not to be confused with a similarly named chain of eateries in California. Long a site of gossiping and politicking as well as, um, squatting and gobbling, this humble diner on the May River Road in town is an indelible part of the local consciousness. Believe it or not, despite the totally unpretentious greasy-spoon ambience—or because of it—the food's actually quite good. They specialize in the usual "American" menu of eggs, bacon, hamburgers, hot dogs, and fries. There's a tie for best thing on the menu—I can't decide whether the Greek pizza is better or the barbecue, so I'll go with both.

Classic Southern
Another beloved Bluffton institution (and Blufftonians love their institutions) is **Pepper's Porch** (1255 May River Rd., 843/757-2295, Tues.–Sun. 11:30 A.M.–9 P.M., $12–20). Housed in an old barn for drying a local herb called deer tongue, this is the kind of distinctly Southern place where they bring out a basket of little corn muffins instead of bread. Entrées include a great stuffed grouper and delicious, fresh-fried shrimp. Don't miss the fried strawberry dessert, which tastes a million times better than it sounds. Weekends see live music and karaoke in the aptly named Back Bar, a favorite local hangout.

Prime rib is the house specialty at **Myrtle's Bar & Grill** (32 Bruin Rd., 843/757-6300, lunch Tues.–Fri. 11:30 A.M.–2:30 P.M., dinner Tues.–Sat. 5–9:30 P.M., brunch Sun. 10 A.M.–2 P.M.), generally served on Tuesday nights. They also do a mean flounder. Housed in the old post office, Myrtle's is a favorite local hangout and has recently begun hosting an interactive murder-mystery dinner theater show.

French

Most dining in Bluffton is pretty casual, but you'll get the white tablecloth treatment at **Claude & Uli's Signature Bistro** (1533 Fording Island Rd., 843/837-3336, lunch Mon.–Fri. 11:30 A.M.–2:30 P.M., dinner Mon.–Sat. starting at 5 P.M., $18–25) just outside of town in Moss Village. Chef Claude has brought his extensive European training and background (including Maxim's in Paris) to this romantic little spot. Claude does a great veal cordon bleu as well as a number of fine seafood entrées, such as an almond-crusted tilapia and an excellent seafood pasta. Don't miss their specialty soufflé for dessert, which

WHO ARE THE GULLAH?

A language, a culture, and a people with a shared history, Gullah is more than that – it's also a state of mind.

Simply put, the Gullah are African Americans of the Sea Islands of South Carolina and Georgia. (In Georgia, the term "Geechee," from the nearby Ogeechee River, is more or less interchangeable.) Protected from outside influence by the isolation of this coastal region after the Civil War, Gullah culture is the closest living cousin to the West African traditions of their ancestors imported as slaves.

While you might hear that "Gullah" is a corruption of "Angola," some linguists think it simply means "people" in a West African language. In any case, the Gullah speak what's known as a "creole" language, i.e., one derived from several sources. Gullah combines elements of Elizabethan English, Jamaican patois, and several West African dialects; for example "goober" (peanut) comes from the Congo *n'guba.*

Another creole element is a word with multiple uses, for example Gullah's *shum* could mean "see them," "see him," "see her," or "see it," in either past or present tense, depending on context.

Though several white writers in the 1900s published collections of Gullah folk tales, for the most part the Gullah tongue was simply considered broken English. That changed with the publication of Lorenzo Dow Turner's groundbreaking *Africanisms in the Gullah Dialect* in 1949. Turner traced elements of the language to Sierra Leone in West Africa and more than 300 Gullah words directly to Africa.

Gullah is typically spoken very rapidly,

which of course only adds to its impenetrability to the outsider. Gullah also relies on colorful turns of phrase. *"E tru mout"* ("He true mouth") means the speaker is referring to someone who doesn't lie. *"Ie een crack muh teet"* ("I didn't even crack my teeth") means "I kept quiet." A forgetful Gullah speaker might say, *"Mah head leab me"* ("My head left me").

Gullah music, as practiced by the world-famous Hallelujah Singers of St. Helena Island, also uses many distinctly African techniques, such as call and response (the folk hymn "Michael Row the Boat Ashore" is a good example).

The most famous Americans with Gullah roots are boxer Joe Frazier (Beaufort), hip-hop star Jazzy Jay (Beaufort), NFL great Jim Brown (St. Simons Island, Georgia), and Supreme Court Justice Clarence Thomas (Pin Point, Georgia, near Savannah).

Upscale development continues to claim more and more traditional Gullah areas, generally by pricing them out through rapidly increasing property values. Today, the major pockets of living Gullah culture in South Carolina are in Beaufort, St. Helena Island, Daufuskie Island, Edisto Island, and a northern section of Hilton Head Island.

The old ways are not as prevalent as they were, but several key institutions are keeping alive the spirit of Gullah: the **Penn Center** (16 Martin Luther King Dr., 843/838-2474, www.penncenter.com, Mon.–Sat. 11 A.M.–4 P.M., $4 adults, $2 seniors and children) on St. Helena Island near Beaufort; the **Avery Research Center** (66 George St., 843/953-7609, www.cofc.edu/avery, Mon.–Fri. 10 A.M.–5 P.M., Sat.

you should order with dinner as it takes almost a half-hour to bake.

Mexican

My favorite restaurant in Bluffton by far is a near-copy of an equally fine Mexican restaurant in Hilton Head, ((**Mi Tierra** (101 Mellichamp Center, 843/757-7200, lunch daily 11 A.M.–4 P.M., dinner Mon.–Fri. 4–9 P.M.,

noon–5 P.M.) at the College of Charleston; and **Geechee Kunda** (622 Ways Temple Rd., 912/884-4440, www.geecheekunda.net) in Riceboro, Georgia, near Midway off U.S. Highway 17.

example of Gullah art: "Baptismal" by artist Allen Fireall at Red Piano Too, an art gallery on St. Helena Island near Beaufort

Sat.–Sun. 4–10 P.M., $3–15). They have very high-quality Tex-Mex-style food in a fun atmosphere at great prices.

Another highly regarded Mexican place in Bluffton is **Amigo's Café Y Cantina** (133 Towne Dr., 843/815-8226, Mon.–Sat. 11 A.M.–9 P.M., $8).

INFORMATION AND SERVICES

You'll find Bluffton's visitors center in the **Heyward House Historic Center** (70 Boundary St., 843/757-6293, www.heyward house.org).

A good Bluffton publication is *Bluffton Today* (www.blufftontoday.com).

If you need postal services, Bluffton also has its own **post office** (32 Bruin Rd., 843/757-3588).

DAUFUSKIE ISLAND

Sitting between Savannah and Hilton Head Island and accessible only by water, Daufuskie Island has about 500 full-time residents, most of whom ride around on golf carts or bikes (there's only one paved road, Haig Point Road, and cars are a rare sight). Once the home of rice and indigo plantations and rich oyster beds—the latter destroyed by pollution and overharvesting—the two upscale residential resort communities on the island, begun in the 1980s, give a clue as to where the future lies, though the recent global economic downturn has slowed development to a standstill.

The area of prime interest to tourists is the unincorporated western portion, or **Historic District,** the old stomping grounds of Pat Conroy during his stint as a teacher of resident African American children. His old two-room schoolhouse of *The Water Is Wide* fame, the **Mary Field School,** is still there, as is the adjacent 140-year-old **Union Baptist Church,** but Daufuskie students now have a surprisingly modern new facility (middle school students are still ferried to mainland schools every day).

Farther north on Haig Point Road is the new **Billie Burn Museum,** housed in the old Mt. Carmel Church and named after the island's resident historian. On the southern end

BEAUFORT

you'll find the **Bloody Point Lighthouse,** named for the vicious battle fought nearby during the Yamasee War of 1815 (the light was actually moved a half-mile inland in the early 1900s). Other areas of interest throughout the island include Native American sites, tabby ruins, the old Baptist Church, and a couple of cemeteries.

Otherwise there's really not much to do on Daufuskie. It's a place where you go to see a slice of Sea Island and Gullah history and relax, relax, relax. While at one time there was an operating resort and spa on the island, as of this writing it was bankrupt and closed, with no clear plans to reopen.

For the freshest island seafood, check out the **Old Daufuskie Crab Company** (Freeport Marina, 843/785-6652, daily 11:30 A.M.–9 P.M., $7–22).

A public ferry to and from Daufuskie from Hilton Head is **Calibogue Cruises** (843/342-8687). It brings you in on the landward side of the island, and from there you can take shuttles or rent golf carts or bikes.

For overnight stays, you can rent a humble cabin at **Freeport Marina** (843/785-8242, rates vary).

BEAUFORT

Points Inland

It's very likely that at some point you'll find yourself traveling inland from Beaufort, given that area's proximity to I-95. While generally more known for offering interstate drivers a bite to eat and a place to rest their heads, there are several spots worth checking out in their own right, especially Walterboro and the Savannah National Wildlife Refuge.

WALTERBORO
The very picture of the slow, moss-drenched Lowcountry town—indeed, the municipal logo is the silhouette of a live oak tree—Walterboro is a delightful, artsy oasis. Right off I-95, Walterboro serves as a gateway of sorts to the Lowcountry, and the cheap commercial sprawl on the interstate shows it. But don't be put off by this ugliness—once you get into town it's as charming as they come, with roots dating back to 1783 and offering the added bonus of being one of the best antiquing locales in South Carolina. Convenient and eminently walkable, the two-block Arts and Antiques District on Washington Street centers on a dozen antiques stores on the town's main drag, interspersed with gift shops and eateries.

Sights
SOUTH CAROLINA ARTISANS CENTER
If in town, don't miss the South Carolina

Artisans Center (334 Wichman St., 843/549-0011, Mon.–Sat. 10 A.M.–6 P.M., Sun. 1–6 P.M., free), an expansive and vibrant collection of the best work of local and regional painters, sculptors, jewelers, and other craftspeople, for sale and for enjoyment. Imagine a big-city folk art gallery, except without the pretension, and you get the idea. It's not on the main drag, but it's only about a block around the corner, so there's no excuse not to drop in.

You can find most any genre represented here, from jewelry to watercolors to shawls to photography to sweetgrass baskets. The Artisans Center hosts numerous receptions, and every third Saturday of the month they hold live artist demonstrations from 11 A.M.–3 P.M.

MUSEUMS
Walterboro and Colleton County boast three museums. The **Colleton Museum** (239 N. Jefferies Blvd., 843/549-2303, www.colletoncounty.org, Tues.–Fri. 10 A.M.–5 P.M., Sat. noon–4 P.M., free) is in the 1855 "Old Jail" downtown, and houses exhibits exploring area history and culture from dinosaurs to the present day. This is also where you can pick up a good self-guided walking tour of the whole town. The **Bedon-Lucas House Museum** (205 Church St., 843/549-9633, tours by appointment, $3 adults, 7 and under free) was built

BEAUFORT

© JIM MOREKIS

the South Carolina Artisans Center

by a local planter in 1820. An example of the local style of "high house," built off the ground to escape mosquitoes and catch the breeze, the house today is a nice mix of period furnishings and unadorned simplicity.

The **Slave Relic Museum** (208 Carn St., 843/549-9130, www.slaverelics.org, Mon.– Thurs. 9:30 A.M.–5 P.M., Sat. 10 A.M.–3 P.M., $6 adults, $5 children) houses the area Center for Research and Preservation of the African American Culture. It features artifacts, photos, and documents detailing the Atlantic passage, slave life, and the Underground Railroad.

TUSKEGEE AIRMEN MEMORIAL
Yes, the Tuskegee Airmen of World War II fame were from Alabama, not South Carolina. But a contingent trained in Walterboro, at the site of the present-day Lowcountry Regional Airport (537 Aviation Way, 843/549-2549) a short ways south of downtown on U.S. 17. Today, on a publicly accessible, low-security area of the airport, stands the Tuskegee Airmen Memorial, an outdoor monument to these brave flyers. There's a bronze statue and several interpretive exhibits.

GREAT SWAMP SANCTUARY
A short ways out of town in the other direction is the Great Swamp Sanctuary (www .thegreatswamp.org, daily dawn–dusk, free), a still-developing ecotourism project focusing on the Lowcountry environment. Located in one of the few braided-creek habitats accessible to the public, the 842-acre Sanctuary has three miles of walking and biking trails, some along the path of the old Charleston-Savannah stagecoach route. Kayakers and canoeists can paddle along over two miles of winding creeks. A 10,000 square-foot interpretive center is in the works.

There are three entry points to the Great Swamp Sanctuary, all off Jefferies Boulevard. Here they are in west-to-east order from I-95: north onto Beach Road, north onto Detreville Street (this is considered the main entrance), and west onto Washington Street.

Accommodations and Food
If you're looking for big-box lodging, the section of Walterboro close to I-95 is chockablock with it. The quality is surprisingly good, perhaps because they tend to cater to northerners on their way to and from Florida.

TUSKEGEE AIRMEN IN WALTERBORO

In a state where all too often African American history is studied in the context of slavery, a refreshing change is the tale of the Tuskegee Airmen, one of the most-lauded American military units of World War II. Though named for their origins at Alabama's Tuskegee Institute, the pilots of the famed 332nd Fighter Group actually completed final training in South Carolina at Walterboro Army Airfield, where the regional airport now sits.

The U.S. military was segregated during World War II, with African Americans mostly relegated to support roles. An interesting exception was the case of the 332nd, formed in 1941 as the 99th Pursuit Squadron by an act of Congress and the only all-black flying unit in the American military at the time. For the most part flying P-47 Thunderbolts and P-51 Mustangs, the pilots of the 332nd had one of the toughest missions of the war: escorting bombers over the skies of Germany and protecting them from Luftwaffe fighters. Though initially viewed with skepticism, the Tuskegee Airmen wasted no time in proving their mettle.

In fact, it wasn't long before U.S. bomber crews – who were, needless to say, all white – specifically requested that they be escorted by the Airmen, who were given the nickname "Red-Tail Angels" because of the distinctive markings of their aircraft. (While legend has it that the 332nd never lost a bomber, this claim has been debunked. But as Tuskegee Airman Bill Holloman said: "The Tuskegee story is about pilots who rose above adversity and discrimination and opened a door once closed to black America, not about whether their record is perfect.") The 332nd's reputation for aggressiveness in air combat was so widely known that the Germans also had a nickname for them – *Schwartze Vogelmenschen*, or "Black Bird Men."

Today Walterboro honors the Airmen with a monument on the grounds of the Lowcountry Regional Airport, on U.S. 17 just northeast of town. In an easily accessible part of the airport grounds, the monument features a bronze statue and several interpretive exhibits. Another place to catch up on Tuskegee Airmen history is at the **Colleton Museum** (239 N. Jefferies Blvd., 843/549-2303, Tues.-Fri. 10 A.M.-5 P.M., Sat. noon-4 P.M., free), which has a permanent exhibit on the pilots and their history in the Walterboro area.

Walterboro Army Airfield's contribution to the war effort was not limited to the Tuskegee Airmen, however. Seven of the famed Doolittle Raiders were trained here, there was a compound for holding German prisoners of war, and it was also the site of the U.S. military's largest camouflage school.

monument to the Tuskegee Airmen at the Walterboro airport

© JIM MOREKIS

A good choice is **Holiday Inn Express & Suites** (1834 Sniders Hwy., 843/538-2700, www.hiexpress.com, $85), or try the **Comfort Inn & Suites** (97 Downs Lane, 843/538-5911, www.choicehotels.com, $95).

If you'd like something with a bit more character, there are two B&Bs on Hampton Street downtown. **Old Academy Bed & Breakfast** (904 Hampton St., 843/549-3232, www.oldacademybandb.com, $80–115) has four rooms housed in Walterboro's first school building. They offer a full Continental breakfast. Note that credit cards are not accepted! Though built recently by local standards, the 1912 **Hampton House Bed and Breakfast** (500 Hampton St., 843/542-9498, www.hamptonhousebandb.com, $125–145) has three well-appointed rooms and offers a full country breakfast. By appointment only, you can see the Forde Doll and Dollhouse Collection, with over 50 dollhouses and oodles of antique dolls.

The story of food in Walterboro revolves around **(Duke's Barbecue** (949 Robertson Blvd., 843/549-1446, $7), one of the best-regarded barbecue spots in the Lowcountry and one of the top two joints named "Duke's" in the state (the other, by common consensus, is in Orangeburg). The pulled pork is delectable, cooked with the indigenous South Carolina mustard-based sauce. Unlike most area barbecue restaurants, some attention is devoted to the veggies, such as collard greens, green beans, and black-eyed peas with rice.

HARDEEVILLE

For most travelers, Hardeeville is known for its plethora of low-budget lodging and garish fireworks stores at the intersection of I-95 and U.S. 17. Truth be told, that's about all that's there.

However, train buffs will enjoy getting a gander at the rare and excellently restored **Narrow Gauge Locomotive** near the intersection of U.S. 17 and Highway 46. Donated by the Argent Lumber Company in 1960, Engine #7 memorializes the role of the timber industry in the area.

If you're hungry in Hardeeville, go straight to **(Mi Tierrita** (U.S. 17 and I-95, 843/784-5011, $5), an excellent, authentic Mexican restaurant near the I-95/U.S. 17 confluence. It's pretty beat-up on the inside, but the food is delicious and many steps above the typical watered-down Tex-Mex you find in the Southeast.

If barbecue's your thing, go on Highway 170A on the "backside" of Hardeeville in the hamlet of Levy to **The Pink Pig** (3508 South Okatie Hwy., 843/784-3635, www.the-pink-pig.com, Tues.–Wed. and Sat. 11 A.M.–3 P.M., Thurs.–Fri. 11 A.M.–3 P.M. and 5–7 P.M., $5–15). They offer three sauces: honey mustard, spicy, and "Gullah." The place is surprisingly hip, with good music piped-in and a suitably cutesy, kid-friendly decor with plenty of the eponymous rosy porcine figures.

SAVANNAH NATIONAL WILDLIFE REFUGE

Roughly equally divided between Georgia and South Carolina, the sprawling, 30,000-acre Savannah National Wildlife Refuge (912/652-4415, www.fws.gov/savannah, daily dawn–dusk, free) is a premier bird-watching and nature-observing locale in the Southeast. As with many refuges in the coastal Southeast, it's located on former plantations. The system of dikes and paddies once used to grow rice now helps make this an attractive stopover for migrating birds.

Bird-watching is best from October–April, with the winter months best for viewing migratory waterfowl. While you can kayak yourself on miles of creeks, you can also call **Swamp Girls Kayak Tours** (843/784-2249, www.swampgirls.com), who work out of nearby Hardeeville, for a guided tour.

To get here, take exit 5 off I-95 onto U.S. 17. Go south to U.S. 170 and look for the Laurel Hill Wildlife Drive. Be sure to stop by the brand-new visitors center.

BEAUFORT

www.moon.com

DESTINATIONS | ACTIVITIES | BLOGS | MAPS | BOOKS

MOON.COM is ready to help plan your next trip! Filled with fresh trip ideas and strategies, author interviews, informative travel blogs, a detailed map library, and descriptions of all the Moon guidebooks, Moon.com is all you need to get out and explore the world—or even places in your own backyard. While at Moon.com, sign up for our monthly e-newsletter for updates on new releases, travel tips, and expert advice from our on-the-go Moon authors. As always, when you travel with Moon, expect an experience that is uncommon and truly unique.

MOON IS ON FACEBOOK—BECOME A FAN!
JOIN THE MOON PHOTO GROUP ON FLICKR

MAP SYMBOLS

▦ Expressway	◖ Highlight	✈ Airport	⚓ Golf Course
═ Primary Road	○ City/Town	✗ Airfield	Ⓟ Parking Area
═ Secondary Road	◉ State Capital	▲ Mountain	▰ Archaeological Site
▩ Unpaved Road	⊛ National Capital	✛ Unique Natural Feature	⛪ Church
▪▪▪ Trail	★ Point of Interest		
▪▪▪ Ferry	• Accommodation	🌀 Waterfall	⛽ Gas Station
▦ Railroad	▾ Restaurant/Bar	⚑ Park	Glacier
▓ Pedestrian Walkway	▪ Other Location	ⓣ Trailhead	Mangrove
▦ Stairs	⅄ Campground	⛷ Skiing Area	Reef
			Swamp

CONVERSION TABLES

°C = (°F - 32) / 1.8
°F = (°C x 1.8) + 32
1 inch = 2.54 centimeters (cm)
1 foot = 0.304 meters (m)
1 yard = 0.914 meters
1 mile = 1.6093 kilometers (km)
1 km = 0.6214 miles
1 fathom = 1.8288 m
1 chain = 20.1168 m
1 furlong = 201.168 m
1 acre = 0.4047 hectares
1 sq km = 100 hectares
1 sq mile = 2.59 square km
1 ounce = 28.35 grams
1 pound = 0.4536 kilograms
1 short ton = 0.90718 metric ton
1 short ton = 2,000 pounds
1 long ton = 1.016 metric tons
1 long ton = 2,240 pounds
1 metric ton = 1,000 kilograms
1 quart = 0.94635 liters
1 US gallon = 3.7854 liters
1 Imperial gallon = 4.5459 liters
1 nautical mile = 1.852 km

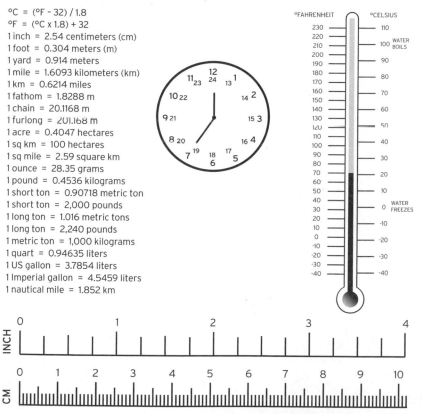

**MOON SPOTLIGHT CHARLESTON &
THE SOUTH CAROLINA LOWCOUNTRY**
Avalon Travel
a member of the Perseus Books Group
1700 Fourth Street
Berkeley, CA 94710, USA
www.moon.com

Editor and Series Manager: Kathryn Ettinger
Copy Editor: Jamie Andrade
Graphics Coordinator: Elizabeth Jang
Production Coordinator: Elizabeth Jang
Cover Designer: Kathryn Osgood
Map Editor: Brice Ticen
Cartographers: Kat Bennett, Chris Markiewicz,
    Allison Rawley

ISBN: 978-1-59880-680-9

Text © 2011 by Jim Morekis.
Maps © 2011 by Avalon Travel.
All rights reserved.

Some photos and illustrations are used by permission
and are the property of the original copyright owners.

ABOUT THE AUTHOR

Jim Morekis

Maybe it's because he was born in the same hospital as Flannery O'Connor – the old St. Joseph's in downtown Savannah – but there's no doubt that Jim Morekis has writing in his blood. As the longtime editor-in-chief of the weekly newspaper *Connect Savannah*, the University of Georgia graduate has written about and experienced pretty much every cultural happening in the area. He credits his love of travel to his mother, Elizabeth, who was John Berendt's travel agent during his stint in Savannah while writing *Midnight in the Garden of Good and Evil*.

Jim currently serves on Savannah's Cultural Affairs Commission, happily spending taxpayer money on the city's many festivals. As for the ongoing debate over which city is better, Charleston or Savannah, Jim calls it a tie: Charleston has better long-term planning, but Savannah has to-go cups (allowing anyone to explore the Historic District with a beer or cocktail in hand).

When not busy writing, Jim enjoys spending time with his two beautiful daughters, Alex and Sophia, and his dear wife, Sonja, who gets his deepest gratitude for opening his eyes to the true wonder and mystery of the Georgia coast.

Jim chronicles the history of the old Morekis family dairy online at www.morekisdairy.com.